# PROGRAMED
# COLLEGE
# VOCABULARY

# Programed College Vocabulary

**FIFTH EDITION**

**George W. Feinstein**
*Pasadena City College*

Prentice Hall, Upper Saddle River, New Jersey 07458

**Library of Congress Cataloging-in-Publication Data**

Feinstein, George W.
    Programed college vocabulary / George w. Feinstein. — 5th ed.
        p.    cm.
    ISBN 0-13-255613-8 (paper)
    1. Vocabulary—Programmed instruction.    I. Title.
PE1449.F38   1997
428.1′07′7—dc21                                                                97-6329
                                                                                    CIP


Editor-in-chief: *Charlyce Jones-Owen*
Acquisition editor: *Maggie Barbieri*
Editorial assistant: *Joan Polk*
Managing editor: *Bonnie Biller*
Production liaison:  *Fran Russello*
Editorial/production supervision: *Publications Development Company of Texas*
Prepress & manufacturing buyer: *Mary Ann Gloriande*
Cover designer: *Bruce Kenselaar*
Cover art: *D, pix, Inc.*
Marketing manager: *Rob Mejia*

This book was set in 10/12 point Times Roman by Publications Development
Company of Texas and was printed and bound by Hamilton Printing.
The cover was printed by Phoenix Color Corp.

 ©1998, 1992, 1986, 1979, 1969 by Prentice-Hall, Inc.
Simon & Schuster/A Viacom Company
Upper Saddle River, New Jersey 07458

Printed in the United States of America

10   9   8   7   6   5   4   3   2   1

ISBN 0-13-255613-8

Prentice-Hall International (UK) Limited, *London*
Prentice-Hall of Australia Pty. Limited, *Sydney*
Prentice-Hall Canada Inc., *Toronto*
Prentice-Hall Hispanoamericana, S.A., *Mexico*
Prentice-Hall of India Private Limited, *New Delhi*
Prentice-Hall of Japan, Inc., *Tokyo*
Simon & Schuster Asia Pte. Ltd., *Singapore*
Editora Prentice-Hall do Brasil, Ltda., *Rio de Janeiro*

**Library of Congress Cataloging-in-Publication Data**

Feinstein, George W.
    Programed college vocabulary / George w. Feinstein. — 5th ed.
        p.    cm.
    ISBN 0-13-255613-8 (paper)
    1. Vocabulary—Programmed instruction.    I. Title.
PE1449.F38    1997
428.1'07'7—dc21                                          97-6329
                                                             CIP


Editor-in-chief: *Charlyce Jones-Owen*
Acquisition editor: *Maggie Barbieri*
Editorial assistant: *Joan Polk*
Managing editor: *Bonnie Biller*
Production liaison:  *Fran Russello*
Editorial/production supervision: *Publications Development Company of Texas*
Prepress & manufacturing buyer: *Mary Ann Gloriande*
Cover designer: *Bruce Kenselaar*
Cover art: *D, pix, Inc.*
Marketing manager: *Rob Mejia*

This book was set in 10/12 point Times Roman by Publications Development
Company of Texas and was printed and bound by Hamilton Printing.
The cover was printed by Phoenix Color Corp.

   ©1998, 1992, 1986, 1979, 1969 by Prentice-Hall, Inc.
Simon & Schuster/A Viacom Company
Upper Saddle River, New Jersey 07458

Printed in the United States of America

10   9   8   7   6   5


**ISBN 0-13-255613-8**

Prentice-Hall International (UK) Limited, *London*
Prentice-Hall of Australia Pty. Limited, *Sydney*
Prentice-Hall Canada Inc., *Toronto*
Prentice-Hall Hispanoamericana, S.A., *Mexico*
Prentice-Hall of India Private Limited, *New Delhi*
Prentice-Hall of Japan, Inc., *Tokyo*
Simon & Schuster Asia Pte. Ltd., *Singapore*
Editora Prentice-Hall do Brasil, Ltda., *Rio de Janeiro*

# Contents

**PART TWO**

# To the Instructor

A student fell in love with his English teacher and sent her a long passionate letter. She returned his letter with unflattering corrections in red ink to his vocabulary and spelling.

One pleasant feature of this programed textbook is that student errors in vocabulary and spelling are discreetly corrected in the margin of each exercise, eliminating any possibility of embarrassment or resentment on the part of a student.

A dentist once claimed that operating on an elephant's teeth was easy except for "getting Jumbo to spit into the little sink." We have had a similar problem, maneuvering a huge bulk of words into a small space. Hundreds of useful words have been added to this fifth edition of *Programed College Vocabulary*. New chapters include Natural Science, also Fine Arts and Philosophy. Thus, this edition exposes students to terms from a broader range of college courses than earlier editions.

Other innovations include Characterization Words and Short Words II. Some of the tests have been revised.

Like a box of soap flakes, this edition could be labeled "new and improved."

Accompanying this edition is a new *Instructor's Manual* that provides chapter tests and review materials.

Psychologists insist that a student can learn practically anything, including the theory of relativity, if only it is broken down into easy steps. But how does an English instructor find enough class time or conference time to help each student individually with the thousand details of composition? Programed learning offers a possible solution, particularly where factual data such as vocabulary must be mastered. Industrial firms and educators have adopted programed techniques with startling success.

*Programed College Vocabulary* has been designed to supplement freshman English. This book differs from most vocabulary textbooks in that (1) it focuses on literary and academic terms, and (2) it is self-instructional. In short, the approach is pragmatic. *Programed College Vocabulary* stresses those words that are particularly useful to college students, and it elicits from each student a stream of active responses with immediate verification, a process that psychologists call *reinforcement*. Furthermore, hundreds of additional responses are called for in the teacher-administered tests accompanying this book, so that even the reinforcement gets reinforced. The system works. The book has now been adopted in more than two hundred colleges and universities, and reports as to the program's effectiveness are extremely encouraging.

Class procedures are flexible. The teacher can leave vocabulary instruction entirely to the programed text itself and simply give chapter tests to the class, as a checkup, at convenient intervals. But the *Instructor's Manual* includes additional study suggestions as well as tests, and the teacher may wish to devote further class time to enrichment of each chapter. Thus, the freshman English course may take on brave new dimensions.

# Acknowledgments

A wag once said, "Be careful when you give advice—somebody might take it." Invaluable advice has been given to me by a throng of careful experts, and I was happy to take it.

I am especially grateful to textbook reviewers Therese Brychta, Truckee Meadows Community College, and Dennis P. Kriewald, Laredo Community College.

For helpful suggestions I am also indebted to English Professors Vivian R. Brown, Patricia B. Gates, Delmar D. Gott, James F. Jester, Ellen Bourland, Barbara Dicey, Mary Alice Hawkins, Charlene Hawks, Patricia A. McDermott, Elizabeth Wahlquist, William F. Woods, and the English staff of Pasadena City College.

Incidentally, if a Hall of Fame is established for outstanding and helpful book editors, I'm going to nominate Nancy Marcus Land of Publications Development Company of Texas; Maggie Barbieri and Joan Polk of the Simon & Schuster Education Group.

I thank my wife Edith for a fruitful remark she made some years ago: "Why write book reviews," she asked, "when you could be writing a book?" We debated the matter. She supplied me with encouragement and tuna sandwiches.

This is the book.

GEORGE W. FEINSTEIN
*Pasadena, California*

# How to Use This Manual

1. Cover the answers at the left side of each page (in the grey area) with a strip of paper or with your hand.

2. Study carefully the definitions and examples at the beginning of each "frame," or word group.

3. Complete each statement—and immediately verify your answer—throughout the rest of the frame. Fill blanks with word choices, letter choices, or completions as indicated, without looking back to the definitions.

4. After completing each statement, uncover enough of the key at the left to check your answer.

5. If your answer is correct, go on to the next statement.

6. If you have made an error, study the explanations again at the top of the frame, or consult a dictionary, before you go on.

7. Take the quizzes and the review tests when you reach them, but wait until you have completed each quiz or review test before checking or grading your answers to it.

8. Throughout this manual, fill in the blanks completely and with correct spelling. The act of writing, as well as the repetition, will help the learning process.

### PRONUNCIATION KEY

| | | | | | | | | | |
|---|---|---|---|---|---|---|---|---|---|
| a | cat | i | hit | oo | took | ü | *as in French* vue |
| ā | hate | ī | kite | oi | coil | zh | *for* si *in* vision |
| â | rare | o | hot | ou | out | ə | *for* a *in* alone |
| ä | far | ō | note | u | up | ṅ | *nasal, as in French* |
| e | men | ô | corn | ū | amuse | | bon |
| ē | evil | ōō | fool | û | burn | | |

# PART ONE

# 1

# Short Words I

| | | |
|---|---|---|
| 1. *ado* | 13. *ewe* | 25. *sod* |
| 2. *aft* | 14. *fax* | 26. *sot* |
| 3. *asp* | 15. *hue* | 27. *spa* |
| 4. *bog* | 16. *ilk* | 28. *urn* |
| 5. *coy* | 17. *ire* | 29. *vex* |
| 6. *cur* | 18. *irk* | 30. *vie* |
| 7. *din* | 19. *lax* | 31. *wag* |
| 8. *dun* | 20. *mot* | 32. *wan* |
| 9. *ebb* | 21. *oaf* | 33. *wen* |
| 10. *eke* | 22. *ode* | 34. *wry* |
| 11. *eon* | 23. *opt* | 35. *yen* |
| 12. *err* | 24. *pry* | 36. *Zen* |

*Mark Twain was paid by the word. In one of his speeches (1906), he said, "I never write 'metropolis' for seven cents, because I can get the same money for 'city.' I never write 'policeman,' because I can get the same price for 'cop.' "*

*Exaggerations aside, Mark Twain is saying that if a short word can do the same work as a long word, the short word is to be preferred. That is good advice. Naturally, when a short word can't do the work of the long word, we use the long one.*

*Our language has a surprising number of short, expressive words in it. Mastery of these short words is essential for writer and speaker. This chapter focuses on three-letter words. Study carefully the definitions at the top of each page. Then fill in the blanks as directed. For more complete definitions, consult a good dictionary.*

*Some of you students are anxious, no doubt, to tackle big words right away. Here then— chew for verbal nourishment on the longest word in Webster's Third International Dictionary:*

*pneumonoultramicroscopicsilicovolcanoconiosises*

*This 47-letter monstrosity refers to a "disease of the lungs caused by breathing extremely fine siliceous dust" (plural). Work that medical freight train into your lunch conversation if you can.*

## EXERCISES

1. **ado:** fuss; excitement; busy activity. "Shakespeare wrote the comedy, *Much Ado About Nothing,* in 1598."
2. **aft:** near the rear of a ship or aircraft. "The mate ordered me to go *aft* and mop the deck."
3. **asp:** a viper; a small poisonous snake. "Cleopatra clutched an *asp* to her breast, committing suicide."
4. **bog:** a swamp; a small marsh. "Thomas Hardy's characters had an unhappy habit of falling into a *bog* or a weir."
5. **coy:** bashful; modest; coquettishly shy. "Gone are the *coy* young women who blushed to expose an ankle."
6. **cur:** a mongrel; a dog of mixed breed; a contemptible fellow. "I was bitten by a mangy *cur,* who seemed to resent me."

Fill the blanks with three-letter words.

coy

asp

cur

bog

aft

ado

■ The _____ (modest) Lady Ashley was about to seat herself on a deck chair right on top of a hissing _____ (poisonous viper). Luckily, a mud-caked _____ (mongrel), which looked as though it had slept in a _____ (swamp), darted _____ (rear of ship) and gobbled the little snake before it could enjoy its deadly mission. Lady Ashley's friends made much _____ (fuss) about the incident, and one of them gratefully threw the heroic dog a stale fish.

ado

coy

■ What an _____ (excitement) at the sorority house! See what's on the finger of _____ (bashful) Betty—a diamond as big as a potato!

bog

asp

■ As Oswald sank deeper into the _____ (marsh), he reached out to save himself and all he could grab was an _____ (viper).

aft

cur

■ I went _____ (to the rear) to use the ship's toilet facilities and found them guarded by a snarling _____ (mongrel), a flea plantation known as White Fang.

Write the letter that indicates the best definition.

1. (d)
2. (e)
3. (f)
4. (b)
5. (a)
6. (c)

(    ) 1. bog        a. fuss; excitement
(    ) 2. cur        b. bashful; artfully shy
(    ) 3. aft         c. a poisonous viper
(    ) 4. coy        d. a swamp or marsh
(    ) 5. ado       e. a mongrel; a contemptible fellow
(    ) 6. asp       f. at the back of the ship

---

7. **din:** a loud confused noise. "I proposed marriage, but Lulu couldn't hear me above the *din* of the rock band."

8. **dun:** to pester for payment of a debt. "Our landlord used to *dun* us for rent—and we were only six months behind."

9. **ebb:** a decline; a flowing back. "His fortunes at low *ebb*, the exbanker now sells apples on a street corner."

10. **eke:** to squeeze by with difficulty. "Old Jim picked up empty beer cans behind the fraternity houses to *eke* out a living."

11. **eon:** millions of years. "It takes an *eon* to develop a condor, ten years to exterminate it."

12. **err:** to make a mistake; go astray. "To *err* is human; to forgive, divine."

Fill the blanks with three-letter words.

dun

eon, din

err

ebb

eke

■ Bill collectors! You've come to _____ (pester) me for payment of debts. By Jove, you've hounded me for an _____ (million years). What a _____ (loud racket) you make, pounding on my door! Yes, I happened to _____ (make a mistake) at the race track, betting my wad on that fugitive from a glue factory; so my cash flow is now at low _____ (decline).

But my luck is changing, gentlemen, and I'll soon _____ (squeeze) out a full settlement for each of you. Just lend me another five hundred—hey, fellows, give me back my wallet!

ebb

eon

■ There the _____ (decline) and flow of the tide went on for many an _____ (countless years).

dun, din

■ So the old goat won't pay child support, Inga? You must _____ (demand payment) him and raise a _____ (clamor).

err

eke

■ Unless I _____ (am mistaken), our star halfback might be able to _____ (squeeze) out a passing grade in Music Appreciation 1A.

---

## Quiz

Write the letter that indicates the best definition.

1. (e)
2. (a)
3. (d)
4. (b)
5. (c)
6. (f)

(    ) 1. ebb         a. millions of years
(    ) 2. eon         b. to make a mistake
(    ) 3. din         c. to keep demanding repayment
(    ) 4. err         d. loud, confused noise
(    ) 5. dun         e. to flow back; decline
(    ) 6. eke         f. to squeeze; barely get by

---

13. **ewe:** a female sheep. "A ram once fell off a cliff and said, 'I didn't see that *ewe* turn.'"
14. **fax:** sending graphic copy electronically. "We'll get the diagrams to your Tokyo office by *fax*."
15. **hue:** a distinctive color. "Roses are of various *hues,* but they all have thorns."
16. **ilk:** same kind or sort. "In prison you will meet burglars, pickpockets, and others of that *ilk*."
17. **ire:** anger; wrath. "Ann said Ed's mouth is so big he can sing duets, and that insult aroused Ed's *ire*."
18. **irk:** to annoy; irritate. "Having to wear socks that didn't quite match never failed to *irk* me."

Fill the blanks with three-letter words.

ewe

ire

irk

ilk, fax

hue

■ I led my _____ (female sheep) across Pete's frozen pond, whereupon Pete shouted with some show of _____ (anger), "Don't pull the wool over my ice." Unfriendly words can _____ (irritate) me, and I decided to avoid Pete and others of his _____ (sort). But an hour later Pete sent me a _____ (electronic note) that said he'd been "kidding," and would I come over for a barbeque. Now that's a horse of a different _____ (color)!

ire

hue

fax

irk

ewe

ilk

■ When Bobby batted his home run through Abner's window, the old man was full of _____ (wrath) and his face took on a purplish _____ (color).

■ For fun Lucy would send a _____ (electronic note) to all her friends, saying, "So sorry to hear about it," which would _____ (irritate) them because they didn't know what the devil she was talking about.

■ The old sheepherder complains that the market price of a _____ (female sheep) is "ba-a-a-d" nowadays because of vegetarians and others of that _____ (sort).

---

**19. lax:** not strict or tight. "Junior shot spitballs at the prettier classmates. Discipline was *lax.*

**20. mot** (mō): a clever saying; witticism; bon mot. "Flo said Tom's teeth looked like a deserted graveyard—what a nasty *mot!*"

**21. oaf:** a stupid, clumsy fellow. "In the midst of those clever, sophisticated people, I felt like an *oaf.*"

**22. ode:** a lyric poem usually in praise of something. "Percy Bysshe Shelley wrote 'Ode to the West Wind' (1820)."

**23. opt:** choose. "If senators can *opt* to give themselves a raise, why can't shoe clerks do it?"

**24. pry:** to try to draw out; extract. "It's easier to raise corn in Death Valley than to *pry* a dollar from my Uncle Phineas."

Fill the blanks with three-letter words.

ode, opt

oaf

mot

pry

lax

■ Oscar Wilde, a brilliant writer, could compose a ballad or an _____ (lyric poem) but what did he _____ (choose) to focus on?—playwriting. One would have to be an _____ (stupid lout) not to enjoy his sophisticated comedies. For instance, one of his characters utters the classic _____ (witticism): "I can resist anything but temptation." Unfortunately, Wilde couldn't resist temptation either. Victorian critics began to _____ (draw out) into his private life, which they considered to be _____ (not strict), and he landed in jail. Some playwrights are tame, but he was Wilde.

pry

mot

oaf

ode

lax

opt

■ Bob's dentist chattered as he tried to _____ (extract) out the molar, and Bob responded with a _____ (witticism) that got lost in the plumbing in his mouth.

■ We knew that an _____ (stupid fellow) like Manny couldn't write this lovely _____ (lyric poem) to the western breeze. He stole it from Shelley.

■ I'm _____ (not strict) about brushing my teeth. I asked my dentist what to do about my yellow teeth, and he said I should _____ (choose) to wear a yellow tie.

## Quiz

Write the letter that indicates the best definition.

1. (c)
2. (f)
3. (d)
4. (b)
5. (a)
6. (e)

(    ) 1. ode      a. a witty remark
(    ) 2. lax      b. a stupid lout
(    ) 3. opt      c. a lyric poem
(    ) 4. oaf      d. to choose
(    ) 5. mot      e. to draw forth
(    ) 6. pry      f. not strict

25. **sod:** a surface layer of earth; turf. "Grandpa sleeps beneath the *sod.*"

26. **sot:** a drunkard. "If it weren't for the olives in his martinis, this *sot* would starve to death."

27. **spa:** a health resort, usually with baths or springs. "Wanda dieted at the *spa* and all she lost was ten days."

28. **urn:** a vase to hold ashes of a cremated body; a big metal coffee dispenser. "John Keats wrote 'Ode on a Grecian *Urn*' (1819)."

29. **vex:** irk; annoy. "The hippies swept rubbish under their carpet, a habit that seemed to *vex* the landlady."

30. **vie:** compete. "Candidates *vie* to make the biggest promises."

Fill the blanks with three-letter words.

■ Nothing could _____ (irritate) Mrs. Jones more than her husband Joe's drinking habits. She dragged him to a _____ (health resort) hoping to dry him out, but all he did

vex

spa

vie

sot

sod

urn

was _____ (compete) with cronies for the alcohol championship. Finally the old _____ (drunkard) was killed by hard drink—a block of ice fell on his head. Instead of burying Joe beneath the _____ (turf), his wife kept his ashes in an _____ (vase). Now and then she flicks cigarette ashes into the burial jar, and friends have asked, "Isn't Joe gaining weight?"

vie

sod

■ Our glorious football teams used to _____ (compete) and break bones on this very _____ (soil).

spa

sot

■ Sir, our _____ (health resort) cures many invalids, but we can't cure a _____ (drunkard).

urn

vex

■ The coffee from this _____ (container) should not _____ (annoy) you. You, too, will be old and weak some day.

---

### Quiz

1. (c)
2. (e)
3. (b)
4. (d)
5. (a)
6. (f)

( ) 1. sot      a. top layer of earth
( ) 2. vex      b. a health resort
( ) 3. spa      c. a drunkard
( ) 4. vie      d. compete
( ) 5. sod      e. annoy
( ) 6. urn      f. a cremation vase

---

31. **wag:** a joker; comical person. "The *wag* asked the hotel clerk to page Mr. Rydus . . . first name, Arthur."
32. **wan:** feeble; sickly pale. "Stay a month in a hospital and you come out *wan* and weak."
33. **wen:** a skin growth; a small tumor, usually on the scalp. "I'll remove the *wen,*" said my surgeon. "Say when."
34. **wry:** twisted; distorted. "Billy shopped for bagels, but came home with a rye bread and a *wry* grin."
35. **yen:** a strong desire. "At two in the morning, his pregnant wife developed a *yen* for red onions."
36. **Zen:** meditation as a key to understanding the universe. "The *Zen* follower sat cross-legged and stared at his belly button."

Fill the blanks with three-letter words.

wag, wry

■ Our village _____ (joker) had a _____ (distorted) sense of humor. He used to tell people that the

wen

_____ (growth) on my scalp was pigeon droppings. But now,

wan

after his heart attack, he looks thin and _____ (sickly pale).

yen

He is dabbling in religion and tells me he has a _____ (de-

Zen

sire) to practice _____ (spiritual meditation).

Zen

■ The follower of _____ (meditation) probably had spiri-

wan

tual health, but he looked like one _____ (sickly pale) and skinny specimen to me.

wag

■ Once popular was the _____ (joker), like Bob Hope, who told thigh-slappers; then came sitcom performers with a more

wry

subtle, _____ (twisted) humor.

wen

■ Little Betty was fascinated by the _____ (skin growth)

yen

on her uncle's forehead and stifled a _____ (desire) to poke at it.

---

## Quiz

Write the letter that indicates the best definition.

1. (c)
2. (e)
3. (a)
4. (f)
5. (d)
6. (b)

(   ) 1. wry      a. a comical person
(   ) 2. Zen      b. pale and feeble
(   ) 3. wag      c. twisted; ironic
(   ) 4. yen      d. a small skin tumor
(   ) 5. wen      e. spiritual meditation
(   ) 6. wan      f. a longing; craving

## REVIEW TEST

Write the three-letter word from this chapter that is defined in the brackets. The first letter of the answer is given.

o _____    1. John Keats wrote an [lyric poem] to a skylark.

s _____    2. Asleep on the train track was the [drunkard].

f _____    3. Send me the facts by [electronic copy].

e _____    4. I'll shear the ram, and you the [female sheep].

d _____    5. Tuning the orchestra created a [loud noise].

a _____    6. Dopey ran [back] and fell off the boat.

o _____    7. Most customers [make a choice] for vanilla.

w _____    8. The [comic fellow] laughed at his own jokes.

e _____    9. The Mets [squeeze] out a victory, 9–8.

d _____    10. Mr. Dunn will [pester] you until you pay.

b _____    11. Out of the [swamp] crawled a lizard.

y _____    12. The addict had a [craving] for a cigarette.

u _____    13. Ernie rests in peace in a lovely [burial vase].

o _____    14. A wrestler isn't necessarily an [stupid lout].

e _____    15. I spent an [million years] in the waiting room.

i _____    16. Films of airborne speeding cars [irritate] Kay.

v _____    17. Winky and Dinky will [compete] for the title.

m _____    18. Wilde's comedy sparkled with many a [witticism].

s _____    19. I can't sleep if a [resort] is too expensive.

i _____    20. Wrong-number phone calls aroused Ed's [wrath].

w _____    21. In the wheelchair sat Juan, sad and [feeble].

c _____    22. Said Herrick to the maiden, "Be not [bashful]."

h _____    23. I wore a tie of unforgivable [color].

e _____    24. Computers don't [make mistakes], but tellers do.

l _____    25. Children may suffer if parents are [not strict].

## Key to Review Test

Check your test answers with the following key. Deduct 4% per error from a possible 100%.

| | | |
|---|---|---|
| 1. ode | 10. dun | 19. spa |
| 2. sot | 11. bog | 20. ire |
| 3. fax | 12. yen | 21. wan |
| 4. ewe | 13. urn | 22. coy |
| 5. din | 14. oaf | 23. hue |
| 6. aft | 15. eon | 24. err |
| 7. opt | 16. irk | 25. lax |
| 8. wag | 17. vie | |
| 9. eke | 18. mot | |

Score: _____ %

# 2

# Short Words II

| | | |
|---|---|---|
| 1. *avid* | 13. *gist* | 25. *quip* |
| 2. *bask* | 14. *goad* | 26. *saga* |
| 3. *bias* | 15. *guru* | 27. *seep* |
| 4. *cloy* | 16. *hoax* | 28. *smug* |
| 5. *coup* | 17. *lank* | 29. *spry* |
| 6. *crux* | 18. *lewd* | 30. *tang* |
| 7. *cult* | 19. *logo* | 31. *teem* |
| 8. *daft* | 20. *lope* | 32. *tome* |
| 9. *dank* | 21. *moot* | 33. *trek* |
| 10. *dote* | 22. *ogle* | 34. *tyro* |
| 11. *elan* | 23. *pate* | 35. *whim* |
| 12. *flux* | 24. *ploy* | 36. *zeal* |

*Tell your friends you are learning some four-letter words and they may snicker. But the laugh is on them. Many of the most useful words in our language have only four letters. Properly used, they can be punchy, precise, and unpretentious.*

*Continue as in Chapter 1.*

*A supplementary list of 160 stubby words will be found at the end of this chapter. Do not underestimate their importance. Like jewels, they are small but valuable.*

## EXERCISES

COVER THIS STRIP

1. **avid** (av′id): very eager; greedy; keenly desirous. "My maiden aunt is an *avid* reader, mostly of love stories."

2. **bask:** to be exposed to pleasant warmth or favor. "Dakotans shovel snow while Californians *bask* in the sun."

3. **bias** (bī′əs): prejudice; partiality; preference. "The referee showed no *bias,* except perhaps to the home team."

4. **cloy:** to weary with too much richness, sweetness, or pleasure. "The chocolates and pastries *cloy* his appetite."

5. **coup** (kōō): an unexpected masterstroke; a brilliant stratagem. "A military *coup* rubbed out the dictator."

6. **crux** (kruks): the basic or crucial point; a baffling difficulty. "Our city has a million cars and only 347 parking spaces—that's the *crux* of our problem."

Fill the blanks with four-letter words.

bask

■ Those who *b*_____ (lie exposed) all day under a hot sun will get a tan and maybe a shot of skin cancer too.

cloy

■ The speaker gushed gallons of sweet talk on the honored guest until the compliments began to *c*_____ (tire).

bias

■ The defendant wore a short skirt, hoping perhaps to *b*_____ (win preference from) the men on the jury.

avid

■ Elmer is such an *a*_____ (eager) follower of country music that he sleeps on a bale of hay.

crux

■ Whether to spend money on bombers or colleges was the *c*_____ (essential point) of the debate.

coup

■ Trading that worn-out pitcher for these two home run hitters was a pennant-winning *c*_____ (masterstroke).

bask

■ Aunt Amy would *b*_____ (lie exposed) under a sunny sky and read those overly sweet romances for which she had an

avid

*a*_____ appetite. Surely the verbal honey would eventually

cloy

*c*_____ or give her diabetes.

**14    Short Words II**

bias

crux

avid

coup

■ We must pick a jury that is without *b*_____ (prejudice).

That is the *c*_____ (central issue) of our problem.

■ Schultz was an *a*_____ (eager) investor, and buying 7-Up when it was five and an eighth was a real *c*_____ (masterstroke).

---

### Quiz

Write the letter that indicates the best definition.

1. (c)
2. (e)
3. (d)
4. (a)
5. (b)
6. (f)

( ) 1. coup   a. prejudice
( ) 2. cloy    b. to recline in warmth
( ) 3. crux    c. a sudden brilliant stroke
( ) 4. bias     d. the vital point
( ) 5. bask    e. to tire of excessive sweetness
( ) 6. avid    f. very eager

---

7. **cult:** a group strongly devoted to a special person, principle, or religious ritual. "The Elvis Presley *cult* decided to meet in Nashville."

8. **daft:** crazy; simple-minded. "Many a genius has been thought to be *daft*."

9. **dank:** unpleasantly moist; damp. "I wasn't happy working in the dark and *dank* sewer system."

10. **dote:** to bestow excessive love or fondness. "I *dote* on figs. Three pounds, please."

11. **élan** (ā-lan′): enthusiasm; dash; vigor. "Our tennis star captured the third set with *élan*."

12. **flux:** continual change. "Stock market prices are in a state of *flux*."

Fill the blanks with four-letter words.

dote

■ My in-laws *d*_____ (lavish their love) on their little boy. Six years old and he goes to the psychiatrist all by himself.

dank

■ I didn't mind that the cave was *d*_____ (unpleasantly moist) and dirty, but I didn't like the bear.

daft

■ Everybody is *d*_____ (crazy) except you and me—and I'm not sure about you.

flux

cult

élan

cult

daft

dote

élan

flux

dank

■ Our weather is in *f*_____ (constant change). Tom put on an overcoat and got sunstroke.

■ Poets with little to say join the *c*_____ (group) of the obscure.

■ Debbie dribbled toward the basket with considerable *é*_____(energy and flair).

■ When I learned that members of the *c*_____ (religious group) gave their entire paychecks to the leader, I thought they were *d*_____ (crazy).

■ Although I *d*_____ (love) on mushrooms and have devoured them with *é*_____ (gusto), my feelings are now in *f*_____ (change) since I nibbled a toadstool that popped up in our *d*_____ (moist) cellar.

### Quiz

Write the letter that indicates the best definition.

1. (e)
2. (f)
3. (b)
4. (c)
5. (a)
6. (d)

(      ) 1. dank      a. insane; silly
(      ) 2. élan      b. continual change
(      ) 3. flux      c. show excessive fondness
(      ) 4. dote      d. a devoted group; sect
(      ) 5. daft      e. repulsively damp
(      ) 6. cult      f. enthusiasm; vigor

13. **gist** (jist): the main part of the matter. "His sermon lasted two hours, and the *gist* of it is that sin is bad."
14. **goad:** to urge on; prod into action. "Cowboys enjoyed using spurs to *goad* a horse, but nobody asked the horse's opinion."
15. **guru** (goo′ roo): a wise leader; spiritual guide. "We sought advice from the city editor, the kindly *guru* of our staff."
16. **hoax:** a practical joke; a mischievous deception. "Many fell for the *hoax* that the Martians had landed."
17. **lank:** lean; long and slender. "Lincoln was gaunt and *lank*, with legs 'long enough to reach the ground.' "
18. **lewd** (lood): obscene; indecent; inciting to lust. "Our beloved evangelist was jailed for *lewd* conduct."

Fill the blanks with four-letter words.

hoax

■ We've bought a fake Rembrandt! We're victims of a h_____ (deception)!

guru

■ The Hindus look to the g_____ for spiritual advice.

lank

■ Our hero was Gary Cooper—l_____ (tall, thin) and handsome.

lewd

■ Movies that were once considered l_____ (obscene) would put a modern audience to sleep.

lank, goad

■ The handsome hero of the western flick dug spurs deep into his l_____ (lean), underfed steed to g_____ (urge on) it toward the trip wire.

gist

■ A book review should give the g_____ (main idea) of a book but not be longer than the book itself.

goad

■ Fathers of Little League players frantically g_____ (urge) the tearful lads to knock home runs.

gist

■ The g_____ (main idea) of the news item was that some-

guru, lewd

body sent the saintly g_____ (spiritual leader) a l_____ (ob-

hoax

scene) film instead of a religious one. What a cruel h_____ (practical joke)!

---

## Quiz

Write the letter that indicates the best definition.

1. (c)
2. (d)
3. (f)
4. (b)
5. (a)
6. (e)

( ) 1. lank       a. a practical joke
( ) 2. goad      b. obscene; lecherous
( ) 3. gist        c. long and slender
( ) 4. lewd      d. to prod; urge on
( ) 5. hoax     e. wise spiritual leader
( ) 6. guru      f. the main point or essence

---

19. **logo** (lô′gō): a trademark. "Every bank, auto, or rat poison has its copyrighted *logo*."
20. **lope:** to run with bounding steps. "Betty watched the health lunatics *lope* through the park."

21. **moot:** debatable; subject to argument. "Whether an honest citizen can get elected to high office is a *moot* question."

22. **ogle:** to stare at with fondness or desire. "The old men sit and *ogle* the bikini-clad girls."

23. **pate:** the head: the top of the head. "Pap's *pate* was as bald as a baby's bottom."

24. **ploy:** a maneuver or trick to gain an advantage. "The beggar developed a limp as a *ploy* to win sympathy."

Fill the blanks with four-letter words.

■ Smith owns one shabby suit which he wears to money-raising affairs—an interesting *pl* _____ (maneuver).

■ The Sleazy Dress Company was sued for copying the *lo* _____ (trademark) of a world-famous designer.

■ Mr. Dooley walks fast, and little Patrick has to *lo* _____ (take bounding steps) to keep up to him.

■ Whether our grandchildren will forgive us for spending trillions of their money is a *mo* _____ (debatable) question.

■ Albert Einstein was remarkable not for the wildness of his hair but for the activity under his *pa* _____ (top of head).

■ You entered a beauty contest? Then don't complain if strangers *og* _____ (stare at) you.

■ The bushy wig on one circus clown's *pa* _____ (head) was his *lo* _____ (trademark). Bozo's favorite *pl* _____ (trick) was to *og* _____ (stare at) a pretty spectator, *lo* _____ (bound) toward her, and pretend to propose. Was she flattered? That's a *mo* _____ (debatable) question.

ploy

logo

lope

moot

pate

ogle

pate
logo, ploy

ogle
lope
moot

## Quiz

Write the letter that indicates the best definition.

1. (f)
2. (d)

(    ) 1. pate      a. a trademark
(    ) 2. moot     b. to eye amorously

3. (a)
4. (c)
5. (e)
6. (b)

(   ) 3. logo     c. to run with bounding steps
(   ) 4. lope     d. arguable; open to question
(   ) 5. ploy     e. a maneuver to take advantage
(   ) 6. ogle     f. the top of the skull

---

**25. quip:** a witty remark, possibly sarcastic. "Remember Shaw's *quip:* 'Fish and relatives begin to smell in three days.' "

**26. saga** (sä'gə): a tale of heroic deeds; a story covering generations. "Zane Grey wrote a *saga* of the American cowboy."

**27. seep:** to ooze; soak. "The cyanides in the landfill began to *seep* into our well water."

**28. smug:** having a confident, self-satisfied air. "He had the *smug* look of a preacher with four aces in his hand."

**29. spry:** nimble; lively. "Felicia is quite *spry* for a woman who won't see eighty again."

**30. tang:** a strong taste or odor. "The garlic powder gave my salad a somewhat regrettable *tang.*"

Fill the blanks with four-letter words.

saga

■ John Galsworthy wrote nine novels in his *sa* _____ (story) of the Forsyte family.

spry

■ At a square dance Grandpa is amazingly *sp* _____ (nimble).

seep

■ Rain water began to *se* _____ (diffuse) through the bed-

smug

room ceiling. "I'll stop that," said Joe with a *sm* _____ (self-satisfied) expression. He opened an umbrella.

quip

■ Consider Woody Allen's *q* _____ (witty comment) about death: "I don't believe in an afterlife, although I am bringing a change of underwear."

tang

■ We added lemon juice to the cat food to give it *ta* _____ (flavor), and now we have a sour puss.

spry

■ The *sp* _____ (agile) old chef assured us with a

smug

*sm* _____ (self-satisfied) smile that his herbs would

seep

*se* _____ (ooze) into the stew and give it an unforgettable

tang

*ta* _____ (flavor).

saga

quip

■ The mile-long 12th century Icelandic s_____ (heroic epic) was serious business, and you won't run into a laugh or a q_____ (witticism) in it anywhere.

## Quiz

Write the letter that indicates the best definition.

1. (b)
2. (c)
3. (f)
4. (e)
5. (d)
6. (a)

| ( | ) 1. saga | a. agile; nimble |
|---|---|---|
| ( | ) 2. quip | b. a chronicle of deeds |
| ( | ) 3. smug | c. a witty comment |
| ( | ) 4. tang | d. to ooze |
| ( | ) 5. seep | e. a strong flavor |
| ( | ) 6. spry | f. self-satisfied and confident |

**31. teem:** to swarm; abound. "On warm summer nights the plazas *teem* with romance-hungry adolescents."

**32. tome:** a heavy, learned book; a ponderous volume. "We found the professor with his nose in a dusty *tome*."

**33. trek:** a long journey, involving difficulties. "The girls started their *trek* across the Sahara on rented camels."

**34. tyro** (tī′rō): a novice; a beginner. "I'm not relaxed when I fly a double loop with a pilot who is a *tyro*."

**35. whim** (hwim): a sudden odd notion; a fanciful impulse. "On a *whim* Ed went on a fruit diet and lost four ounces."

**36. zeal:** enthusiastic devotion to a cause. "Carrie Chapman Catt raided saloons and smashed whiskey bottles with *zeal*."

Fill the blanks with four-letter words.

tome

■ The earthquake caused an ancient *to*_____ (volume) to drop upon my pate.

teem

■ The landlord said the rooms were empty, but actually they *te*_____ (swarm) with roaches.

whim

■ This may be a *wh*_____ (fanciful notion) but I believe the rock band gave up melody for Lent.

tyro

■ The schoolboy, who looked like a *ty*_____ (beginner), took all of twelve moves to checkmate me.

trek

zeal

whim

tome

tyro

zeal, trek

teem

■ The explorer took a six-month *tr*_____ (journey) where, in his words, "The hand of man had never set foot."

■ The country preacher spoke with such *ze*_____ (fervor) that he converted eleven farmers and a cow.

■ Apparently on a *w*_____ (impulse), because I was tardy, my history teacher assigned me a two-thousand page *t*_____ (fat volume) to read and report on by next morning.

■ As an explorer, Stanley was a *ty*_____ (novice), yet he undertook with *z*_____ (enthusiasm) the *tr*_____ (journey)—through jungles that *te*_____ (swarm) with dangers—to find Livingston.

## Quiz

Write the letter that indicates the best definition.

1. (d)
2. (b)
3. (e)
4. (a)
5. (f)
6. (c)

(   ) 1. trek       a. a heavy old book
(   ) 2. teem      b. to swarm
(   ) 3. zeal       c. a fanciful notion
(   ) 4. tome      d. a long, difficult journey
(   ) 5. tyro       e. enthusiastic devotion
(   ) 6. whim     f. a beginner

Write the four-letter word from this chapter that is defined in the brackets. The first letter of the answer is given.

*s* _____    1. Norway spawned many a [tale of heroes and demigods].

*t* _____    2. Covered wagons began the slow [hard journey] westward.

*g* _____    3. Scan the novel and you'll get the [main idea] of the plot.

*t* _____    4. Something added to the punch gave it an exceptional [taste].

*d* _____    5. You bet on Slopoke? You must be [insane].

*b* _____    6. Every mother thinks her baby is beautiful—so much for [prejudice].

*b* _____    7. The coal miner's dream was to [lie exposed] in the sun.

*t* _____    8. The county assessor consulted a huge [heavy volume].

*d* _____    9. The hobo slept in the [unpleasantly moist] weeds.

*l* _____    10. I recognized the familiar cola [trademark] in Dublin.

*m* _____    11. Cut budget or raise taxes? It's a [arguable] issue.

*q* _____    12. Dorothy Parker was famous for many a [witticism].

*p* _____    13. The freebie is the peddler's [trick] to get inside.

*c* _____    14. The shaky government was toppled by a military [sudden stroke].

*t* _____    15. Her first serve was an ace. She was no [beginner]!

*h* _____    16. Ponzi's get-rich-quick scheme was a [deception].

*f* _____    17. Better, worse, better, worse—her health is in [change].

*l* _____    18. Watch our forwards [run with a bound] toward the basket!

*g* _____    19. "Be unselfish," advised our [spiritual leader], who owned five Cadillacs.

*l* _____    20. The rap singer was arrested for using [obscene] lyrics.

*a* _____    21. Boys read the Alger books with [very eager] interest.

*t* _____    22. These lakes [swarm] with dive-bomber mosquitoes.

*c* _____    23. Help!—I'm a slave in a weird religious [group].

*z* _____    24. Ed attacked the steak with great [enthusiasm].

*p* _____    25. Our Nuke Lotion will grow hair on a bald [scalp] or even on a brick. Only $79.95.

## Key to Review Test

Check your test answers with the following key. Deduct 4% per error from a possible 100%.

| | | |
|---|---|---|
| 1. saga | 10. logo | 19. guru |
| 2. trek | 11. moot | 20. lewd |
| 3. gist | 12. quip | 21. avid |
| 4. tang | 13. ploy | 22. teem |
| 5. daft | 14. coup | 23. cult |
| 6. bias | 15. tyro | 24. zest |
| 7. bask | 16. hoax | 25. pate |
| 8. tome | 17. flux | |
| 9. dank | 18. lope | |

Score: _____ %

## SUPPLEMENTARY LIST

You are familiar with most of these short words. Use your dictionary to check words about which you are doubtful.

*Class Exercise:* Divide into panel groups. Each group will be responsible for discussing and clarifying a segment of the following list for the benefit of the rest of the class.

| | | | |
|---|---|---|---|
| 1. apt | 41. abet | 81. gait | 121. oust |
| 2. awe | 42. ague | 82. gird | 122. pact |
| 3. awl | 43. amok | 83. glum | 123. pang |
| 4. ban | 44. apex | 84. glut | 124. pelt |
| 5. boa | 45. aria | 85. gory | 125. pert |
| 6. cud | 46. aura | 86. grit | 126. plod |
| 7. cue | 47. aver | 87. halo | 127. pomp |
| 8. doe | 48. balk | 88. heft | 128. pout |
| 9. duo | 49. bevy | 89. hone | 129. prim |
| 10. era | 50. bilk | 90. icon | 130. prod |
| 11. erg | 51. bloc | 91. jeer | 131. pyre |
| 12. fez | 52. buff | 92. jilt | 132. ramp |
| 13. foe | 53. buss | 93. jowl | 133. rapt |
| 14. fop | 54. cant | 94. kiln | 134. ream |
| 15. hew | 55. cede | 95. leer | 135. rift |
| 16. hod | 56. chic | 96. lieu | 136. sage |
| 17. hub | 57. cite | 97. lisp | 137. scan |
| 18. ion | 58. cope | 98. loam | 138. sear |
| 19. lee | 59. crag | 99. loge | 139. sect |
| 20. lei | 60. curt | 100. loll | 140. seer |
| 21. lob | 61. cyst | 101. lout | 141. serf |
| 22. mar | 62. daub | 102. lull | 142. sham |
| 23. nee | 63. diva | 103. lure | 143. silt |
| 24. nib | 64. drab | 104. lush | 144. slur |
| 25. nil | 65. drub | 105. lust | 145. snub |
| 26. ohm | 66. dune | 106. maim | 146. sulk |
| 27. orb | 67. emit | 107. meek | 147. tact |
| 28. pod | 68. epee | 108. menu | 148. tint |
| 29. pun | 69. ergo | 109. mesa | 149. tory |
| 30. sac | 70. etch | 110. mime | 150. tram |
| 31. sip | 71. fang | 111. moat | 151. turf |
| 32. sou | 72. fete | 112. muse | 152. veto |
| 33. soy | 73. feud | 113. mute | 153. visa |
| 34. sty | 74. fiat | 114. myth | 154. void |
| 35. tic | 75. flaw | 115. nape | 155. wane |
| 36. via | 76. foal | 116. nyet | 156. wary |
| 37. vim | 77. foil | 117. oboe | 157. welt |
| 38. vow | 78. fret | 118. ogre | 158. wilt |
| 39. wan | 79. fume | 119. omen | 159. yoke |
| 40. yam | 80. gaff | 120. opus | 160. zest |

# 3

# Words Often Confused I

| | | |
|---|---|---|
| *accept,* **1** | *continuously,* **20** | *imply,* **33** |
| *adapt,* **3** | *decent,* **21** | *infer,* **34** |
| *adopt,* **4** | *descent,* **22** | *instance,* **35** |
| *advice,* **5** | *desert,* **23** | *instants,* **36** |
| *advise,* **6** | *dessert,* **24** | *it's,* **38** |
| *affect,* **7** | *disinterested,* **25** | *its,* **37** |
| *allusion,* **9** | *dual,* **27** | *ladder,* **39** |
| *amount,* **11** | *duel,* **28** | *later,* **40** |
| *brake,* **13** | *effect,* **8** | *latter,* **41** |
| *break,* **14** | *every body,* **29** | *leave,* **42** |
| *capital,* **15** | *everybody,* **30** | *let,* **43** |
| *capitol,* **16** | *except,* **2** | *number,* **12** |
| *complement,* **17** | *foreword,* **31** | *uninterested,* **26** |
| *compliment,* **18** | *forward,* **32** | |
| *continually,* **19** | *illusion,* **10** | |

*To use a medicine because it looks "something like" the one you need can lead to trouble. To use a word because it sounds "something like" the one you need also leads to trouble.*

*Some common words, with their frame numbers, are listed above. These words look as harmless as old luggage, yet each should be handled as if it held a little bomb. "A sandy* desert*" is hardly the same as "a sandy* dessert*," and "marital* music*" is hardly the same as "martial* music*"; so be sure you know your homonyms.*

*Most of the word pairs in this chapter sound alike or are very similar in sound. You should train both your ear and your eye to notice the slight difference in sound or spelling in each pair, so that you will choose the correct word.*

*Study carefully the words at the top of each frame. Then fill each blank with the correct word. As always, keep a dictionary near you. A dictionary is bound to be useful, and that's not just a pun.*

*Enough* foreword—*now go* forward!

COVER THIS STRIP

_____

**1. accept** (ak-sept´): to take or receive. "*Accept* the lemons of life, and make lemonade."

**2. except** (ik-sept´): all but; excluding. "This singer has everything *except* talent." *Except* has to do with an *exception*.

accept

except

■ The church will *ac*_____ all your paintings *ex*_____ the nude.

except, accept

■ Every teacher _____ Smedley will _____ the two percent raise.

accept

except

■ The opera singer was glad to _____ the gift package, which was quite ordinary _____ for its ticking sound.

except

accept, except

■ Flem had no coins _____ a wooden nickel, yet he would never _____ a free drink— _____ when he was awake.

_____

**3. adapt:** to fit for a new use; to adjust to a new situation. "Can man *adapt* to life on the moon?" "This play is an *adaptation* of a novel."

**4. adopt:** to take into one's family; to pick up and use as one's own. "They found me in a trash barrel and *adopted* me."

adapt

■ I could *ad*_____ to army life if they'd let me sleep till noon.

adopt

adapt

■ If we _____ a bright chimpanzee, it would probably _____ quickly to California life.

adapt

adopt

■ Hollywood wants to _____ your life story to film. Better _____ a pseudonym because this movie may be X-rated.

adopt

■ Who deserves little Ignatz—his natural mother or the couple who happened to _____ and raise him?

_____

5. **advice** (ad-vīs′): *Noun*—counsel. "Dad gives me *advice,* not money."

6. **advise** (ad-vīz′): *Verb*—to counsel; to recommend. "Please *advise* me."

advice ■ As a young singer I asked a vocal critic for *ad*_____.

advise He said: "I _____ you to sell fish."

advice ■ Joe's _____ costs nothing, and it's worth it.

advise, advice ■ I _____ you to take teacher's _____.

advise ■ My friends _____ me to forget my lost sweetheart. Be-

advise, advice lieve me, it's easier to _____ than to take _____.

Advice, advise ■ _____ rhymes with "ice"; _____ rhymes with "eyes."

---

7. **affect** (ə-fect′): *Verb*—to produce a change; to influence. "The damp air may *affect* Joe's lungs."

8. **effect** (i-fect′): *Noun*—result. "Physicists study cause and *effect.*" *Verb*—to cause or bring about. "Dad tried to *effect* a change in my study habits."

affect ■ Marriage will _____ Tony's career. [Verb: means "to influence."]

effect ■ Marriage will have an excellent _____ on Tony. [Noun: means "result."]

effect ■ Marriage will _____ an improvement in Tony's habits. [Verb: means "to bring about."]

affect ■ The concussion did not _____ my academic grades, which were low anyhow, and seemed to have no lasting

effect _____.

effect ■ Baseball representatives can probably _____ a compro-

effect mise, but they must consider the _____ on the box office.

effect ■ Drugs had a tragic _____; his hallucinations

affect still _____ him day and night.

---

Write the letter that indicates the best definition.

| | |
|---|---|
| ( ) 1. advise | a. to receive something offered |
| ( ) 2. except | b. a result |
| ( ) 3. adopt | c. to recommend; to give opinion |
| ( ) 4. accept | d. to take into one's family |
| ( ) 5. effect (*n.*) | e. all but |
| ( ) 6. advice | f. to produce a change; influence |
| ( ) 7. adapt | g. an opinion or recommendation |
| ( ) 8. affect | h. to adjust to a new use |

1. (c)
2. (e)
3. (d)
4. (a)
5. (b)
6. (g)
7. (h)
8. (f)

---

9. **allusion:** a casual reference. "Flaky resented my *allusion* to his driving record."

10. **illusion:** a misleading image; a misconception; delusion. "The hundred-dollar bill was an optical *illusion*."

■ I crawled across the hot sand, and horrors! The lake was an _____ .

*illusion*

■ When I made an _____ to a ghost I had seen, Tom turned pale. "I've seen it, too," he said. "Then it's not an _____ . That's the spirit!"

*allusion*

*illusion*

■ Louie had the _____ that he'd get better grades if he dropped a casual _____ now and then to Bill Shakespeare or Hank Longfellow.

*illusion*

*allusion*

■ The bully made a nasty _____ to my maternal ancestry, and I, unfortunately, was under the _____ that I could knock him down.

*allusion*

*illusion*

---

11. **amount:** quantity; mass.

12. **number:** refers to countable objects. "Joe ate a huge *amount* of ice cream and a small *number* [not *amount*] of doughnuts."

Write *amount* or *number*.

■ Sheila collected an unusual _____ of mosquito bites.

*number*

■ The mugger separated me from a large _____ of credit cards and a small _____ of cash.

*number*

*amount*

number

■ The sink had no drainpipe, so I washed a great _____ of dishes and my feet at the same time.

number

amount

■ St. Patrick chased a vast _____ of snakes out of Ireland, but they return to those who drink a certain _____ of whiskey.

---

**13. brake:** a device for stopping a vehicle. "Step on the *brake*."

**14. break:** to shatter. "*Break* the glass."

brake

■ All my car needs is *br*_____ pads and a new motor.

brake, break

■ Hit the _____, or we'll _____ our necks!

break

■ "Waiter," I asked, "did this chicken _____ its leg?" "You wanna eat it, mister, or dance with it?"

brake

break

■ The emergency _____ stopped us in time. Now let's drive so that we don't _____ the law.

break

■ The drug addict couldn't _____ his dangerous habit.

---

### Quiz

Write the letter that indicates the best definition.

1. (d)
2. (a)
3. (e)
4. (f)
5. (c)
6. (b)

( ) 1. illusion     a. countable objects (ex., eggs)
( ) 2. number     b. to crack into pieces
( ) 3. brake     c. a reference to something
( ) 4. amount     d. a mistaken impression
( ) 5. allusion     e. a car-stopper
( ) 6. break     f. quantity (ex., dirt)

---

**15. capital:** *Adjective*—excellent; written with large letters; involving execution. "She is against *capital* punishment." *Noun*—accumulated assets; a city which is the seat of government. "The *capital* of Alabama is Montgomery."

**16. capitol:** the statehouse; the building where legislators meet. "The governor stood on the steps of the *capitol*."

capital, capital

■ A backer of *cap*_____ punishment says he has a _____ idea: "Suspend the criminal instead of the sentence."

| | |
|---|---|
| capitol | ■ Rain leaked through the roof of the _____ and soaked a senator making a dry speech. |
| capitol | ■ "We can repair the dome of this _____," said the |
| capital | senator, "but that will take _____." |
| capital | ■ Printed in _____ letters above the main entrance |
| capitol | to the _____ was the word LEGISLATURE. |

---

17. **complement:** *Noun*—that which completes a thing; the counterpart. "Her white shoes serve as a *complement* to her black dress." *Verb*—to complete. "Her shoes *complement* her dress."

18. **compliment:** *Noun*—words of praise. "Thanks for the *compliment*." *Verb*—to praise. "Such a dessert! Let me *compliment* the chef."

| | |
|---|---|
| complement | ■ Gardens *comp* _____ the tidy English cottages. |
| compliment | ■ "You have brains, Gwendolyn, and that's not an idle _____," |
| complement | said Mother. "You'll be the perfect _____ to Sir Percy, who is a shmoe." |
| complement | ■ "Here's a rosy apple, teacher, to _____ your |
| compliment | cheeks."—"What a sweet _____, Archy! I hope you |
| complement | can earn an *A* today to _____ that *F* you got yesterday." |
| compliment | ■ Like perfume, a _____ should be inhaled, not swallowed. |

---

19. **continually:** often repeated; again and again. "Football players are *continually* breaking arms and legs."

20. **continuously:** without stopping. "The chairman spoke *continuously* for ninety minutes and never grazed a fresh idea."

| | |
|---|---|
| continually | ■ George Bernard Shaw quoted himself *con*_____, claiming, "It adds spice to my conversation." |
| continually | ■ Blizzards strike Montana *con*_____, and one storm |
| continuously | raged *con*_____ for three days. |
| continuously | ■ A mountain road winds _____ from Crestville to |
| continually | Helengone, and accidents occur on it _____. |

continually

continuously

■ Louie the Loafer is _____ fired from his jobs, and he has never held one job _____ for six months.

---

**21. decent:** proper and fitting. "Joe had a *decent* burial."

**22. descent:** a coming down; ancestry. "A man of Irish *descent* made a *descent* into the cellar."

descent

■ The elevator's rapid *de*_____ made my stomach hit my tonsils.

decent

■ Mary thinks I'm not making a _____ salary as a custodian, but I'm cleaning up.

descent

decent

■ The parachute slowed Edna's _____, and she made a fairly _____ landing in an elm tree.

descent

decent

■ Hugo is of Austrian _____, and he bakes a very _____ apple strudel.

---

### Quiz

Write the letter that indicates the best definition.

( ) 1. continually     a. in good taste; respectable
( ) 2. descent         b. assets; involving execution
( ) 3. complement      c. words of praise
( ) 4. capital         d. without stopping
( ) 5. continuously    e. the statehouse
( ) 6. decent          f. a going down; ancestry
( ) 7. compliment      g. the counterpart; that which completes
( ) 8. capitol         h. repeatedly; again and again

---

**23. desert:** *Noun* (dez'ərt)—a dry wasteland. *Verb* (dizûrt')—to abandon one's post or duty. "She's rich. He won't *desert* her."

**24. dessert:** a delicacy served at the end of a meal.

desert

dessert

■ "Only a rat would *des*_____," said our sergeant, as he cut a slab of apple pie for _____. "Pass me the cheese."

desert

dessert

■ Crossing the sandy _____, we had dates for _____.

desert

■ I'll never _____ my ship," said the brave captain, "glub . . . glub . . . ."

dessert

■ What has a double portion of *s*'s and calories? _____ .

---

**25. disinterested:** impartial; not biased. "A jury should be made up of *disinterested* citizens."

**26. uninterested:** not interested. "Grandma was *uninterested* in the soccer game."

uninterested

■ I tried to explain calculus to the baby, but she seemed _____ .

disinterested

■ We prefer an honest referee if such exists—a truly _____ fellow.

uninterested

■ I don't blame you if you're _____, but please don't yawn in my face.

fair-minded

■ A disinterested judge is _____ [excitable / fair minded];

bored

an uninterested judge is probably _____ [bored / alert].

---

**27. dual:** *Adjective*—double; twofold.

**28. duel:** *Noun*—a combat between two antagonists.

duel

■ Macbeth and Macduff have a *du*_____ to the death.

dual

■ In a warplane with _____ wings, the Red Baron won

duel

many a fiery _____ .

dual

■ Dmitri has a _____ personality. You never know

duel

whether he's going to embrace you or _____ with you.

duel

■ When challenged to a _____, Mark Twain told

duel

the gunslinger, "How about a _____ with water pistols at sixty paces?"

dual

■ With _____ exhaust pipes you can pollute the air twice as fast.

---

Write the letter that indicates the best definition.

1. (e)
2. (c)
3. (d)
4. (f)
5. (a)
6. (b)

(    ) 1. uninterested     a. not prejudiced
(    ) 2. duel     b. pie, ice cream, etc.
(    ) 3. desert (*n.*)     c. a fight between two rivals
(    ) 4. dual     d. a dry, sandy region
(    ) 5. disinterested     e. bored
(    ) 6. dessert     f. double

---

**29. every body:** each separate body. "*Every body* had bruises on it."
**30. everybody:** every person. "*Everybody* is welcome."

every body

■ The surgeon examined *ev*_____ as it was carried in.

Everybody

■ *Ev*_____ who is a nonreader is a threat to civilization.

everybody

■ At ballet school *ev*_____ exercises daily, and

every body

*ev*_____ is attractive in its proportions.

everybody

■ The butchers killed the pigs, and then _____ got

every body

busy cutting _____ into ham, bacon, and knuckles.

(b)

■ *Everybody, anybody, and somebody* refer to (a) bodies, (b) persons. (    )

(a)

■ *Every body, any body,* and *some body* refer to (a) bodies, (b) persons. (    )

---

**31. foreword:** a preface; introductory note.
**32. forward:** onward; toward what lies ahead.

forward

■ Our nation will go *for*_____, according to the author

foreword

in his *for*_____ .

forward

■ Volunteers, please step *for*_____ .

foreword

■ Read the _____ of a technical book before plunging

forward

_____ into the chapters ahead.

forward

■ My mule is backward about going _____ .

forward

■ All _____ motion isn't progress, if your brakes don't work.

foreword

■ The introduction or "before" word of a book is known as the _____ .

---

**33. imply** (im-plī′): to hint at; to suggest without stating; to signify.

**34. infer** (in-fûr′): to draw a conclusion.

imply

infer

■ These bloodstains *im*_____ that the victim may have been knifed. What do you *in*_____ ?

imply

■ Her high grades *i*_____ unusual intelligence.

infer

imply

■ From various evidence I *i*_____ that the baseball fans no longer admire Lefty Smeeby. Their jeers *i*_____ that they have lost confidence in him.

imply, infer

■ Melvin's smiles _____ success. We can _____ that Betty has accepted his marriage proposal.

inferred

■ Hot tar was spilled at the intersection, from which the police _____*ed* that there was dirty work at the crossroads.

---

**35. instance:** an example. "She recalled an *instance* of wifebeating in the bridal suite."

**36. instants:** moments. "Tragedy struck within *instants.*"

instance

■ The playboy cited an *inst*_____ of a New Year's party that broke up in March.

instants

■ The three sprinters hit the tape within *inst*_____ of each other.

instance

instants

■ I was worried, for *in*_____, when the old plane shook for several *in*_____ and a voice said: "This is your pilot, Orville Wright."

instance

■ Using my toothbrush to clean his typewriter keys was another _____ of poor manners.

instants

■ The lights turned green, and _____ later the horns were honking up a storm.

---

**Quiz**

Write the letter that indicates the best definition.

1. (e)
2. (g)
3. (h)
4. (c)
5. (f)
6. (a)
7. (d)
8. (b)

( ) 1. instance    a. moments
( ) 2. forward    b. each person
( ) 3. imply    c. a preface to a book
( ) 4. foreword    d. to judge from evidence; conclude
( ) 5. every body    e. an example; case
( ) 6. instants    f. each of the bodies
( ) 7. infer    g. toward what is ahead
( ) 8. everybody    h. to hint or suggest

---

**37. its** (possessive): "The basset hound stepped on *its* ear."

**38. it's** (contraction): it is. "Frankly, *it's* a hot dog."

it's

its

■ Surely *it*_____ no fun for a rabbit to be held by *it*_____ ears. (Hint: Write *it's* only if "it is" can be substituted for it.)

it's

its

■ As for this camel, *i*_____ a poor specimen; it has bumps on *i*_____ back.

its, its

■ I wanted to be a lion tamer, but when the circus lion bared _____ fangs and _____ claws, I decided to become a clown.

its

its

■ This lake is perfect, except that _____ fish are tiny and _____ mosquitoes are big as eagles.

it's

it's

■ Truly _____ lucky to own a shiny penny—if _____ wrapped in fifty-dollar bills.

it's

its

■ "If _____ true that the cow jumped over the moon," Junior asked teacher, "how did it get _____ thrust?"

---

**39. ladder:** a device with steps for climbing. "Climb a *ladder* and get up in the world."

**40. later:** afterwards; more late. "He returned *later*."

**41. latter:** the last mentioned. "Stephen Douglas or Abe Lincoln? Mary Todd married the *latter*."

later  ■ It's *lat*_____ than you think.

ladder

latter, ladder  ■ Moe held the *la*_____ for Curly and Jack, and the

later  *la*_____ fell off the *la*_____ a

minute *la*_____ .

ladder, latter  ■ On his deathbed my grandfather bargained with Sid and Max and

sold his old *la*_____ to the *la*_____ .

latter  ■ We're out of dates and figs, but we'll have the _____

later  a little _____ .

later  ■ An hour _____ I knocked the paint bucket off

ladder  my _____ onto the new Persian rug. Mr. and Mrs.

latter  Schultz seemed quite unhappy, especially the _____ .

---

**42. leave:** to depart. "We will *leave* at dawn."

**43. let:** to allow. "Please *let* us help."

let  ■ Society must *le*_____ women develop to their full
potential.

leave, let  ■ Before we *le*_____ , *le*_____ us come
to an understanding.

let  ■ The hostess will _____ you kiss her when

leave  you _____ .

let, leave  ■ The pacifist would not _____ his son _____
for the front.

---

**Quiz**

Write the letter that indicates the best definition.

| | | |
|---|---|---|
| 1. (e) | (    ) 1. let | a. the last one mentioned |
| 2. (f) | (    ) 2. later | b. it is |
| 3. (g) | (    ) 3. leave | c. a climbing device |
| 4. (d) | (    ) 4. its | d. belonging to it |
| 5. (c) | (    ) 5. ladder | e. to permit; allow |
| 6. (a) | (    ) 6. latter | f. afterward |
| 7. (b) | (    ) 7. it's | g. to go away |

**REVIEW TEST**

Write in full the word that is indicated in brackets.

_____ 1. My new diet allows me one prune for [des-rt].

_____ 2. Buffalo Bill killed the herd and let [ev-body] rot.

_____ 3. He warned me [contin-ly] not to play Ping-Pong with my mouth open.

_____ 4. Drugs have a bad [-fect] on brains, if you have any.

_____ 5. I [adv-e] against selling jewelry on credit to hoboes.

_____ 6. "Pay up," snarled Flem, "or we [br-k] your fingers."

_____ 7. The yodeler was of Swiss [d-c-nt].

_____ 8. Two little scholars fought a [du-l] with spitballs.

_____ 9. I read the book from [for-rd] to index.

_____ 10. A [compl-m-nt] a day keeps divorce away.

_____ 11. Spend the interest, but don't touch the [cap-t-l].

_____ 12. The orphanage was sure nobody would [ad-pt] me.

_____ 13. Ben wanted to play chess, but Fifi was [-interested].

_____ 14. Life is an elevator. It has [it-] ups and downs.

_____ 15. Would sudden wealth [-fect] me? I'll never find out.

_____ 16. The grateful native offered me his pet boa constrictor, but I didn't [-cept] it.

_____ 17. Free [advi-e] is often worth what you pay for it.

_____ 18. Presidents have walked the floors of our [cap-t-l].

_____ 19. Slavery was an [instan-] of low minimum wages.

_____ 20. Felicia made an [-lusion] to her Mayflower ancestor.

---

Write the correct word in full.

_____ 21. Don't [leave / let] Junior play with those razors.

_____ 22. Medical tests [imply / infer] that I may last until Sunday.

_____ 23. Fay got rid of 279 ugly pounds—[its / it's] her husband.

_____ 24. Our hen had an optical [illusion /allusion] and sat on a snowball.

_____ 25. I ate a large [amount / number] of watermelon slices and my ears got washed.

---

**Words Often Confused I     37**

## Key to Review Test

Check your test answers with the following key. Deduct 4% per error from a possible 100%.

| | | |
|---|---|---|
| 1. dessert | 10. compliment | 19. instance |
| 2. every body | 11. capital | 20. allusion |
| 3. continually | 12. adopt | 21. let |
| 4. effect | 13. uninterested | 22. imply |
| 5. advise | 14. its | 23. it's |
| 6. break | 15. affect | 24. illusion |
| 7. descent | 16. accept | 25. number |
| 8. duel | 17. advice | |
| 9. foreword | 18. capitol | |

Score: _____ %

# 4

# Words Often Confused II

| | | |
|---|---|---|
| *loose,* **1** | *past,* **16** | *than,* **31** |
| *lose,* **2** | *personal,* **17** | *their,* **33** |
| *marital,* **3** | *personnel,* **18** | *then,* **32** |
| *martial,* **4** | *plain,* **19** | *there,* **34** |
| *medal,* **5** | *plane,* **20** | *they're,* **35** |
| *metal,* **6** | *principal,* **21** | *weak,* **36** |
| *miner,* **7** | *principle,* **22** | *weather,* **38** |
| *minor,* **8** | *quiet,* **23** | *week,* **37** |
| *moral,* **9** | *quite,* **24** | *whether,* **39** |
| *morale,* **10** | *shone,* **25** | *who's,* **40** |
| *nauseated,* **11** | *shown,* **26** | *whose,* **41** |
| *nauseous,* **12** | *stake,* **27** | *your,* **42** |
| *naval,* **13** | *stationary,* **29** | *you're,* **43** |
| *navel,* **14** | *stationery,* **30** | |
| *passed,* **15** | *steak,* **28** | |

*Continue as in the previous chapter. Study the homonyms at the top of each frame.* They're
there *to be studied, not admired, so notice* their *differences.*

*As always, be sure to cover the answers in the left-hand column until you have completed
the frame. (If you* peek *before you write, you won't reach the* peak *of your potential.)*

COVER THIS STRIP

_____

**1. loose** (rhymes with *goose*):  not tight; unfastened.

**2. lose:**  to suffer a loss.

loose, lose

■ The goose is *lo* _____ ! We must not *lo* _____ it.

loose

lose

■ In time of war a *lo* _____ tongue can cause us to *lo* _____ a troopship.

lose, loose

■ When I _____ weight, my pants hang _____ .

lose

■ Not only did I _____ the fight, but I may

lose, loose

also _____ this _____ tooth.

loose

■ The word *goose* rhymes with the word *l* _____ .

_____

**3. marital:**  pertaining to marriage.

**4. martial:**  pertaining to war.

marital

■ "Thanks to my husband for three years of *mar* _____ bliss," said Mrs. Roe on her golden anniversary.

martial

■ Will nations abolish *mar* _____ conflict or will

martial

*mar* _____ conflict abolish nations?

marital

■ Love one another, if you want _____ happiness.

marital

■ Wagner's "Wedding March" is _____ music;

martial

"Marine's Hymn" is _____ music.

_____

**5. medal:**  a decorative award for a distinguished act.

**6. metal:**  a substance such as silver, tin, or steel.

medal

■ Goering wore many a *me* _____ on his uniform and probably on his pajamas.

metal

■ Gold is a precious *me* _____ , and Olympic win-

medal

ners are awarded a gold *me* _____ . Those in second

medal

place are awarded a silver *me* _____ .

metal

■ Ben's mouth, with its _____ fillings, looks like mother lode country.

medal

metal

■ I was to receive a _____ for being Most Careful Driver, but on the way I hit a _____ post.

---

7. **miner:** somebody who works in a mine.

8. **minor:** somebody who is below legal age; of lesser importance.

miner

■ "Gold! I found gold!" whispered the dying *min*_____.

miner, minor

■ The old *mi*_____ sang in a *mi*_____ key about a goat.

minor

minor

■ A draftee complains, "As a _____ I can die for my country, yet as a _____ I cannot vote."

miner

minor

■ At the end of a hard day a coal _____ does not look like Snow White. However, that to him is of _____ importance.

---

## Quiz

Write the letter that indicates the best definition.

1. (c)
2. (f)
3. (e)
4. (g)
5. (b)
6. (h)
7. (a)
8. (d)

( ) 1. minor          a. iron, tin, etc.
( ) 2. medal          b. untied; not bound together
( ) 3. martial        c. a youth; less important
( ) 4. miner          d. to suffer a loss
( ) 5. loose          e. concerning war
( ) 6. marital        f. a decoration, as for heroism
( ) 7. metal          g. a mine worker
( ) 8. lose           h. concerning marriage

---

9. **moral** (mor'əl): *Adjective*—virtuous; of good character, as in "a *moral,* law-abiding family"; virtual—"a *moral* victory." *Noun*—the lesson in a story.

10. **morale** (mər-al'): *Noun*—state of mind as to confidence and enthusiasm.

morale

■ After ten losses our team was low in *mor*_____, and

moral

this tie was like a *mor*_____ victory.

| | |
|---|---|
| moral | ■ Some people are *mo* _____ only because they've never been tempted. |
| moral | ■ A pox on any film of violence whose only _____ is "Shoot first!" |
| morale | ■ Malaria can damage one's _____ . |
| morale | ■ High _____ is desirable, but to succeed you also |
| moral | need talent, skills, and _____ character. |

---

**11. nauseated:** sickened; disgusted; ill at the stomach. "Those unhappy people at the ship rail are *nauseated.*"

**12. nauseous:** sickening; disgusting; causing to vomit. "The over-ripe fruit was rotting and *nauseous.*"

| | |
|---|---|
| nauseous | ■ Disgusting things are *nau* _____ . People sickened |
| nauseated | by such things are *nau* _____ . |
| nauseated | ■ Several strikers were *na* _____ when struck by a |
| nauseous | stinkbomb with an extremely *na* _____ odor. |
| nauseous | ■ The contaminated salmon at "Hepatitis Hotel" was _____ , |
| nauseated | and several members of the wedding party were _____ . |
| nauseated | ■ Norma was _____ to see the baby seals clubbed to |
| nauseous | death. "What a _____ sight!" she moaned. |

---

**13. naval:** pertaining to a navy.

**14. navel:** umbilicus; "belly button."

| | |
|---|---|
| naval | ■ In 1588 England won a great *nav* _____ victory. |
| naval | ■ One sailor on the *na* _____ vessel was stripped to |
| navel | the waist and scratching his *na* _____ . |
| navel | ■ An orange that has a scar on it like a human _____ |
| navel | is called a _____ orange. |
| naval | ■ After a lengthy parade honoring our _____ fleet, |
| navel | one flagbearer complained of an enlarged _____ . |

---

**15. passed:** went by (verb, past tense of *pass*). "The gassy truck *passed* the joggers."

**16. past:** beyond; earlier; an earlier period. (*Past* is not a verb.) "During the *past* minute, six gassy trucks have gone *past* the joggers."

Write *passed* or *past*.

passed

■ Tony *pa*_____ the tavern. (Here Tony is the subject of a missing verb, and the verb ends in *ed*.)

past

■ Tony walked *pa*_____ the tavern. (Here Tony is the subject of the verb *walked,* and the missing word is not a verb.)

past

passed

■ Some years in the *p*_____ Tom wanted to be a barber. He took a licensing test and *p*_____ by a hair.

past

passed

passed

■ The bullet screamed _____ my ear, and I heard it twice; first, when it _____ me, and then when I _____ it.

past

passed

■ At half-_____ ten Mary bid six spades, and I _____ .

---

## Quiz

Circle the choice that results in the more acceptable sentence.

1. nauseated

2. past
   morale

3. moral

4. navel

1. Sue ate too much health food and became [nauseous / nauseated].
2. Every boy [past / passed] five is told he'll be president, and the threat is bad for his [moral / morale].
3. Except for the orgies, they were [moral / morale] citizens.
4. At the deli a caraway seed got lodged in Art's [naval / navel].

---

**17. personal:** *Adjective*—private. "It's a *personal* problem."

**18. personnel** (accent on *nel*): the people employed in a business. "Miss Boe is in charge of *personnel*."

personnel

personal

■ Any business can succeed if the *per*_____ take a *per*_____ interest in their work.

| | |
|---|---|
| personal | ■ I made a p_____ application for a job at the mortu- |
| personnel | ary, but the p_____ manager said business was dead. |
| personal | ■ My _____ opinion is that when the head |
| personnel, personal | of _____ calls me a nerd, he's getting too _____. |
| personnel | ■ Our office _____ have gear trouble: They talk in |
| | high and think in low. |

**19. plain:** *Adjective*—clear; common looking. *Noun*—a prairie.

**20. plane:** *Noun*—an airplane; a flat, two-dimensional surface.

| | |
|---|---|
| plain | ■ We need pla_____ talk between nations, not |
| plane | a pl_____ loaded with bombs. |
| plain | ■ The rain in Spain fell on the grassy pl_____. |
| plane | ■ Our baby, Wayne, born on a speeding _____, |
| plain | looks rather _____, but we can't complain. |
| plane, plain | ■ Gus studied _____ geometry, and the _____ |
| | fact is that he didn't like it. |
| plain | ■ Abraham Lincoln was a _____ man and he |
| plain | used _____ words. |

**21. principal:** main; head of a school; chief actor or doer; a capital sum. "'Spend the interest and save the *principal*'—that was the *principal* lesson that the school *principal* taught us."

**22. principle:** a rule of action or conduct. (Note that *principle* and *rule* both end in *le*.) "Isaac Newton worked out the *principle* of gravitation."

| | |
|---|---|
| principle | ■ The professor explained a basic *prin*_____ of |
| | thermodynamics. (Refers to a *rule*.) |
| principal | ■ The *prin*_____ cause of divorce is marriage. |
| principal, principal | ■ The high school *pr*_____ played the *pr*_____ |
| | role in the faculty comedy. |

principle

principal

principal

principle

■ Jane Pittman was a woman of lofty _____, and that is a _____ reason we honor her.

■ My _____ objection is to speech courses that stress the questionable _____, "Say it with sincerity, whether you believe it or not."

---

**23. quiet** (kwī′-ət): silent; silence.
**24. quite** (kwīt): really; entirely.

quiet, quite

■ To be *qui*_____ is often *qu*_____ as important as to talk.

quite

quiet

■ Since Albert broke his stereo, our house is *q*_____ *q*_____.

quiet

■ The baby is _____. Go see what's the matter.

quite

quiet

■ Slim told _____ a few jokes, but we stifled our laughs and remained _____.

---

### Quiz

Write the letter that indicates the best definition.

1. (f)
2. (g)
3. (e)
4. (a)
5. (c)
6. (d)
7. (b)
8. (h)

(   ) 1. principal     a. silent
(   ) 2. plane     b. private
(   ) 3. personnel     c. a prairie; ordinary looking
(   ) 4. quiet     d. a rule of conduct
(   ) 5. plain     e. a staff of employees
(   ) 6. principle     f. the head of a high school
(   ) 7. personal     g. an aircraft
(   ) 8. quite     h. really; entirely

---

**25. shone** (past tense of *shine*): "The sun *shone*."
**26. shown** is related to *show*. "I was *shown* the fish."

shone

■ The moon *sho*_____ at night, according to Abner, when we needed it most.

shown

■ She smoked too much. I was *sho*_____ her new-born baby, and it had yellow fingernails.

shone

shown

■ The pirate's eyes *sho*_____ when he was

*sho*_____ the treasure chest.

shown

■ Such a doctor! Break an ankle and you'll be _____
how to limp.

shown

shone, shown

■ The customer was _____ twelve pairs of shoes, but

suddenly his face _____ when he was _____
the yellow oxfords.

shone

■ The candle _____ like a good deed in a naughty world.

27. **stake:** a stick or post; something wagered or risked.
28. **steak:** a slice of meat or fish.

stake

■ Joan of Arc was burned at the *st*_____ .

stake

■ We have a *st*_____ in the future of our nation.

steak

■ Grandpa ate a fat, oily *s*_____ , and he doesn't squeak
any more.

stake

stake

■ The prospector drove a _____ into the ground

to _____ his claim.

steak

steak

■ I used to order a _____ rare. Now I order

a _____ rarely.

stake

steak

■ "I'll _____ a dollar," muttered the waitress, "that

this health nut orders the halibut _____ ."

29. **stationary:** not moving.
30. **stationery:** writing paper.

stationery

■ At Christmas I got six boxes of *sta*_____ .

stationery

stationary

■ Stanley buys *st*_____ ; then he sits

*st*_____ in front of his typewriter.

stationery

■ The word "paper" has an *er* in it, and so does the word

_____ .

stationary

■ Is that hydrant really _____ , or did it move out and hit my fender?

stationery

■ On official _____ Clarence confessed: "If an irre-

stationary

sistible force hits a _____ object, I'm probably the driver."

---

**31. than** (used in comparisons). "Fido bites harder *than* Rover."

**32. then:** at that time. "We were younger and thinner *then*."

then

■ Now and *th*_____ Junior loses a tooth.

than

■ The wrestler's nose was flatter *th*_____ a bicycle seat.

then

■ Our government operated on a smaller budget _____

than

_____ now.

then

■ The shepherd saw her sweater and _____ realized

than

that the wool looked better on the girl _____ on the sheep.

than

■ The word _____ suggests a comparison; the

then

word _____ suggests time.

---

### Quiz

Write the letter that indicates the best definition.

1. (f)
2. (c)
3. (e)
4. (g)
5. (b)
6. (h)
7. (a)
8. (d)

(    ) 1. stationery    a. at that time
(    ) 2. shown    b. compared with
(    ) 3. steak    c. displayed; exhibited
(    ) 4. shone    d. writing paper
(    ) 5. than    e. a slice of meat
(    ) 6. stake    f. not moving
(    ) 7. then    g. was shining
(    ) 8. stationary    h. a post; something wagered

---

**33. their** (possessive). "*Their* dog has fleas."

**34. there:** in that place. "Sit *there* and wait."

**35. they're:** they are. "*They're* sleeping."

their

■ The dentist will have to straighten *th*_____ teeth,

they're

because *th*_____ not going to straighten themselves.

there

their

they're, their

there

they're

their

■ Soon the three wise men arrived *th* _____

on *th* _____ camels.

■ The old folks say _____ happy in _____ merry Oldsmobile.

■ The salesmen over _____ are live wires. A widow wants a burial suit for her husband, and _____

selling her _____ best silk suit with two pairs of pants.

---

**36. weak:** lacking in strength; feeble.

**37. week:** a seven-day period.

week, weak

■ After a *we* _____ of fasting, I was as *we* _____ as a baby.

week

■ "God created man at the end of the *we* _____," says Mark Twain, "when God was tired."

weak

week

■ The strong have oppressed the _____, not just for a day or a _____ but for centuries.

weak

■ "Don't sneer at our coffee," said the waiter. "You, too, will be old and _____ some day."

---

**38. weather:** *Noun*—atmospheric conditions. "Stormy *weather!*" *Verb*—to wear away; to survive.

**39. whether:** if. "He'll decide *whether* to operate."

weather, whether

■ We predict the *w* _____, but I doubt *w* _____ we can control it.

weather

■ Fred has a thirty percent chance of becoming a *w* _____ forecaster.

whether

■ Worries, worries! Rich people must decide _____ to drive the Rolls or the Cadillac.

weather, whether

■ You'll love Dakota's winter _____, _____ you prefer twenty below or forty below.

whether, weather   ■ I doubt _____ we could _____ the

weather    rigors of Klondike _____ .

---

**40. who's:** who is. "*Who's* calling, please?"
**41. whose** (possessive). "*Whose* shoes are these?"

whose    ■ Find out *wh*_____ car was smashed and

who's    *wh*_____ to blame. (Hint: Write *who's* only if "who is" would be correct in the blank.)

whose    ■ The aged alumni, *wh*_____ class reunion this is, are

who's    getting together to see *wh*_____ falling apart.

who's    ■ Mr. Bigmouth wants to know _____ marry-

whose    ing _____ daughter.

who's    ■ A girl _____ fit as a fiddle should have a beau.

who's    ■ "I'd like to catch the actor _____ careless,"

whose    said Hamlet, "and _____ spear keeps jabbing me in the third act."

whose    ■ The word _____ is possessive; the word

who's    _____ means "who is."

---

**42. your** (possessive). "Put on *your* gas mask."
**43. you're:** you are. "*You're* beautiful."

your, you're    ■ Hold *yo*_____ horses—*yo*_____ traveling too fast.

you're    ■ Until April 15 *yo*_____ deep in the heart of taxes.

your    ■ Wilhelm,_____ poems are so sweet

you're, your    that _____ making _____ readers throw up.

you're    ■ When _____ famous, the public takes an in-

your    terest in _____ sins.

you're, your    ■ If *y*_____ going to break *y*_____

your    leg on *y*_____ motorcycle, don't come running to me.

you're

your

your

■ "Listen," said Barnum to Tom Thumb, "_____

so little that you have to stand on _____ chair

to brush _____ teeth."

---

## Quiz

Circle the choice that results in the more acceptable sentence.

1. who's
2. you're
3. there
4. weak
5. weather

1. Sam sang, "I wonder [whose / who's] kissing her now."
2. Read constantly, or [you're / your] wasting time in college.
3. All my friends were [there / their / they're]—both of them.
4. After seven days without water, I was [weak / week].
5. Twenty below zero—that was our warmest [weather / whether].

---

## REVIEW TEST

Write in full the word that is indicated in brackets.

_____  1. Sheila is prettier [th-n] a tax refund.

_____  2. The homesick soldier sniffed the perfumed [stat-n-ry].

_____  3. Ulysses came back when twenty years had [pas-].

_____  4. Hamlet debated [w-th-r] to be or not to be alive.

_____  5. John Paul Jones won a [na-l] victory.

_____  6. An arrow whistled [past / passed] General Custer.

_____  7. Luke sang in [min-r] key of his untrue lover.

_____  8. Art started at the bottom and stayed [th-r-].

_____  9. The baby is [qui-]. Go see if he is sick.

_____ 10. Find out [who-] toupee fell from the balcony.

_____ 11. Now that I can afford a T-bone [st-], I have no teeth.

_____ 12. To buy on credit is a dangerous [princ-p-].

_____ 13. A gangster's bullet hit Nick in the [nav-l].

_____ 14. A [l-se] tooth is driving me to extraction.

_____ 15. To ask your hostess her age is a bit [pers-n-l].

_____ 16. After a [we-k] my sweatsuit stood up by itself.

_____ 17. Getting fired didn't help my [mo-r-l].

_____ 18. At a gory movie, I feel [nause-].

Write the correct word in full.

_____ 19. Their [marital / martial] life was happy until they left the altar.

_____ 20. The solar-powered cars moved when the sun [shone / shown].

_____ 21. The Martians landed and [there / their / they're] leader saluted a gas pump.

_____ 22. The tavern won't sell liquor to a [miner / minor].

_____ 23. If the chute won't open, say [your / you're] prayers.

_____ 24. In a laziness contest, Ken wins the gold [medal / metal].

_____ 25. Jim's books come in a [plain / plane] wrapper.

**Words Often Confused II**    51

## Key to Review Test

Check your test answers with the following key. Deduct 4% per error from a possible 100%.

| | | |
|---|---|---|
| 1. than | 10. whose | 19. marital |
| 2. stationery | 11. steak | 20. shone |
| 3. passed | 12. principle | 21. their |
| 4. whether | 13. navel | 22. minor |
| 5. naval | 14. loose | 23. your |
| 6. past | 15. personal | 24. medal |
| 7. minor | 16. week | 25. plain |
| 8. there | 17. morale | |
| 9. quiet | 18. nauseated | |

Score: _____ %

## SUPPLEMENTARY LIST

*Class Exercise:* Divide into panel groups. Each group will be responsible for discussing and clarifying a segment of the following list for the benefit of the rest of the class.

| | | | |
|---|---|---|---|
| 1. addition, edition | 18. cereal, serial | 31. envelop, envelope | 48. pail, pale |
| 2. aisle, isle | 19. chord, cord | 32. fair, fare | 49. peace, piece |
| 3. alley, ally | 20. coarse, course | 33. flea, flee | 50. picture, pitcher |
| 4. allowed, aloud | 21. council, counsel | 34. flour, flower | 51. pole, poll |
| 5. altar, alter | 22. costume, custom | 35. forth, fourth | 52. pore, pour |
| 6. anecdote, antidote | 23. dairy, diary | 36. foul, fowl | 53. profit, prophet |
| 7. angel, angle | 24. dammed, damned | 37. heal, heel | 54. prophecy, prophesy |
| 8. ascent, assent | 25. dear, deer | 38. hear, here | 55. respectfully, respectively |
| 9. bare, bear | 26. deceased, diseased | 39. hoarse, horse | 56. ring, wring |
| 10. base, bass | 27. device, devise | 40. hole, whole | 57. sail, sale |
| 11. beach, beech | 28. disinterested, uninterested | 41. holey, holy | 58. steal, steel |
| 12. beat, beet | 29. dyeing, dying | 42. incidence, incidents | 59. summary, summery |
| 13. berth, birth | 30. emigrate, immigrate | 43. knew, new | 60. threw, through |
| 14. board, bored | | 44. lessen, lesson | |
| 15. boarder, border | | 45. liable, libel | |
| 16. bridal, bridle | | 46. mantel, mantle | |
| 17. censor, censure | | 47. meat, meet | |

# 5

# Latin Derivatives I

---

ROOTS

---

1. *am, amat*
2. *ann, enn*
3. *aqu*
4. *aud, audit*
5. *capit*
6. *cent*
7. *cred, credit*
8. *dic, dict*
9. *duc, duct*

10. *fid*
11. *frater*
12. *greg*
13. *litera*
14. *loc*
15. *loqu, locut*
16. *mal*
17. *man*
18. *mater, matr, metr*

19. *mit, miss*
20. *mor, mort*
21. *mov, mot, mob*
22. *nov*
23. *omni*
24. *ped*
25. *pon, posit*

*Latin derivatives make up at least half of our language. A student without this half of English vocabulary would be like a sprinter with one leg. Luckily you are already familiar with hordes of useful Latin derivatives and by one technique or another you can learn hundreds more. Taking six years of classical Latin is an excellent method, but if that route is inconvenient, you can study common Latin roots and prefixes that have enriched our English language.*

*Chapters 5 and 6 focus on fifty important Latin roots and their clusters of derivatives. Chapter 7 reviews Latin prefixes.*

*First, memorize the Latin term and its definition, given at the beginning of each frame. Next, note carefully the example derivatives that follow in italics. Try to understand the connection between each of these derivatives and its Latin root. Then fill in the blanks.*

## Roots

___

### 1. am, amat: love.

Derivatives: *amateur, amative, amatory, amiable, amity, amorist, amours.*

loving

■ Since *amat* means *love,* an *amative* young man is _____ [hostile / loving].

love

■ An *amateur* golfer plays for _____ [love / the fat fees] of the game.

■ The two letters in the words *amorist* and *amatory* that suggest *love*

*am*

are _____ .

amorist

■ The Casanova devoted to *love*-making is an _____ [atheist / amorist], and he has _____ [amatory / mandatory] adventures.

amatory

amours

■ Cleopatra's *love* affairs are her _____ *rs.*

amity

■ Warm friendship between nations is international _____ [animosity / amity].

amiable

■ Friendly people are _____ [amiable / alienated].

___

### 2. ann, enn: year.

Derivatives: *annals, anniversary, annual, annuity, biennial, centennial, millennium, perennial, superannuated.*

■ The three letters in the words *annals* and *annual* that suggest *year*

*ann*

are _____ .

year

■ *Per annum* means per _____ [month / year].

annuity

■ *Yearly* income from a fund is called an _____ [excise / annuity].

superannuated

■ A man who has lived many *years* is said to be _____ [superannuated / supercilious].

■ In some words, like *biennial*, *centennial*, and *perennial*, the Latin root for *year* is _____ [*ial* / *enn*].

### 3. aqu: water.

Derivatives: *acquacade, aqualung, aquamarine, aquaplane, aqua regia, aquarium, aquatint, aqua vitae, aqueduct, aqueous humor, aquiculture, subaqueous.*

■ To make an *aqueous* solution you dissolve something in _____ [alcohol / water].

■ The three letters in *aqualung* and *aquiculture* that suggest *water* are _____ .

■ An *aquaplane* is towed on _____ [snow / water / rocks].

■ A *water* festival which involves swimming and diving is sometimes called an _____ *cade.*

■ Small fish may be kept in an _____ *ium.*

■ The sign of the zodiac that represents a *water* bearer is _____ [Aquarius / Taurus].

■ The *watery* fluid between the cornea and the lens of the eye is known as _____ [aqueous / amorous] humor.

### 4. aud, audit: hear.

Derivatives: *audible, audience, audile, audio-frequency, audiophile, audio-visual, audiphone, audit, audition, auditor, auditorium, auditory.*

■ You can assume that *auditory* nerves help you to _____ [hear / see], since the five-letter Latin root for *hear* is _____ [*ditor* / *audit*].

■ After a successful critical *hearing,* or _____ *ion,* a singer might entertain an _____ *ce* in an _____ *ium.*

An *audiometer* is an instrument which measures sensitivity of

hearing

_____ [hearing / sight].

hi-fi

An *audiophile* is enthusiastic about _____
[stamps /hi-fi].

Which word has no business being in the following list? *audible,*

adenoids

*audiphone, audio-frequency, adenoids, auditor* _____ .

---

### 5. capit: head.

Derivatives: *cap, capital, capitalism, capitate, capitol, caption, decapitate, per capita, recapitulate.*

head

*Capit* is a root that means *h*_____ ; so the *heading*

caption

of a chapter or an article is called a _____ [decoction / caption].

head

*Capitation* is a tax or fee on each _____ [head / foot].

head

A per *capita* tax is assessed as so much per *h*_____ .

*capit*

The Latin root for *head* is _____ .

capital

In Paris, the _____ *al* of France, King Louis XVI

decapitated

got a sovereign cure for headaches—he was *de*_____ .

recapitulate

Newscasters sometimes *re*_____ the day's news;
such a *recapitulation* literally restates the news (a) in full, (b) by

(b)

headings. ( )

---

### Quiz

Write the meaning of each boldface Latin root.

1. hear
2. head
3. water
4. love
5. year

1. **aud**ience        *h* _____
2. **cap**itol         *h* _____
3. sub**aqu**eous      *w* _____
4. **am**atory         *l* _____
5. a**nn**iversary     *y* _____

**6. cent:** hundred.

Derivatives: *cent, centavo, centenarian, centenary, centennial, centigrade, centigram, centiliter, centime, centimeter, centipede, centuple, centurion, century, tercentennial.*

*cent*

hundred

century

■ The Latin root for *hundred* is *c*_____; thus, a *centenarian* has lived a _____ years, in other words, an entire _____*ury*.

centigrade

■ There are one *hundred* degrees between the freezing and boiling points of water on the _____ [Fahrenheit / centigrade] thermometer.

centimeter

■ One-*hundredth* of a meter is a _____ [centimeter / kilometer].

centigram

■ One-*hundredth* of a gram is a _____.

centiliter

■ One-*hundredth* of a liter is a _____.

centennial

hundred

■ A *centenary,* or _____*ial,* is celebrated after one _____ years.

2076

■ Since **tri** means *three,* the **tri***centennial* of the Declaration of Independence should occur in the year _____ [2076 / 2776]. You are all invited.

---

**7. cred, credit:** believe; trust.

Derivatives: *accredit, credence, credentials, credible, credit, creditable, creditor, credo, credulity, credulous, creed, discredit.*

*cred*

believable

■ Since the Latin root for *believe* is _____ [cred / crud], a *credible* story is _____ [believable / absurd].

(b)

■ Your *creed,* or *credo,* is what you (a) fight, (b) believe in. (    )

believe

■ To give *credence* to a rumor is to _____ [deny / believe] it.

accredited

credentials

■ An *ac*_____ college hires only those teachers who have proper _____*ials.*

believe

■ Your *credulity* is your readiness to _____ [love / believe].

incredulous

■ Sometimes news is so amazing that you are_____ [cretinous/ incredulous].

---

### 8. dic, dict: say.

Derivatives: *addict, benediction, contradict, dictaphone, dictate, diction, dictograph, dictum, edict, indicative, indict, interdict, jurisdiction, malediction, predicate, predict, valedictorian, verdict.*

*dict*

■ The four-letter Latin root of *dictate* and *dictum* is _____

say

and it means *s*_____ .

predict

■ To *say* what will happen, or foretell, is to *pre*_____ .

edict

■ An order issued by an absolute ruler is an _____ [edict/audit].

verdict

■ The judgment of a jury is a *v*_____ .

predicate

■ The part of a sentence which *says* something about the subject is the *pre*_____ .

indicative

■ The mood of a verb that merely states a fact is _____ [subjunctive / indicative].

duck

■ *Dictaphone, contradict, indicate, duck, addict*—which word floated in by mistake? _____

---

### 9. duc, duct: lead.

Derivatives: *abduct, aqueduct, conducive, conduct, deduce, duchess, duct, ductility, duke, educate, educe, Il Duce, induce, introduce, produce, reduce, reproduce, seduction, traduce.*

*duc*, lead

■ To *educate* is literally to "lead out." The three-letter root of *education* is *d*_____ and it means *l*_____ .

Leader

■ Mussolini was called *Il Duce,* which means "The _____*er*."

dukes

■ Europe has had many princely *leaders* known as _____ [schlemiels / dukes], but America's democratic climate is hardly

| | |
|---|---|
| conducive | *con* _____ to the growth of a crop of *dukes* and their |
| duchesses | wives, _____ *es*. |
| aqueduct | ■ Water is sometimes *led* into a city through an *aq* _____ . |
| seducer | ■ An innocent girl may be *led* astray by a _____ [seducer / centuple]. |
| ductility | ■ The ability of a metal to be *led* into various shapes is called _____ [motility / ductility]. |

---

**10. fid:** faith; trust.

Derivatives: *affidavit, confidant, confide, confidence, confidential, diffident, fidelity, fiduciary, infidel, perfidious, perfidy.*

| | |
|---|---|
| faith | ■ To *confide* in a stranger is an act of _____ [leading / faith]. |
| *fid* | ■ The Latin root for *faith* is *f* _____ . |
| unfaithfulness | ■ *Infidelity* means _____ [unfaithfulness / inability to provide]. |
| perfidious | ■ In betraying his *trust*, Benedict Arnold did a _____ [perfervid / perfidious] thing. |
| perfidy | ■ In fact, Benedict Arnold committed an act of _____ [perfidy / persiflage]. |
| confident | ■ A prizefighter who has *faith* in himself is said to be *con* _____ . |
| diffident | ■ A lad who is shy and lacks *faith* in himself is said to be _____ [amative / diffident]. |

---

**Quiz**

Write the meaning of each boldface Latin root.

| | | | |
|---|---|---|---|
| 1. lead | 1. de**duct**ion | *l* | _____ |
| 2. hundred | 2. **cent**ury | *h* | _____ |
| 3. believe | 3. **cred**ential | *b* | _____ |

4. faith

5. say

4. af**fid**avit      *f* _____

5. bene**dic**tion     *s* _____

---

**11. frater:** brother.

> Derivatives: *confraternity, frater, fraternal, fraternity, fraternize, fratricide.*

brother

■ *Frater* means *b* _____ .

brotherly

■ *Fraternal* obligations are _____ [fatherly / brotherly].

fraternize

■ To mingle with conquered people in a social or *brotherly* way is to _____ *nize* with them.

fratricide

■ Killing one's own *brother* is called _____ cide.

brother

■ A girls' club should not be called a *fraternity* because *frater* means _____ .

confraternity

■ A *brotherly* group devoted to charitable work is sometimes called a _____ [fiduciary / confraternity].

---

**12. greg:** flock.

> Derivatives: *aggregation, congregate, egregious, gregarious, segregate.*

*greg*

■ The Latin root for *flock* is *g* _____ .

congregation

■ A minister's *flock* is called a *con* _____ .

segregation

■ Separation from the main group or *flock* is *se* _____ .

flock

society

■ Since *greg* means *f* _____ , we may assume that *gregarious* people like _____ [solitude / society].

egregious

■ Insulting your teacher during examination week might stand out from your *flock* of lesser mistakes as an _____ [egregious / diffident] blunder.

aggregation

■ Bismuth is ineligible to play with the football _____ [aggravation / aggregation].

---

**13. litera:** letter.

Derivatives: *alliteration, literacy, literal, literalism, literally, literary, literate, literati, literature, litterateur, transliteration.*

litera
letter

■ The Latin root of the word *literary* is *l*_____, and it means *l*_____.

literal

■ Translating *letter* for *letter* results in a _____*al* translation.

illiterate

■ A person who can't read or write is *unlettered,* or _____ [illegitimate / illiterate].

literate
literature

■ The person who reads and writes is _____ [literate / libelous] and possibly enjoys _____*ure.*

realistically

■ *Literalism* in art means drawing things to the *letter,* that is, _____ [realistically / imaginatively].

(b)

■ A *litterateur* is (a) a man who keeps rabbits, (b) a man of letters. ( )

**14. loc:** place.

Derivatives: *allocate, dislocate, locale, localism, locality, localize, location, locative,* loco citato, *locus, relocate.*

loc

■ A three-letter Latin root that means *place* is *l*_____.

place

■ The *locale* of a train wreck refers to the _____ [place / cause].

locality, localism

■ An expression that is used only in a certain *place,* or _____*ty,* is called a _____ [barbarism / localism].

locus
loci

■ In mathematics the set of points or *places* which satisfy a given condition is called the _____*us.* The plural of *locus* is _____ [locusts / loci].

place

■ In footnotes *loco citato* is abbreviated as *loc. cit.* and means "in the *p*_____ cited."

place

■ In Latin and Greek grammar the *locative* case denotes _____ [time / place].

### 15. loqu, locut: talk.

Derivatives: *allocution, circumlocution, colloquial, colloquium, colloquy, elocution, eloquent, grandiloquent, interlocutor, loquacious, prolocutor, soliloquy.*

talkative

■ A *loquacious* child is _____ [sulky / talkative].

colloquial

■ Most people talk informally, that is, in _____ [literary / colloquial] English.

■ In *interlocutor* and *locution* the five-letter root that suggests *talk* is

*locut*

*l*_____ .

eloquent

■ Webster was an inspired *talker,* in fact, he was often

*el*_____ .

grandiloquent

■ A windy orator who uses grand, phony expressions is _____ [magnanimous / grandiloquent].

■ Saying a thing in a roundabout way is known as

circumlocution

_____ [circumspection / circumlocution].

■ Hamlet's "To be or not to be," spoken alone on stage, is a

soliloquy

_____ [solecism / soliloquy].

### Quiz

Write the meaning of each boldface Latin root.

1. letter
2. talk
3. brother
4. place
5. flock

1. al**liter**ation    *l* _____
2. col**loqu**ium    *t* _____
3. **frater**nal    *b* _____
4. dis**locat**e    *p* _____
5. ag**greg**ate    *f* _____

## 16. mal: bad.

Derivatives: *maladjusted, maladminister, maladroit, malaise, malapropos, malaria, malcontent,* mal de mer, *malediction, malefactor, malevolent, malfeasance, malformed, malice, malign, malignant, malinger, malnutrition, malocclusion, malodorous, malpractice.*

bad

■ *Malfeasance* in office refers to _____ [bad / admirable] conduct.

bad

■ *Mal* means b_____ .

malignant

■ The truly *bad* tumors are the _____ [benign / malignant] ones.

(b)

■ To hurl *maledictions* is to fling (a) small rocks, (b) evil words or curses. (    )

malevolent

■ Evil wishers are _____ [benevolent / malevolent].

bad

■ *Malaise* is physical discomfort that hints of _____ [good / bad] health.

maladroit

■ A clumsy child is said to be _____ [maladroit / adroit].

malnutrition

■ A badly nourished child suffers from _____*tion.*

malodorous

■ Goats don't smell good; they are _____*odorous.*

---

## 17. man: hand.

Derivatives: *amanuensis, manacle, manage, mandate, mandatory, maneuver, manicure, manifest, manifesto, manipulate, manual, manufacture, manumit, manuscript.*

hands

■ *Manacles* are worn on the _____ [eyes / hands].

*man*

■ The Latin root for *hand* is m_____ .

manicure

■ *Hands* with ugly nails should be given a _____ [manicure / pedicure].

hand

■ Both *emancipate* and *manumit* mean to set free, that is, to let go from the h_____ .

hand

■ An *amanuensis* is a copyist—he works with his _____ [jaw / hand].

*man*

manuscript

■ Another word derived from the root _____ , meaning *hand*, is _____ [amnesia / amenity / enema / manuscript].

---

18. **mater, matr, metr:** mother.

Derivatives: *alma mater, maternal, maternity, matriarch, matricide, matriculate, matrilineal, matrimony, matrix, matron, metronymic, metropolis.*

matriarch

■ A *mother* who rules a family or tribe is a _____ [matriarch / patriarch].

*matr,* mother

■ In the words *matrix* and *matrimony* the four-letter Latin root is _____ , and it means *m*_____ .

matricide

■ Slaying one's own *mother*, an ungrateful business, is known as _____ [uxoricide / matricide].

mater

matriculate

■ Our college is our alma *m*_____ (fostering mother). To enroll is to _____*ate*.

matron

maternity

■ A hospital _____*on* supervises the care of expectant *mothers* in the _____*ty* ward.

mother

■ *Matrilineal* descent refers to kinship through the _____ [father / mother].

metronymic

■ Henry Cabot Lodge derived his middle name from the maiden name of his mother; therefore for him the name *Cabot* is a _____ [metronymic / patronymic].

---

19. **mit, miss:** send.

Derivatives: *admissible, admit, commissary, commit, emissary, emit, intermittent, mission, missionary, missive, omission, permit, premise, promise, remit, submit, transmit.*

*miss*

send

■ The Latin root in *mission* is _____ and it means *s*_____ .

missionary

emissary

missive

*mit*

intermittent

■ The person we *send* to convert the heathens is called a mi_____ .

■ The diplomat we *send* out is an _____ [emissary / auditor].

■ A tourist usually *sends* his home-town friends a _____ [missive / missile].

■ Which three letters in *remit* mean *send?* _____

■ Shots *sent* out at intervals are said to be _____ [interdicted / intermittent].

---

**20. mor, mort:** death.

Derivatives: *immortal, moribund, mortal, mortality, mortgage, mortician, mortify, mortuary, post-mortem,* rigor mortis.

death

■ The root *mort* suggests that a *mortician* is concerned with _____ [birth / death].

mortuary

*mortis*

■ The *mortician* operates a funeral home, which is known as a _____ ry, and he is, no doubt, acquainted with the *stiffness of death* known as *rigor m*_____ .

dying

immortal

■ Greeting card sellers complain that the custom of sending valentines is *moribund*—that is, _____ [too lively / dying]. If the custom never died, it would be _____ [immortal / immoral].

(a)

■ If you develop gangrene, your flesh *mortifies;* this means that it a) decays and dies, (b) glows with health. (     )

---

**Quiz**

Write the meaning of each boldface Latin root.

1. hand
2. mother
3. death
4. send
5. bad

1. **man**ual          h _____
2. **mater**nal       m _____
3. **mort**gage      d _____
4. e**miss**ion       s _____
5. **mal**efactor     b _____

---

## 21. mov, mot, mob: move.

Derivatives: *automobile, commotion, demote, emotion, immobile, immovable, locomotive, mobile, mobility, motile, motion, motivation, motor, promote, remote, remove.*

*mov*

*mot, mob*

move

■ Give the root of *movable:* _____ ; of *motor:* _____ ; of *mobile:* _____ .

These variant Latin roots mean _____ .

move

■ From the letters mot it's a safe guess that *motile* cells are able to _____ [talk / move].

move

mobility

■ An army's ability to *move* is referred to as its _____ [stability / mobility].

motivation

■ Whatever *moves* one to study or marry or assassinate is one's _____ [innovation / motivation].

emotions

■ You are often *moved,* or stirred, by _____ [emotions / omissions].

promotion

■ Another word derived from the root meaning *move* is _____ [mother / matador / promotion / smote].

## 22. nov: new.

Derivatives: *innovation, nova, Nova Scotia, novel, novelette, novella, novelty, novice, novitiate, novocain, renovate.*

new

■ The letters *nov* in *novelty* mean n_____ .

new

■ An *innovation* is a _____ [crazy / new] idea or custom.

novice

novitiate

■ In a religious order a *new* member is called a _____ice and the probationary period is a _____ate.

(b)

■ A *nova* star is (a) a faithful old planet, (b) a brilliant new exploding star. ( )

novel

■ A hint of something *new* also occurs in the word _____ [naval / novel / venerable / Navaho].

renovate

new

■ When our landlord promises to _____ *ate* our apartment, we hope he knows that the word-root *nov* means _____ [air / new].

---

**23. omni:** all.

> Derivatives: *omniactive, omnibenevolent, omnibus, omniferous, omnipotent, omnipresent, omniprevalent, omniscient, omnium-gatherum, omnivorous.*

*omni*

■ In the words *omniscient* (all-knowing) and *omnipotent* (all-powerful) the four-letter root that means *all* is _____.

many

■ An *omnium-gatherum* is a collection of _____ [many / one or two] different things.

omniferous

■ A tree that produces *all* varieties is _____ [mellifluous / omniferous].

all

(b)

■ Because *omni* means _____ [all / small], we can assume that an *omnivorous* reader reads (a) only the funnies, (b) practically everything. ( )

omnibuses

■ To transport loads of students, a school usually buys _____ [compacts / omnibuses].

---

**24. ped:** foot.

> Derivatives: *biped, centipede, expedient, expedite, expedition, impediment, pedal, pedestal, pedestrian, pedometer, quadruped, sesquipedalian.*

foot

■ A *pedestrian* travels by _____ [foot / jet plane].

*ped*

■ The three-letter word-root meaning *foot* is p_____.

walked

■ A *pedometer* measures the distance _____ [driven / walked].

biped

■ A man has two *feet* and so according to Aristotle man is a featherless _____ [biped / slob].

feet

■ An *impediment* is literally something that obstructs or hinders the _____ [feet / meals].

(a)

feet

■ To *expedite* means, in a sense, to free the *feet,* hence, (a) to speed up the action, (b) to snarl things up. (    )

■ Since *sesqui* means "one and a half," a *sesquipedalian* is a word that is supposedly about one and a half _____ [feet / years] long.

---

**25. pon, posit:** place.

Derivatives: *apposite, appositive, component, composition, depose, deposit, dispose, exponent, expose, impose, interpose, juxtapose, opponent, position, positive, postpone, proponent, propose, repository.*

*posit,* place

■ The words *position, deposit,* and *appositive* all contain the five-letter root _____ , which means *p* _____ .

*pon*

■ Another root that means *place* is _____ [*pan / pon*].

components

■ Stereo set parts that must be *placed* together are called _____ [compartments / components].

juxtaposed

■ Objects *placed* alongside each other are _____ [juxtaposed / coincident].

repository

dispose

■ You can *place* old books in a _____ [repertory / repository] or otherwise *dis* _____ of them.

exponent

■ One who sets forth, or advocates, a doctrine is its _____ [expatriate / exponent].

apposite

■ Appropriate or *well-placed* remarks are said to be _____ [apposite / appellate].

---

**Quiz**

Write the meaning of each boldface Latin root.

1. foot
2. new
3. place
4. all
5. move

1. **ped**al          *f* _____
2. **nov**elette      *n* _____
3. com**posit**ion    *p* _____
4. **omni**present    *a* _____
5. de**mote**         *m* _____

---

# REVIEW TEST

Write *True* or *False*.

_____ 1. A *pedestrian* is one who walks.

_____ 2. An *innovation* is something newly introduced.

_____ 3. A *localism* is a universally popular pet phrase.

_____ 4. A *missive* is a small female ballet dancer.

_____ 5. A *literal* translation follows the original very closely.

_____ 6. In a *matriarchy* the mother rules the family or tribe.

_____ 7. A *dictum* is someone injured in an accident.

_____ 8. *Loquacity* refers to talkativeness.

_____ 9. To *mobilize* means to hypnotize and to stop action.

_____ 10. The name *Il Duce* means the "deuce" or "two-spot."

Write the meaning of each boldface Latin root. The first letter of each answer is given.

11. a **frater**nity of poets                b _____

12. guilty of **mal**practice               b _____

13. **aqu**atic sports                       w _____

14. an in**cred**ible plot                   b _____

15. a Robert Frost **cent**ennial            h _____

16. an **am**orous sonnet                    l _____

17. the im**mort**al Chaucer                 d _____

18. an e**greg**ious idiot                   f _____

19. an illuminated **man**uscript            h _____

20. dis**posit**ion of funds                 p _____

Write the letter that indicates the best completion.

(    ) 21. An *infidel* is one who has no (a) married parents, (b) schooling, (c) musical ability, (d) religious faith.

(    ) 22. An *audible* kiss is one that (a) lasts a long time, (b) can be seen, (c) can be heard, (d) gives off steam.

( ) 23. That which is *omnipresent* is (a) nowhere, (b) everywhere, (c) a welcome gift, (d) invisible.

( ) 24. The Latin root for *head* is used in which word?—(a) aquatint, (b) caption, (c) deception, (d) amour.

( ) 25. The Latin root for *year* is used in which word?—(a) perennial, (b) banana, (c) birthday, (d) decade.

## Key to Review Test

Check your test answers with the following key. Deduct 4% per error from a possible 100%.

| | | |
|---|---|---|
| 1. True | 10. False | 19. hand |
| 2. True | 11. brother | 20. place |
| 3. False | 12. bad | 21. (d) |
| 4. False | 13. water | 22. (c) |
| 5. True | 14. believe | 23. (b) |
| 6. True | 15. hundred | 24. (b) |
| 7. False | 16. love | 25. (a) |
| 8. True | 17. death | |
| 9. False | 18. flock | |

Score: _____ %

# 6

# Latin Derivatives II

ROOTS

1. *port, portat*
2. *prim*
3. *reg*
4. *rupt*
5. *sanct*
6. *scrib, script*
7. *seg, sect*
8. *sequ, secut*
9. *sign*

10. *sol*
11. *son*
12. *spec, spect*
13. *spir, spirat*
14. *tempor*
15. *terra*
16. *tort*
17. *tract*
18. *turb*

19. *urb*
20. *vac*
21. *vers, vert*
22. *vid, vis*
23. *vinc, vict*
24. *vit, viv*
25. *voc, vocat*

*Chapter 6 continues our study of Latin roots and their derivatives. Follow the same procedure as in Chapter 5.*

**Roots**

---

**1. port, portat:** carry.

> Derivatives: *comport, deport, disport, export, import, portable, portage, portfolio, porter, portmanteau, purport, rapport, report, support, transport.*

*port*

*carry*

■ The words *porter, export,* and *purport* all have the root _____, which means c _____ .

transport, portable

portfolio

portmanteau

■ One can easily *trans* _____ a _____ *able* typewriter, a _____ *io* (brief case), or a _____ *teau* (leather suitcase that opens into two compartments like a book).

(a)

■ To make a *portage* between lakes means (a) to carry gear, (b) to stop for lunch. (     )

deportment

■ Your _____ *ment* is your behavior or way of *carrying* yourself.

---

**2. prim:** first.

> Derivatives: *prima donna, primal, primarily, primary, primate, prime, prime minister, primer, primeval, primitive, primitivism, primogeniture, primordial, primrose, primula.*

prime

■ The *first* or top statesman in England is the _____ minister.

prima

■ The *first* female singer in opera is the _____ *a* donna.

primula, primrose

*prim*

■ We can assume that the *first* flowers of spring include the _____ *ula*—also called _____ *rose*— because the Latin root _____ means "first."

primary

primer

■ We *first* went to a _____ *ry* school, and our *first* book was a _____ *er.*

primates
primitive

■ Human beings, known as _____ tes, have progressed from _____ ve cave to fancy condominium.

■ The system of *primogeniture* provided that one's estate and title

first

went to the son who was born _____ [first / last].

primarily

■ Breathing through your nose is wise, _____ ly (mainly) because it keeps your mouth shut.

---

### 3. reg: rule.

Derivatives: *interregnum, irregular, regal, regalia, regency, regent, regicide, regime, regiment, Regina, region, regular, regulate, regulation.*

regulation
(a)

■ A soldier must obey an army _____ tion because the *reg* in *regulation* means (a) "rule," (b) "fool around." (    )

regiment

■ If you join our _____ ment, you must wear

regalia

our _____ ia (official decorations).

Regina

■ Elizabeth _____ na (Queen) *ruled* the entire

region, regal

_____ on in a _____ al (royal) manner.

regicide

■ In 1649 King Charles I was beheaded, an act of _____ ide

irregular

as *ir* _____ as it was barbaric.

regimen

■ My doctor ordered me to follow a _____ men (health system) of tasteless food and hard exercise.

■ The period between two successive reigns or *rulers* is known as an

interregnum

*int* _____ .

■ The *regents* evidently run a university, because the three-letter

reg

Latin root _____ means "rule."

---

### 4. rupt: break.

Derivatives: *corrupt, disrupt, erupt, interrupt, rupture.*

interrupt

■ You're *breaking* into our conversation. Please don't *int* _____ us.

| | |
|---|---|
| corrupt | ■ Bribed? Then "Honest Abe" Jones is *co*_____! |
| *rupt* | ■ The Latin root for *break* is _____. |
| erupt | ■ Soon this rumbling volcano will *e*_____ (break out). |
| rupture | ■ Uncle Rudy dug deep and managed to _____*re* (break) a gas main. For good measure, the heavy lifting gave Rudy an |
| rupture | abdominal _____*re*. |
| disrupt | ■ Hecklers may *dis*_____ the political rally. |

---

**5. sanct:** holy.

Derivatives: *sanctified, sanctify, sanctimonious, sanctimony, sanction, sanctitude, sanctity, sanctuary, sanctum, sanctorum.*

| | |
|---|---|
| sanctified | ■ The Normandy beach is *holy* ground, _____*ied* by the blood of American soldiers. |
| sanctitude | ■ The priest had an air of _____*ude* (holiness). |
| holy | ■ Since *sanct* means _____ [drowned / holy], we refer to |
| sanctum, sanctorum | the *holy* of *holies* as the _____*um*_____*um*. |
| sanctuary | ■ A church is a true _____*ry* (holy refuge). |
| sanction | ■ Slavery? How can any nation _____*n* (approve) it? |
| sanctimonious | ■ Tartuffe speaks _____*ous* (pretending to be holy) words, but what a difference between the hypocrite's |
| sanctimony, sanctity | _____*ny* and genuine _____*ty!* |

---

### Quiz

Write the meaning of each boldface Latin root.

| | | |
|---|---|---|
| 1. rule | 1. **reg**ulation | *r* _____ |
| 2. first | 2. **prim**itive | *f* _____ |
| 3. holy | 3. **sanct**uary | *h* _____ |

4. break

5. carry

<br />

4. inter**rupt**    b _____

5. **port**able    c _____

---

**6. scrib, script:** write.

Derivatives: *ascribe, circumscribe, conscription, describe, inscribe, manuscript, nondescript, postscript, prescribe, proscribe, scribble, scribe, scripture, subscribe, transcribe, typescript.*

■ The five-letter root of *subscribe, proscribe,* and *inscribe* is _____, and it means *w*_____.

*scrib, write*

■ An afterthought *written* at the end of a letter is a *p*_____.

postscript

■ The army draft, or enrollment, is known as *con*_____.

conscription

■ The Scriptures were so named because they were _____ [sung / written], possibly _____ [transfused / transcribed] into beautiful *manu*_____ by industrious _____ [porters / scribes].

written

transcribed

manuscripts

scribes

■ My doctor peered at my tongue, then hastily wrote a *pre*_____.

prescription

■ A *nondescript* dog is (a) a very individual type, (b) hardly individual enough to be written about. (    )

(b)

---

**7. seg, sect:** cut.

Derivatives: *antivivisection, bisect, dissect, intersect, sect, sectarian, section, sector, segment, trisect, vivisection.*

■ Our streets *cut* across one another, so let's meet where they *int*_____.

intersect

■ *Cut* angle A into two equal parts and angle B into three equal parts; in other words, *b*_____ angle A and *tr*_____ angle B.

bisect, trisect

■ The butcher *cut* off a _____ *ent* of salami, then began to *di*_____ my chicken.

segment

dissect

| | |
|---|---|
| sect | ■ Members of a strange religious _____ (cult) live |
| section | in my _____ *on* (part) of town. |
| | ■ Splitting away from the main church are several small |
| sectarian | _____ *ian* groups. |
| | ■ *Cutting* into a live animal for medical research is known as |
| vivisection | *viv*_____ ; opposition to such experiments |
| antivivisection | is *ant*_____ . |

---

### 8. sequ, secut: follow.

Derivatives: *consecutive, consequently, execution, executive, obsequies, obsequious, persecute, prosecute, sequel, sequence, subsequently.*

| | |
|---|---|
| subsequently | ■ *Tom Sawyer* was a success, and *sub*_____ (at a fol- |
| sequel | lowing time) Mark Twain wrote a _____ *el* (follow-up) about Huck Finn. |
| consecutive | ■ If this baseball team loses three *con*_____ (in a row) games, these fans will hang the coach and won't even attend the |
| obsequies | *ob*_____ (funeral rites). |
| (a) | ■ The roots *sequ, secut* mean (a) follow; (b) sexy. (  ) |
| executive | ■ The person who *follows* up on company plans is the *ex*_____, |
| execution | responsible for *ex*_____ of the board's decisions. |
| obsequious | ■ Lord Bigmouth had a *following* of *ob*_____ (submissive) servants. |
| sequence | ■ Shakespeare describes the seven ages of man in *se*_____ (order), from infancy to feeble old age. |
| Consequently | ■ Gravitation works day and night. *Con*_____ (as a result), my lawn is covered with oak leaves. |
| prosecute | ■ In America we may *pro*_____ (put on trial) a per- |
| persecute | son in court; but we do not *per*_____ (cruelly harass) our citizens. |

---

**9. sign:** sign.

Derivatives: *assign, consign, countersign, design, designate, ensign, insignia, resign, signal, signalize, signatory, signature, signet, significant, signify.*

sign, sign

■ In the words *signalize, countersign,* and *designate* the root is _____ , and—who'd guess it?—it means _____ .

signature

■ *Sign* the check with your own _____*ture.*

significant

■ One's *signature* on a document is very _____ [sagacious

signifies

/ significant] since it _____ [beclouds / signifies] one's intentions.

signet

■ An initial or other special *sign* is carried on a _____ [signet / garnet] ring.

an ensign

■ A military banner or other *sign* of authority is known as _____ [lasagne / an ensign].

signatory

■ Countries that have *signed* a treaty are _____ [secessionist / signatory] nations.

sign

■ Remember that the Latin root *sign* means _____ .

assignment

If necessary, repeat it ten times—what an _____*ment!*

---

**10. sol:** alone.

Derivatives: *desolation, isolate, sole, soliloquy, solitaire, solitary, solitude, solo.*

solitaire

■ Boomer sat *alone,* playing _____*re.*

solitary

■ The vicious prisoner was put in _____*y* confinement.

solo, solitude

■ I warbled my _____*o,* "In my _____*de* I dream of you"—and my canary threw seeds at me.

isolate

■ Smallpox? Then we must *is*_____ you!

desolation

■ The fire left behind it a scene of utter *de* _____ (loneliness and ruin).

sole

soliloquy

■ Macbeth was now the _____ character on stage.
As though thinking aloud, he began his _____ y.

## Quiz

Write the meaning of each boldface Latin root.

1. cut
2. holy
3. alone
4. sign
5. follow

1. bi**sect**          c _____
2. **sanct**uary       h _____
3. **isol**ate         a _____
4. in**sign**ia        s _____
5. con**secut**ive     f _____

**11. son:** sound.

> Derivatives: *assonance, consonance, resonance, sonar, sonata, sonatina, sonic, sonics, sonnet, sonorous, supersonic.*

sonic

supersonic

■ The plane burst through the *sound* barrier, letting out a _____ boom, and accelerated to *sup* _____ (faster than sound) speeds.

dissonance

■ Such discordant *sounds!* Such *dis* _____ !

sonata

sonatina

resonance

■ Yasha pounded out a four-movement Mozart _____ *ta* and a short _____ *na,* then told us our piano had fine *re* _____ (vibrant sound).

sound

■ The Latin root *son* means _____ [boy / sound].

sonar

■ We located the sunken ship by means of *sound*-wave apparatus called _____ *r.*

sonnet, sonorous

■ The poet read his _____ *t* in a rich _____ *ous* (deep and vibrant) voice.

assonance

■ Imperfect rhyme involving identical vowel sounds (e.g., fame-lake, hope-boat) is known as *as* _____ ; imperfect rhyme involving identical consonant sounds (e.g., dog-dig, live-love) is

| | |
|---|---|
| consonance | known as *con*_____. (See "Poetry," Chapter 20, frames 16–17.) |

---

**12. spec, spect:** look.

Derivatives: *aspect, circumspect, inspect, introspection, perspective, prospect, respect, retrospect, spectacle, specter, spectroscope, spectrum.*

| | |
|---|---|
| *spect* | ■ The root in *inspect, aspect,* and *prospect* is _____, |
| look | and it means *l*_____. |
| circumspect | ■ To be cautious and *look* around before acting is to be _____ [circumspect / circumscript]. |
| introspection | ■ Marcel Proust had a habit of *looking* into his mind and memories—he was given to _____ [introspection / interdiction]. |
| retrospect | ■ *Looking* back he saw things in *ret*_____. |
| perspective | ■ Another viewpoint would have given him a different *per*_____. |
| (d) | ■ One word that did *not* develop from the root for *look* is (a) specter, (b) spectrum, (c) spectacles, (d) spaghetti. (    ) |

---

**13. spir, spirat:** breathe.

Derivatives: *aspirate, aspire, conspire, expire, inspire, perspire, respiration, spiracle, spirit, spirometer.*

| | |
|---|---|
| breathe | ■ *Spirat* means _____ [spin / breathe]. |
| respiration | ■ To *breathe* through the lungs is called *resp*_____; |
| perspiration | to *breathe*—or seep—through the skin is *per*_____. |
| spiracle | ■ The zoological term for a whale's breathing hole is _____ [spiracle / oracle]. |
| spirit | ■ In the sea battle Captain Ahab yielded up his _____ *it* |
| expired | and *ex*_____. |

■ A machine which measures one's lung capacity, or *breath*, is

spirometer

called a _____ [spectroscope / spirometer].

(a)

■ Poetic *inspiration* was originally thought to be (a) a breathing in of a divine influence, (b) the product of indigestion. (    )

---

**14. tempor:** time.

Derivatives: *contemporary, contretemps, extemporaneous, extempore, extemporize, pro tem, tempo, temporal, temporary, temporize.*

■ Emerson and Thoreau lived at the same *time*—they were

contemporary

_____ [congruent / contemporary] writers.

*tempor*

■ The root _____ means *time*.

time

■ To be chairman *pro tem* means "for the _____ being,"

temporarily

or _____ *ily*.

■ Talks or remarks made at the *time* without preparation are said to

extemporaneous

be _____ [extenuating / extemporaneous].

■ To delay, or consume *time*, by needless discussions is to

temporize

_____ [temporize / expedite].

■ An inopportune or embarrassing occurrence is known as a

contretemps

_____ [nondescript / contretemps].

tempo

■ Parade music has a brisk _____ *o.*

---

**15. terra:** earth.

Derivatives: *disinter, inter, terrace, terra cotta, terra firma, terramycin, terraqueous, terrazzo, terrestrial, terrier, territory.*

terramycin

■ One antibiotic derived from the *earth* is called _____ *mycin.*

*terra*

■ The Latin root for *earth* is *t* _____ .

earth

■ *Terra firma* refers to firm _____ [water / earth].

terra

■ Unglazed, brown-red *earthenware* is known as *t* _____ cotta.

(a)

■ *Terrain* has to do with (a) land surfaces, (b) ammunition. (    )

terrestrial

■ The *earth's land* as distinct from water is _____ [global / terrestrial].

terrier

■ A small hunting dog which burrowed into the *earth* for small game was called a _____ *ier.*

(b)

■ A body that is *interred* has been (a) cremated, (b) buried. (    )

---

## Quiz

Write the meaning of each boldface Latin root.

1. earth          1. **terr**itory          *e* _____
2. sound          2. super**son**ic         *s* _____
3. look           3. per**spect**ive        *l* _____
4. time           4. con**tempor**ary       *t* _____
5. breathe        5. in**spir**e            *b* _____

---

**16. tort:** twist.

Derivatives: *contortion, distort, retort, tort, tortoise, tortuous, torture.*

distort

■ Scowls will *d*_____ your face, so smile.

contortion

■ The acrobat *twisted* into an odd *con*_____.

retort

■ Groucho was quick with a *ret*_____ (witty reply).

torture

■ *Twisting* the limbs to encourage confessions or religious conversion was a type of medieval _____ *re.*

*tort*

■ The Latin root *t*_____ means "twist."

twist

■ Tabloids are guilty of *distortions.* This means that they _____ [verify / twist] the facts.

tort

■ In law, an injury for which you can sue is a _____ [tort / sanct].

tortuous
tortoise

■ The road was so steep and _____ous (twisted) that a _____se passed us twice.

---

**17. tract:** draw, pull.

Derivatives: *attract, attractive, contract, detract, distract, extract, protract, retract, subtract, tract, tractable, tractate, traction, tractor.*

tractor
traction

■ The farmer's _____r, which was *pulling* a plow, got stuck in mud and lost _____n (drawing power).

tractable

■ The bronco was tamed and is now quite _____ble (easily handled).

distract
extract

■ The dentist tried to *dis*_____ (draw attention away) me with questions about politics, while trying to *e*_____ my molar.

draw
attractive

■ *Tract* means _____ [draw / repel], and boys find Lisa very _____ve.

protract
contract

■ If you *pr*_____ (draw out) this strike, you'll be breaking your *c*_____ (agreement).

detract

■ Nothing you say can *d*_____ (take away) from Amy's splendid reputation.

retract

■ Better *re*_____ (take back) that statement, or he'll punch your nose.

tractate
tract

■ The minister referred to his essay as a _____ate, or religious _____ .

---

**18. turb:** agitate, whirl.

Derivatives: *disturb, disturbance, imperturbable, perturbation, perturbed, turbid, turbine, turbojet, turbulent.*

disturb

■ Even earthquakes don't *dis*_____ Joe's slumber.

| | |
|---|---|
| perturbed | ■ Much *per*_____ by the accusations, Ignatz leaped |
| turbulent | into the _____*nt* waters. |
| | |
| (b) | ■ The Latin root *turb* refers to (a) gutter edging, (b) agitation. ( ) |
| | ■ The Missouri is muddied by its current; so the water is |
| turbid | _____*id* (cloudy and agitated). |
| | |
| disturbance | ■ A hive of bees caused a *dis*_____ at our picnic. |
| | |
| imperturbable | ■ With bases loaded, the *imp*_____ (calm) Casey swung his bat—and struck out. |
| | |
| | ■ A motor driven to rotation by the thrust of fluids or gases is called |
| turbine | a _____*ne*. |
| | |
| | ■ A jet engine using a turbine to drive an air compressor is |
| turbojet | a _____*jet*. |

---

### 19. urb: city.

Derivatives: *interurban, suburban, suburbanite, suburbs, urban, urbane, urbanism, urbanite, urbanity, urbanize.*

| | |
|---|---|
| city | ■ To *urbanize* a district is to make it become like a _____ [city / farm]. |
| | |
| *urb* | ■ The three-letter Latin root that means *city* is *u*_____. |
| | |
| interurban | ■ Buses that travel between *cities* are *inter*_____. |
| | |
| suburbs | ■ On the outskirts of the *cities* lie the _____ [subways / suburbs]. |
| | |
| (a) | ■ An *urbane* fellow is (a) polished and suave, (b) countrified and crude. ( ) He is accustomed to those *citified* refinements of man- |
| urbanities | ners known as the _____ [gaucheries / urbanities]. |

---

### 20. vac: empty.

Derivatives: *evacuate, vacancy, vacant, vacate, vacation, vacuity, vacuous, vacuum.*

evacuate

vacation

vacate

*vac*

vacuum

vacancy

vacant

vacuous

(b)

■ Floods made us *e*_____ our homes.

■ It rained during our _____*on* abroad, and in the hotels we got soaked in more ways than one.

■ "Pay for your room or _____*te*," growled the manager.

■ The three-letter root _____ means *empty*, and nothing is *emptier* than a _____*um*.

■ As soon as the landlord has a _____*y*, he'll rent us the _____*t* apartment.

■ Look alert. The professor will throw questions at you if you wear a _____*s* expression.

■ A reference to your "mental *vacuity*" should be taken as (a) a compliment, (b) criticism. (    )

---

**Quiz**

Write the meaning of each boldface Latin root.

1. city
2. agitate
3. twist
4. draw
5. empty

1. inter**urb**an        *c* _____
2. **turb**ulent         *a* _____
3. **tort**uous          *t* _____
4. pro**tract**          *d* _____
5. **vac**uity           *e* _____

---

**21. vers, vert:** turn.

Derivatives: *conversation, convert, diversion, extrovert, introvert, inverted, perversion, reverse, revert, subvert, versatile, verse, version, versus, vertebra, vertebrate, vertex, vertical, vertigo.*

introvert

extrovert

■ Shy Sherlock, who *turns* to his inner thoughts and feelings, is an *in*_____ . Sociable Sophie, who *turns* to outer activities, is an *ex*_____ .

versatile

■ Diane *turns* to art, to music, and to sports. In fact, she's very _____*le.*

| | |
|---|---|
| vertebra | ◼ Helping you to *turn* your spine is your _____ *ra*. |
| vertebrate | ◼ You have a spinal column, so you're a _____ *te*. |
| revert | ◼ Some drug addicts are "cured," then *re* _____ , (turn back) to their old habits. |
| vertex | ◼ When I reached the _____ *x* (top) of the mountain, |
| vertigo | things seemed to *turn* dizzily. I had _____ *go*. |
| subvert | ◼ Traitors may *su* _____ (overturn) the government. |
| | ◼ A line that *turns* at right angles to a horizontal line |
| vertical | is _____ *l*. |
| convert | ◼ Killer Kane *turned* to the church and became a *c* _____ . |
| perversion | ◼ *Turning* to abnormal sexual behavior is called *per* _____ . |

---

### 22. vid, vis: see.

Derivatives: *advise, envision, evidence, improvisator, invidious, providence, revise, supervise, visible, visionary, visit, vista, visualize.*

◼ The words *visible, visit,* and *supervise* have the same three-letter

| | |
|---|---|
| *vis*, see | root _____ , which means *s* _____ . |
| view | ◼ A *vista* is a _____ [view / southern mansion]. |
| | ◼ The words *evidence* and *providence* have the same three-letter |
| *vid*, see | root _____ , which also means _____ . |
| | ◼ To the Puritans *divine providence* meant that God would |
| foresee | _____ [ignore them / foresee]. |
| | ◼ Comparisons which are unfair and offensive to our sight |
| invidious | are _____ [invaluable / invidious]. |

---

### 23. vinc, vict: conquer.

Derivatives: *convict, conviction, convince, evince, invincible, victim, victimize, victor, Victorian, victorious, victory.*

**Latin Derivatives II    85**

victory

invincible

■ The Nazis expected to win a _____ ry, but the Allies were *in* _____ (unconquerable).

convict

■ Defeated by the evidence, Bugsy became a prison *c* _____ .

victor

victim

■ Jungle beasts fight to the death. The _____ r (conqueror) does not spare the _____ *m.*

convince

victimize

■ Old Ned was easy to *con* _____ (conquer by argument), and any swindler who peddled gold bricks could _____ *ize* him.

conquer
(b)

■ *Vict* means _____ , and to *evict* tenants is to (a) reward them, (b) remove them. (    )

conviction

victorious

■ I have a *con* _____ (strong belief) that our soccer team will be _____ *ous.*

Victorian

■ Flourishing during the reign of Queen Victoria were the somewhat prudish *V* _____ writers such as Charles Dickens.

evince

■ Lefty held four aces, but his face did not *e* _____ (reveal) any emotion.

## 24. vit, viv: life.

Derivatives: *convivial, devitalized, revive, vital, vitality, vitals, vitamin, vivace, vivacious, vivid, vivify, viviparous, vivisection.*

vital

■ Desdemona was _____ *al* (essential) to his happiness, and because she was dead, Othello stabbed himself in the

vitals

_____ *ls* (heart, lungs, etc.).

devitalized

vitamin

■ If you eat *de* _____ (energy-deprived) foods, you'd better take _____ *in* pills.

vitality

■ Buster is a bundle of _____ *ty* (energy).

convivial

■ Flo and Moe love food, friends, and *life.* In other words, they're *con* _____ people.

*vit, viv*

■ Two Latin roots, only three letters long, that are full of *life* are _____ and _____ .

vivid, vivacious

vivace

■ I have a _____d (lifelike) memory of my _____ous (lively) grandmother tootling the _____ce (lively) movement of a Sousa march on her piccolo.

viviparous

■ Most mammals bring forth *living* young rather than eggs; in other words, they are _____ous.

vivisection

revive

■ My pet was a laboratory victim of _____on (cutting a live animal). We were unable to re_____ my beloved cat.

---

### 25. voc, vocat: call.

Derivatives: *advocate, avocation, convocation, equivocal, evoke, invoke, irrevocable, provoke, revoke, vocable, vocabulary, vocal, vocation, vociferous.*

convocation

■ A *calling* together of students to assembly is a _____ [convocation / convection].

spoken

call

■ *Vocal* promises are _____ [written / spoken]; after all, the root *voc* means c_____ .

vocation

■ Your career job, or *calling,* is your _____ion.

avocation

■ Your hobby is your *av*_____ .

advocate

■ I *ad*_____ (recommend) that you choose your field of specialization wisely because by commencement day that decision

irrevocable

will be practically _____ [irrepressible / irrevocable].

invokes

■ At the beginning of his epic, the poet Homer _____ [invokes / inspires] the gods.

invocation

■ Today a minister usually gives the *in*_____ .

equivocal

■ A sentence which seems to say two opposite things is said to be _____ [omniscient / equivocal].

---

## Quiz

Write the meaning of each boldface Latin root.

| | |
|---|---|
| 1. conquer | 1. in**vinc**ible    _c_ _____ |
| 2. life | 2. **viv**acious    _l_ _____ |
| 3. see | 3. super**vise**    _s_ _____ |
| 4. turn | 4. extro**vert**    _t_ _____ |
| 5. call | 5. **voca**tion    _c_ _____ |

# REVIEW TEST

Write *True* or *False*.

_____ 1. A *sanctuary* is a fairly safe place.

_____ 2. The *primrose* is a late bloomer.

_____ 3. *Nondescript* houses are quite undistinguished.

_____ 4. *Tractable* animals are rather tame.

_____ 5. A *circumspect* fellow is reckless.

_____ 6. An *obsequious* person has a regal manner.

_____ 7. *Imperturbable* people are calm and cool.

_____ 8. To *temporize* is to delay.

_____ 9. *Vertigo* involves a dizzy feeling.

_____ 10. An *equivocal* remark is clear and vivid.

Write the meaning of each boldface Latin root. The first letter of each answer is given.

11. con**vinc**e the jury          *c* _____

12. a **rupt**ured lung           *b* _____

13. dis**tort**ed features         *t* _____

14. a game of **sol**itaire        *a* _____

15. good re**son**ance            *s* _____

16. **urb**an problems            *c* _____

17. a Republican **reg**ime        *r* _____

18. super**vis**e the class         *s* _____

19. to e**vac**uate the city         *e* _____

20. inter**sect**ing highways       *c* _____

Write the letter that indicates the best completion.

(    ) 21. *Respiration* refers to (a) the heart, (b) sweat, (c) first aid, (d) breathing.

(    ) 22. An example of a *viviparous* creature is (a) an eagle, (b) a rabbit, (c) a chicken, (d) a butterfly.

(    ) 23. To *disinter* a body is to take it out of (a) the water, (b) the earth, (c) a hospital, (d) wreckage.

**Latin Derivatives II**    89

(    ) 24. *Portable* television sets are, by definition, (a) in color, (b) solid state, (c) able to be carried, (d) manufactured abroad.

(    ) 25. A *signet* ring has on it (a) a sign, (b) an emerald, (c) a diamond, (d) a curse.

## Key to Review Test

Check your test answers with the following key. Deduct 4% per error from a possible 100%.

| | | |
|---|---|---|
| 1. True | 10. False | 19. empty |
| 2. False | 11. conquer | 20. cut |
| 3. True | 12. break | 21. (d) |
| 4. True | 13. twist | 22. (b) |
| 5. False | 14. alone | 23. (b) |
| 6. False | 15. sound | 24. (c) |
| 7. True | 16. city | 25. (a) |
| 8. True | 17. rule | |
| 9. True | 18. see | |

Score: _____ %

# 7

# Latin Derivatives III

PREFIXES

1. *ad*
2. *ante*
3. *bi*
4. *circum*
5. *co*
6. *contra, contro, counter*
7. *de*
8. *inter*
9. *intra, intro*
10. *mis*
11. *multi*
12. *post*
13. *pre*
14. *pro*
15. *quadr*
16. *quasi*
17. *quint*
18. *retro*
19. *semi*
20. *sub*
21. *super*
22. *trans*
23. *tri*
24. *ultra*
25. *uni*

*A knowledge of Latin prefixes is indispensable to a mastery of English vocabulary. Prefixes multiply the use we make of roots.*

*For example, we have seen that* scrib, script *means "write," and that with prefixes we get combinations like* circumscribe, conscription, describe, inscribe, nondescript, postscript, prescribe, proscribe, subscribe, *and* transcribe. *These prefixes are a key to the meaning of such combinations.*

*Sometimes the spelling of a prefix is modified for the sake of pronunciation. For instance, the prefix* sub, *meaning "under," changes to* suc *in* succinct *and to* sup *in* supplant; *the prefix* ad, *meaning "to," changes to* af *in* affiliate *and to* an *in* annul. *The process is called assimilation.*

*Time has a way of changing the spelling, meaning, and application of words; so we should be ready to supplement our analysis of word parts by consulting a dictionary.*

*In this chapter we will focus on twenty-five basic prefixes and their most common meanings.*

## EXERCISES

### Prefixes

COVER THIS STRIP

**1. ad:** to; toward.

Examples: *adhesive, admissible, advocate.*

adhesive

■ A substance such as tape that sticks *to* other things is _____ *ve.*

advocate

■ To speak in favor of a measure is to _____ [advocate / deprecate] it.

may

■ *Admissible* evidence _____ [may / may not] be brought into a court case.

■ The prefix *ad* is slippery and often changes to an "assimilated" form. It appears, for example, as *ac* in *accord* (because *adcord* would be hard to pronounce). Other assimilated forms of *ad* include *ag* in

*al, an*

*aggressive,* _____ in *allude,* _____ in

*as*

*annex,* and _____ in *assign.*

**2. ante:** before.

Examples: *antebellum, antedate, anterior.*

before

■ *Antebellum* days came _____ [before / after] the Civil War.

antedated

■ The Civil War _____ [antedated / succeeded] the first World War.

■ That which is toward the front or which comes *before* is

anterior

_____ [anterior / posterior].

**3. bi:** two.

Examples: *bicameral, bifocal, bipartisan.*

two

■ A *bicameral* legislature has _____ [one / two] chambers.

bifocals

■ Glasses with *two* different focal lengths are called _____ [monocles / bifocals].

| | |
|---|---|
| bipartisan | ■ A committee which represents *two* parties is _____ [bipartisan / partisan]. |

**4. circum:** around.

Examples: *circa, circumference, circumvent.*

| | |
|---|---|
| circumference | ■ The line *around* a circle is the _____ [circumference / diameter]. |
| (a) | ■ To *circumvent* the villain is (a) to get around him and outwit him, (b) to fall into his trap. (    ) |
| about | ■ Dante's *Divine Comedy* was written *circa* 1320, that is, _____ [after / about] 1320. |

**5. co:** together.

Examples: *coagulate, coeducation, coexistence, coincidence.*

| | |
|---|---|
| (a) | ■ When blood or any other fluid *coagulates,* it (a) clumps together, (b) gets thinner. (    ) |
| together | ■ *Coeducation* refers to the teaching of male and female students _____ [together / separately]. |
| coexistence | ■ People of different religions and ideologies should strive for peaceful _____ *ce* (living together). |
| coincidence | ■ My birthday and my bypass operation on the same day? What a *co* _____ ! |
| con, cor | ■ The prefix *co* is assimilated as *com* in *compassion,* as *col* in *collate,* as _____ in *congenital,* and as _____ in *correlate.* |

### Quiz

Write the meaning of each boldface Latin prefix.

| | | |
|---|---|---|
| 1. two | 1. **bi**nominal | *t* _____ |
| 2. to | 2. **ad**vantage | *t* _____ |
| 3. together | 3. **co**operation | *t* _____ |

| | |
|---|---|
| 4. around | 4. **circum**navigate    *a* _____ |
| 5. before | 5. **ante**cedent       *b* _____ |

**6. contra, contro, counter:** against.

    Examples: *contraband, controvert, countercharge.*

(b)

■ A *countercharge* is (a) an admission of guilt, (b) a charge by the accused against his accuser. (   )

controvert

■ To argue *against* a certain idea is to _____ [corroborate / controvert] it.

illegal

■ *Contraband* is _____ [legal / illegal] merchandise.

**7. de:** away; down.

    Examples: *degradation, delusion, derision.*

down

■ Those who live in *degradation* are usually far _____ [up / down] on the socio-economic ladder.

delusions

■ The lunatic was lured *away* from reality by _____ [delusions / allusions] of grandeur.

(a)

■ An object of *derision,* Fulton was greeted by (a) jeers and ridicule, (b) warm applause. (   )

**8. inter:** between.

    Examples: *intercultural, interlinear, interregnum.*

between

■ An *interlinear* translation has the meaning inserted _____ [opposite / between] the lines.

between

■ The *interregnum* is the period _____ [during / between] the rule of kings.

intercultural

■ Relations *between* cultural groups are said to be _____ [intercultural / subcultural].

**9. intra, intro:** within.

    Examples: *intramuscular, intrastate, intravenous.*

| | |
|---|---|
| within | ■ *Intramuscular* pains are _____ [between / within] the muscles. |
| intravenous | ■ An injection *within* a vein is _____ [intervenous / intravenous]. |
| Albany | ■ *Intrastate* commerce goes on between New York City and _____ [Chicago / Albany]. |

**10. mis:** wrong, bad.

Examples: *misadventure, misdemeanor, misnomer.*

| | |
|---|---|
| misadventure | ■ We enjoyed our picnic, except for the _____ *ure* (accident) involving the rattlesnake. |
| (a) | ■ Overtime parking is *wrong* behavior of a minor sort. It is therefore classed as a (a) misdemeanor, (b) felony. ( ) |
| (b) | ■ Our plumber is called Speedy, but that's a *misnomer* (wrong name). He is actually very (a) fast, (b) slow. ( ) |

## Quiz

Write the meaning of each boldface Latin prefix.

| | | | |
|---|---|---|---|
| 1. between | 1. **inter**linear | *b* | _____ |
| 2. wrong | 2. **mis**represent | *w* | _____ |
| 3. against | 3. **contra**dict | *a* | _____ |
| 4. away | 4. **de**tour | *a* | _____ |
| 5. within | 5. **intra**mural | *w* | _____ |

**11. multi:** many.

Examples: *multimillionaire, multiped, multitude.*

| | |
|---|---|
| many | ■ A *multiped* insect has _____ [many / two] feet. |
| are not | ■ If your possessions are worth $3,469.12, you _____ [are / are not] a *multimillionaire*. |
| multitude | ■ The ninety thousand frantic spectators at a soccer game are quite a _____ [multitude / solitude]. |

**12. post:** after.

Examples: *posterior, posterity, posthumous.*

after

posterity

posterior

■ Mark Twain's *The Mysterious Stranger* was published *posthumously,* that is, _____ [before / after] his death.

■ Those generations which come *after* us are our _____ [ancestors / posterity].

■ That part of us which comes *after* us is our _____ *ior.*

---

**13. pre:** before.

Examples: *preamble, precedence, prejudice.*

before

before

preamble

■ That which has *precedence* comes _____ [before/ after] the rest.

■ The word *prejudice* implies that a judgment is made _____ [before / after] the facts are studied.

■ The beginning of a constitution is a good place for the _____ [amendments / preamble].

---

**14. pro:** forward; favoring.

Examples: *progeny, prognosis, prolabor.*

prognosis

progeny
(a)

prolabor

■ The doctor noted gloomily that I had contracted leprosy and gave me his _____ *is* (medical forecast).

■ Those interested in their _____ *ny* (offspring) tend to look (a) forward, (b) backward. (    )

■ Gary and Mary argue constantly because he is promanagement and she is _____ *or* (favorable to workers).

---

**15. quadr:** four.

Examples: *quadrangle, quadrant, quadruplets.*

quadrants

■ The pie graph was equally divided into four _____ *ts.*

■ After taking a fertility drug the woman gave birth to

**quadruplets**

_____ *ts.*

**four**

■ A *quadrangle,* as on a college campus, is an area with _____

**four**

sides and _____ angles.

### Quiz

Write the meaning of each boldface Latin prefix.

1. after
2. many
3. four
4. forward
5. before

1. **post**pone       *a* _____
2. **multi**tude       *m* _____
3. **quadr**illion      *f* _____
4. **pro**pulsion      *f* _____
5. **pre**natal        *b* _____

**16. quasi** (kwā′sī): seemingly but not actually.

  Examples: *quasi-antique, quasi-poetry, quasi-scientific.*

**does not**

■ A writer who refers to "the *quasi-scientific* mumbo-jumbo of astrology" _____ [does / does not] believe that astrology is a true science.

**quasi-poetry**

■ At Gettysburg, Lincoln's words—noble and rhythmical—were _____-*poetry.*

**(b)**

■ Sandstorms battered our new desert home, quickly turning it into (a) a genuine antique, (b) a quasi-antique. (    )

**17. quint:** five.

  Examples: *quintessence, quintet, quintuplets.*

**quintet**

■ Our woodwind _____*t* (five musicians) played Mozart, and I think Mozart lost.

**fifth**

■ Their first kiss was the *quintessence*—that is, the ultimate or _____ [third / fifth] essence—of happiness.

quintuplets

■ "I'm pooped," said the stork. "I just brought Mrs. Shlep a set of _____ *ts*" (five offspring).

**18. retro:** back.

Examples: *retroactive, retrogress, retrorocket.*

(b)

■ If civilization is *retrogressing,* it is (a) improving, (b) going back to a worse condition. (     )

retard

■ A *retrorocket* tends to _____ [speed up / retard] a space ship.

retroactive

■ A law or ruling which affects an earlier period is _____ [retroactive / radioactive].

**19. semi:** half.

Examples: *semicentennial, semidiameter, semilunar.*

half

■ A *semilunar* shape is like that of the _____ [full / half] moon.

fifty

■ *Semicentennials* celebrate a period of _____ years.

radius

■ The *semidiameter* of a circle is equal to its _____ [radius / circumference].

**20. sub:** under.

Examples: *subconscious, subcutaneous, subtrahend.*

under

■ The *subconscious* operates _____ [within / under] the conscious mind.

under

■ A *subcutaneous* infection is _____ [on / under] the skin.

subtrahend

■ In subtraction the number written *under* the other number is called the _____ [subtrahend / minuend].

## Quiz

Write the meaning of each boldface Latin prefix.

1. half
2. back
3. under
4. five or fifth
5. not actually

1. **semi**tone     h _____
2. **retro**spect     b _____
3. **sub**marginal     u _____
4. **quint**ile     f _____
5. **quasi**-bargain     n _____ a _____

---

**21. super:** above; beyond.

     Examples: *supersensory, supersonic, superstructure.*

beyond

■ *Supersensory* impressions are _____ [within / beyond] the normal limits of the senses.

above

■ The *superstructure* of a warship is _____ [above / below] the main deck.

supersonic

■ Speeds *beyond* the speed of sound are _____ *sonic.*

---

**22. trans:** across.

     Examples: *transgress, transpolar, transversal.*

across

■ A *transpolar* flight goes _____ [around / across] the pole.

transversal

■ In geometry a line that cuts *across* two other lines is called a _____ [tangent / transversal].

(b)

■ To *transgress* is (a) to respect the rules, (b) to step across the rules or violate them. ( )

---

**23. tri:** three.

     Examples: *tricuspid, trilingual, triplicate.*

triplicate

■ Two copies weren't enough for my boss. No, everything had to be in _____ *te* (three copies).

tricuspid

■ Dr. Pullem, my dentist, triumphantly held up a bloody, *three*-pointed tooth known as a _____ *id*.

trilingual

■ My Swiss friend speaks French, German, and English. He's _____ *al*.

---

**24. ultra:** very; beyond.

Examples: *ultraconservative, ultramodern, ultraviolet.*

beyond

■ *Ultraviolet* rays are invisible because they lie _____ [beyond / inside] the violet end of the visible spectrum.

■ Mr. Skraggs bitterly fought equal pay for women, social security, "and all them other radical notions." Skraggs was an

ultraconservative

_____ *tive*.

ultramodern

■ The Gelts had a dream kitchen—the latest in _____ *modern* equipment—but they always ate out.

---

**25. uni:** one.

Examples: *unicameral, unicorn, unicycle.*

unicameral

■ A legislature with *one* chamber is _____ [unicameral / bicameral].

one

■ The horns on a *unicorn* reach the grand total of _____ .

■ A tricycle has three wheels; a bicycle has two wheels; a

unicycle

_____ has *one* wheel.

---

**Quiz**

Write the meaning of each boldface Latin prefix.

1. across
2. three
3. above
4. one
5. very

1. **trans**fusion       *a* _____
2. **tri**pod            *t* _____
3. **super**saturated    *a* _____
4. **uni**son            *o* _____
5. **ultra**fastidious   *v* _____

---

# REVIEW TEST

Write *True* or *False*.

_____ 1. To *advocate* a policy is to speak against it.

_____ 2. The Revolutionary War *antedated* the War of 1812.

_____ 3. A *semimonthly* magazine comes out twice a month.

_____ 4. To *retrogress* is to go back to an earlier condition.

_____ 5. Opera stars strive to win the audience's *derision*.

_____ 6. *Binoculars* are used by two eyes at the same time.

_____ 7. *Profeminists* usually favor women's rights.

_____ 8. Phone calls from Boston to Seattle are *intercontinental*.

_____ 9. *Quasi-Chinese* music is the native music of China.

_____ 10. The killer's nickname, "Gentle John," is a *misnomer*.

Write the meaning of each boldface Latin prefix. The first letter of each answer is given.

11. an unusual **circum**stance     *a* _____

12. **com**passion for the blind     *t* _____

13. a **contro**versial issue     *a* _____

14. problems in **tri**gonometry     *t* _____

15. a **multi**tude of unpaid bills     *m* _____

16. **quint**essence of greed     *f* _____

17. Chapman's **trans**lation     *a* _____

18. to run **inter**ference     *b* _____

19. **sub**zero weather     *u* _____

20. the campus **quad**rangle     *f* _____

Write the letter that indicates the best completion.

(   ) 21. A *post-mortem* is held on a person who is (a) old, (b) dead, (c) diseased, (d) dying.

(   ) 22. The *preamble* to a document comes (a) at the beginning, (b) in the middle, (c) at the end, (d) in the amendments.

(     ) 23. The Latin prefix for *above* is used in which word?—(a) anteroom, (b) supernatural, (c) retrorocket, (d) submerge.

(     ) 24. The prefix in *united* and in *unification* means (a) nation, (b) states, (c) one, (d) peace.

(     ) 25. The Latin prefix for *beyond* is used in what word?—(a) navigate, (b) submit, (c) infrared, (d) ultraviolet.

## Key to Review Test

Check your test answers with the following key. Deduct 4% per error from a possible 100%.

| | | |
|---|---|---|
| 1. False | 10. True | 19. under |
| 2. True | 11. around | 20. four |
| 3. True | 12. together | 21. (b) |
| 4. True | 13. against | 22. (a) |
| 5. False | 14. three | 23. (b) |
| 6. True | 15. many | 24. (c) |
| 7. True | 16. five, fifth | 25. (d) |
| 8. False | 17. across | |
| 9. False | 18. between | |

Score: _____ %

# LATIN DERIVATIVES

## Supplementary Exercise 1

One derivative of each Latin root is given. Write three more derivatives. If in doubt about a word, check its etymology in a dictionary.

| ROOT | MEANING | DERIVATIVES |
|------|---------|-------------|
| 1. *ac, acr* | sharp | acrimony, _____, _____, _____ |
| 2. *aer* | air | aerial, _____, _____, _____ |
| 3. *agr* | field | agrarian, _____, _____, _____ |
| 4. *ali* | another | alias, _____, _____, _____ |
| 5. *alter, altr* | change | alternate, _____, _____, _____ |
| 6. *anim* | spirit | animosity, _____, _____, _____ |
| 7. *apt, ept* | adjust | aptitude, _____, _____, _____ |
| 8. *arm* | weapon | armistice, _____, _____, _____ |
| 9. *art* | craft | artificial, _____, _____, _____ |
| 10. *avi* | bird | aviary, _____, _____, _____ |
| 11. *bel, bell* | war | rebel, _____, _____, _____ |
| 12. *ben, bene* | well | benefit, _____, _____, _____ |
| 13. *brev* | short | abbreviate, _____, _____, _____ |
| 14. *carn* | flesh | incarnate, _____, _____, _____ |
| 15. *cid, cis* | kill; cut | precise, _____, _____, _____ |
| 16. *civ* | citizen | civil, _____, _____, _____ |
| 17. *clam* | shout | exclaim, _____, _____, _____ |
| 18. *claud, claus* | close | closet, _____, _____, _____ |
| 19. *cogn* | know | incognito, _____, _____, _____ |
| 20. *cord* | heart | cordial, _____, _____, _____ |

## Supplementary Exercise 2

One derivative of each Latin root is given. Write three more derivatives. If in doubt about a word, check its etymology in a dictionary.

| ROOT | MEANING | DERIVATIVES |
|------|---------|-------------|
| 1. *corp* | body | corpse, _____, _____, _____ |
| 2. *cruc* | cross | crux, _____, _____, _____ |
| 3. *dent* | tooth | indent, _____, _____, _____ |
| 4. *dign* | worthy | dignity, _____, _____, _____ |
| 5. *doc, doct* | teach | doctor, _____, _____, _____ |
| 6. *dom* | master | domineer, _____, _____, _____ |

**Latin Derivatives III    103**

|     | ROOT | MEANING |  |
|-----|------|---------|--|
| 7.  | *don* | bestow | donate, _____, _____, _____ |
| 8.  | *du* | two | duet, _____, _____, _____ |
| 9.  | *ego* | I | egotist, _____, _____, _____ |
| 10. | *err* | wander | error, _____, _____, _____ |
| 11. | *fin* | end; limit | define, _____, _____, _____ |
| 12. | *fort* | strong | fortify, _____, _____, _____ |
| 13. | *fus* | pour | effusive, _____, _____, _____ |
| 14. | *gen* | birth; race | progeny, _____, _____, _____ |
| 15. | *grat* | please | gratify, _____, _____, _____ |
| 16. | *grav* | heavy | gravity, _____, _____, _____ |
| 17. | *jac, ject* | throw | eject, _____, _____, _____ |
| 18. | *junct* | join | adjunct, _____, _____, _____ |
| 19. | *labor* | work | elaborate, _____, _____, _____ |
| 20. | *leg* | law | legal, _____, _____, _____ |

## Supplementary Exercise 3

One derivative of each Latin root is given. Write three more derivatives. If in doubt about a word, check its etymology in a dictionary.

|     | ROOT | MEANING | DERIVATIVES |
|-----|------|---------|-------------|
| 1.  | *lev* | lift | levity, _____, _____, _____ |
| 2.  | *lib* | book | libel, _____, _____, _____ |
| 3.  | *luc* | light | elucidate, _____, _____, _____ |
| 4.  | *magn* | large | magnify, _____, _____, _____ |
| 5.  | *mar* | sea | mariner, _____, _____, _____ |
| 6.  | *medi* | middle | medium, _____, _____, _____ |
| 7.  | *min* | little; less | minimum, _____, _____, _____ |
| 8.  | *mon, monit* | warn | premonition, _____, _____, _____ |
| 9.  | *mor* | custom | moral, _____, _____, _____ |
| 10. | *mut* | change | mutation, _____, _____, _____ |
| 11. | *nav* | ship | navigator, _____, _____, _____ |
| 12. | *nomen, nomin* | name | nominee, _____, _____, _____ |
| 13. | *ocul* | eye | monocle, _____, _____, _____ |
| 14. | *par* | equal | parity, _____, _____, _____ |
| 15. | *pater, patr* | father | patron, _____, _____, _____ |
| 16. | *rat, ration* | reason | rational, _____, _____, _____ |
| 17. | *rect* | right | direct, _____, _____, _____ |
| 18. | *simil* | like | simile, _____, _____, _____ |
| 19. | *struct* | build | construct, _____, _____, _____ |
| 20. | *ten* | hold | tenacious, _____, _____, _____ |

# 8

# Greek Derivatives I

| | | |
|---|---|---|
| 1. *anthrop* | 10. *dec* | 19. *metr, meter* |
| 2. *astr* | 11. *dem* | 20. *morph* |
| 3. *auto* | 12. *derm* | 21. *neur* |
| 4. *bibli* | 13. *dyn* | 22. *orth* |
| 5. *bio* | 14. *gram, graph* | 23. *paleo* |
| 6. *chrom* | 15. *hetero* | 24. *pan* |
| 7. *chron* | 16. *homo* | 25. *path* |
| 8. *crypt* | 17. *hydr* | |
| 9. *cycl* | 18. *log* | |

*Socrates never heard of a* telephone *or an* astronaut *or* psychiatry—*and yet those words are derived from Greek roots. As more scientific discoveries are made year after year, the chances are good that new names will continue to be built on the old Greek stems and prefixes. Knowing the meaning of these Greek forms can throw a high-wattage light on many English words.*

*Historically, Greek and Latin came flooding into our language in three waves: (1) religious terms at the beginning of the Christian era; (2) literary and cultural terms during the Renaissance, the revival of learning of the fifteenth and sixteenth centuries; and (3) scientific terms in recent centuries.*

*Chapters 8 and 9 focus on fifty important Greek terms and their clusters of derivatives. First, memorize the Greek term and its definition, given at the beginning of each frame. Next, note carefully the example derivatives that follow. Try to understand the connection between each of these derivatives and its Greek root. Then fill in the blanks.*

## Roots

---

### 1. anthrop: man.

Derivatives: *anthropocentric, anthropogenesis, anthropogeography, anthropoid, anthropology, anthropometry, anthropophagy, misanthropy, philanthropy.*

anthropoids

■ The *man*-like apes are called _____*poids.*

*anthrop*

■ The Greek root for *man* is *a_____* .

anthropology

■ The study of *man* is _____ [philology / anthropology].

anthropophagy

■ Cannibalism, or the eating of man's flesh, is known as _____ [anthropophagy / herbivorousness].

man

■ *Anthrop* means _____ .

anthropocentric

■ A *man*-centered universe is obviously _____*ic.*

misanthrope

■ One who hates *mankind* is a _____ [misanthrope / metronymic].

philanthropist

■ A charitable fellow is a _____*ist* (from *phil,* meaning

*anthrop,* man

loving and *a_____* , meaning *m_____*).

---

### 2. astr: star.

Derivatives: *aster, asterisk, asteroid, astral, astrobiology, astrodome, astrogate, astrolabe, astrology, astrometry, astronaut, astronomy, astrophysics, disaster.*

stars

■ *Asteroids* are tiny planets that look like _____ [apes / stars].

*astr*

■ The Greek root for *star* is *a_____* .

astronomy

■ The scientific study of the *stars* is _____*my,* and

astrology

fortune-telling by the *stars* is _____*gy.*

■ Those who fly toward the *stars* are said not to navigate but

astrogate

to _____ *gate*, and the fliers themselves are

astronauts

called _____ [dreadnaughts / astronauts].

■ Printer's *stars* (as in H\*Y\*M\*A\*N  K\*A\*P\*L\*A\*N) are

asterisks

called _____ *ks*.

disaster

■ The word *dis* _____ hints that the *stars* were contrary.

---

### 3. auto: self.

Derivatives: *autobiography, autocrat, autogenesis, autograph, autohypnosis, autoinfection, automat, automation, automaton, automobile, autopsy, autosuggestion.*

self

■ An *autobiography* is written by one's _____ [critic / self].

self

■ *Autosuggestion* is given by one's _____ [doctor / self].

*auto*

■ The Greek root for *self* is *a* _____ .

automation

■ A system of *self*-operating machinery is called _____ *ion*.

automat

■ A *self*-operating restaurant service is an _____ *at*.

autocrat

■ I can't admire any _____ *crat* (dictator, having *self*-

automobile

power) riding in his bullet-proof _____ , but I might ask

autograph

him for his _____ (*self*-written name).

---

### 4. bibli: book.

Derivatives: *Bible, Biblicist, bibliofilm, bibliography, bibliolatry, bibliomania, bibliophile, bibliopole, bibliotheca.*

*bibli*

■ The Greek root for *book* is *b* _____ .

bibliography

■ A list of *book* sources is called a _____ *phy*.

a bibliotheca

■ A library or *book* collection is sometimes called _____ [volumetrics / a bibliotheca].

bibliomania

■ A craze for collecting *books* is _____ [numismatics / bibliomania].

bibliophile
bibliopole

■ The _____ _phile_ (book-lover) gets _books_ from a _____ _pole_ (book-dealer).

■ Scholars record rare _books_ on special microfilm known

bibliofilm

as _____ [movifilm / bibliofilm].

book

■ The root _bibli_ means _____ .

---

**5. bio:** life.

Derivatives: _biochemist, biodynamics, biogenesis, biography, biology, biolysis, biometrics, biophysics, biopsy._

life

■ _Biology_ deals with plant and animal _____ [life / fiction].

_bio_

■ The three-letter Greek root for _life_ is _____ .

biography

■ The written account of a _life_ is a _____ _phy._

■ The diagnostic examination by microscope of a piece of _living_ tis-

biopsy

sue is a _____ _psy._

■ The calculation of the probable span of human _life_ is called

biometrics

_____ [kinematics / biometrics].

■ The branch of physics that deals with _living_ matter is

biophysics

_____ _cs._

■ The branch of chemistry that deals with _life_ processes is

biochemistry

_____ _try._

■ _Biogenesis_ is the theory that living things can come from (a) living

(a)

things only, (b) lifeless matter. (        )

---

## Quiz

Write the meaning of each boldface Greek root.

1. book
2. self
3. man
4. star
5. life

1. **bibli**omania        *b* _____
2. **auto**infection      *s* _____
3. **anthrop**ocentric    *m* _____
4. **astr**al             *s* _____
5. anti**biot**ics        *l* _____

---

**6. chrom:** color.

Derivatives: *chromatic, chromatology, chrome, chromium, chromosome, chromosphere, panchromatic, polychrome.*

polychromatic

■ A many-colored print is _____ [polyglot / polychromatic].

color

■ A lens with *chromatic* aberration distorts _____ [sound / color].

*chrom*

■ The Greek root for *color* is *ch* _____ .

■ The *colorful* gases seen around the sun during a total eclipse are

chromosphere

called the _____ [biolysis / chromosphere].

color

■ *Chrom* means _____ .

chromosomes

■ Our hereditary markings depend on tiny _____*somes.*

---

**7. chron:** time.

Derivatives: *chronic, chronicle, chronograph, chronological, chronology, chronometer, chronometry, chronoscope, synchronize.*

time

■ *Chronological* order is _____ [time / place] order.

time

■ *Chron* means *t* _____ .

■ A motion picture film and its sound effects should be *timed* to-

synchronized

gether, or *syn* _____ .

| | |
|---|---|
| chronometer | ■ A watch or clock is sometimes called a _____ *meter,* and |
| chronometry | the scientific measurement of *time* is _____ *try.* |
| *chron* | ■ The Greek root for *time* is _____ . |
| chronic | ■ If your back aches for a long *time* you have a _____ backache. |

---

**8. crypt:** secret.

Derivatives: *crypt, cryptic, cryptogram, cryptographer, cryptography, cryptology, cryptonym.*

| | |
|---|---|
| secret | ■ A *cryptic* remark has a _____ [clear / secret] meaning. |
| *crypt* | ■ The Greek root for *secret* is cr_____ . |
| cryptogram | ■ A *secret,* coded message is a _____ *gram,* and the fellow |
| cryptographer | who decodes it is a _____ *er.* |
| cryptonym | ■ A *secret* name is a _____ [cognomen / cryptonym]. |
| crypt | ■ Bodies were often hidden away in a _____ [chromosphere / crypt]. |

---

**9. cycl:** circle; wheel.

Derivatives: *cycle, cyclograph, cycloid, cyclometer, cyclone, cyclorama, cyclotron, encyclical, encyclopedia.*

| | |
|---|---|
| (b) | ■ An *encyclopedia* gives instruction in (a) science only, (b) the *circle* of arts and sciences. (     ) |
| *cycl* | ■ The Greek root for *circle* or *wheel* is c_____ . |
| cyclone | ■ A storm that has *circling* winds is called a _____ . |
| cyclorama | ■ A *circular* room with large pictures is a _____ *ama.* |
| cyclotron | ■ An apparatus that accelerates atomic particles in *circles* is a _____ *on.* |

wheel

motorcycle

■ A *cyclometer* measures _____ [wheel / Russian] revolutions and might be useful on a _____ [foot / motorcycle].

---

**10. dec:** ten.

Derivatives: *decade, decagon, decaliter, Decalogue, Decameron, decameter, decasyllable, decathlon, decennial, decimal, decimate.*

decade

decaliter

decameter

■ *Ten* years equal a _____ *de,* ten liters equal a _____ *er;* ten meters equal a _____ *er.*

*dec*

■ The Greek root for *ten* is *d*_____ .

ten

■ A *decathlon* consists of _____ [five / ten] athletic events.

ten

■ A *decennial* celebrates _____ years.

Decalogue

■ The *Ten* Commandments are called the _____ [Heptateuch / Decalogue].

Decameron

■ Boccaccio's tales were supposedly told during a plague by *ten* people on *ten* days—hence, they are entitled the _____ Pentateuch / *Decameron*].

---

**Quiz**

Write the meaning of each boldface Greek root.

1. secret
2. wheel
3. ten
4. color
5. time

1. **crypt**ogram    *s* _____
2. bi**cycle**    *w* _____
3. **dec**imal    *t* _____
4. **chrom**atism    *c* _____
5. **chron**ology    *t* _____

---

**11. dem:** people.

Derivatives: *demagogue, demiurge, democracy, democrat, demography, endemic, epidemic, pandemic.*

| | |
|---|---|
| democracy | ■ Government by the *people* is called _____ *cy*. |
| demagogue | ■ One who uses false claims and emotional appeals to stir up the common *people* is a _____ *gue*. |
| people | ■ The Greek root *dem* means _____ . |
| endemic | ■ A disease restricted to *people* in one locality is _____ [endemic / cycloid]. |
| epidemic | ■ A disease that spreads among *people* is *epi* _____ , and |
| pandemic | if it hits *people* over a very wide area it is _____ [panoramic / pandemic]. |
| people | ■ *Demography* is a study of how _____ [people / cattle] are distributed. |
| *dem* | ■ The Greek root for *people* is _____ . |

### 12. derm: skin.

Derivatives: *dermatitis, dermatoid, dermatologist, dermatophyte, epidermis, hypodermic, pachyderm.*

| | |
|---|---|
| skin | ■ *Dermatitis* is an inflammation of the _____ [joints / skin]. |
| dermatologist | ■ A *skin* infection should be treated by a _____ *ist*. |
| *derm* | ■ The Greek root for *skin* is *d* _____ . |
| pachyderms | ■ Thick-*skinned* animals, like elephants and rhinoceroses, are _____ [anthropoids / pachyderms]. |
| epidermis | ■ Our outermost layer of *skin* is the *epi* _____ . |
| hypodermic | ■ An under-the-*skin* injection is a *hypo* _____ . |

### 13. dyn: power.

Derivatives: *dynamic, dynamism, dynamite, dynamo, dynamometer, dynasty, dyne, electrodynamics, hydrodynamics, thermodynamics.*

| | |
|---|---|
| (b) | ■ A *dyne* is a unit of (a) time, (b) force or power. (   ) |
| dynamometer | ■ Mechanical *power* can be measured by a _____ *meter.* |
| *dyn* | ■ The Greek root for *power* is *d*_____ . |
| dynamic | ■ An energetic person is said to be _____ *ic.* |
| dynasty | ■ A *powerful* family which has ruled for some generations is a _____ *sty.* |
| power | ■ *Dyn* means _____ . |
| power | ■ The *dynamos* at Niagara produce electrical _____ . |
| dynamite | ■ One *powerful* explosive is _____ . |

### 14. gram, graph: write.

Derivatives: *autograph, biography, calligraphy, cryptogram, diagram, epigram, geography, graffiti, gramophone, grammar, graphic, graphite, graphology, holograph, lithograph, mimeograph, photograph, seismograph, telegram, typography.*

| | |
|---|---|
| writing | ■ A *mimeograph* makes duplicates of _____ [secrets / writing]. |
| writing | ■ *Graphite* is used in pencils for _____ [erasing / writing]. |
| write | ■ The Greek roots *gram* and *graph* mean _____ [heavy / write]. |
| calligraphy | ■ One's penmanship, or *handwriting,* is called _____ [calliope / calligraphy]. |
| seismograph | ■ Seismic disturbances, or earthquakes, are *recorded* on the *seis*_____ . |
| (b) | ■ *Graphology* tries to analyze character by means of (a) head bumps, (b) handwriting. (   ) |
| (b) | ■ The *graffiti* found on walls are (a) insects, (b) rude sketches and writing. (   ) |

grandma

■ Which word wandered into the wrong line-up?—*epigram, telegram, grammar, grandma, lithograph.* _____

---

**15. hetero:** other.

Derivatives: *heterodox, heterodyne, heterogeneous, heterograft, heteromorphic, heteronym, heteroplasty, heterosexual.*

other
(a)

■ *Hetero* means _____ . Members of a *heterogeneous* group are (a) of various types, (b) all alike. (    )

other

■ A *heterosexual* person is attracted to the _____ [same / other] sex.

heterodox

■ Religious or political beliefs that are *other* than the usual kind are _____ *dox.*

heteroplasty

■ Surgery in which the grafted tissue comes from *another* person is called _____*plasty* or

heterograft

_____ *graft.*

---

**Quiz**

Write the meaning of each boldface Greek root.

1. people
2. write
3. power
4. other
5. skin

1. **dem**ocrat          *p* _____
2. litho**graph**        *w* _____
3. **dyn**amism          *p* _____
4. **hetero**geneity     *o* _____
5. pachy**derm**         *s* _____

---

**16. homo:** same.

Derivatives: *homeopathy, homochromatic, homogamy, homogeneous, homogenize, homograft, homologous, homonym, homosexual.*

homogeneous

■ If those in a group are the *same,* that group is _____ [homogeneous / heterogeneous].

| | |
|---|---|
| homonyms | ■ Words that have the *same* sound, like "bare" and "bear," are called _____ [antonyms / homonyms]. |
| *homo* | ■ The Greek root for *same* is h_____. |
| color | ■ *Chrom* means _____ , and flowers which are all the *same* |
| homochromatic | color are _____ [homochromatic / heterochromatic]. |
| homogenized | ■ Milk which is uniformly of the *same* texture has been _____ *ed*. |
| homosexual | ■ One who has sexual desire for those of the *same* sex is _____ [homosexual / heterosexual]. |

### 17. hydr: water.

Derivatives: *hydraulics, hydrocarbon, hydrocephaly, hydrogen, hydrography, hydrokinetics, hydrometer, hydropathy, hydrophobia, hydroponics, hydrotherapy.*

| | |
|---|---|
| water | ■ *Hydraulics* deals with the mechanical properties of *w*_____ and other liquids. |
| water | ■ *Hydropathy* and *hydrotherapy* involve treatment of disease by use of *w*_____. |
| *hydr* | ■ The Greek root for *water* is h_____. |
| hydrophobia | ■ Because rabies brings on a fear of *water,* the disease is also known as _____ *bia*. |
| hydrocephaly | ■ Excessive fluid in the skull is called _____ [hydrocephaly / heteroplasty]. |
| fluids | ■ *Hydroponics* is the science of growing plants in _____ [sand / fluids]. |

### 18. log: word; study.

Derivatives: *apology, biology, decalogue, dialogue, doxology, embryology, eulogy, geology, hydrology, logic, logorrhea, mineralogy, monologue, philology, prologue, tautology, theology.*

| | |
|---|---|
| study | ■ *Biology* is the _____ [breeding / study] of plant and animal life. |
| study | ■ *Mineralogy* is the s_____ of minerals. |
| *log* | ■ The Greek root for *study* is l_____ . |
| hydrology | ■ The *study* of water and its distribution is _____ [hydrolysis / hydrology]. |
| embryology | ■ The *study* of embryo development is _____ [embryology / embryectomy]. |
| word | ■ The root *log,* as in *monologue, dialogue,* and *eulogy,* means _____ [word / log]. |
| words | ■ A *tautology*—as in "small little midget"—uses too many w_____ . |
| words | ■ A person with *logorrhea* pours out too many w_____ . |

---

**19. metr, meter:** measure.

Derivatives: *ammeter, barometer, centimeter, chronometer, geometry, hexameter, hydrometer, metrology, metronome, micrometer, pentameter, seismometer, speedometer, thermometer, trigonometry.*

| | |
|---|---|
| measure | ■ A *barometer* is used to _____ [measure / lower] air pressure. |
| measure | ■ A *chronometer* is used to m_____ time. |
| micrometer | ■ One instrument which *measures* tiny distances is the _____ [micrometer / microcosm]. |
| geometry, trigonometry *metr* | ■ Mathematics courses that deal with *measurement* include geo_____ and trig_____. In these two words the root that means *measure* is _____ . |
| (b) | ■ *Metrology* is the science of (a) metals, (b) weights and measures. (    ) |

---

**20. morph:** form.

> Derivatives: *amorphous, anthropomorphic, isomorph, metamorphosis, Morpheus, morphine, morphology.*

■ Ovid's *Metamorphoses* tells how the gods caused people to change their (a) financial condition, (b) form or shape. ( )

(b)

■ *Morph* means f_____ .

form

■ In linguistics the study of the internal structure and *form* of words is called _____ *ology.*

morphology

■ *Formless* sulphur is _____ [amorphous / crystalline].

amorphous

■ *Morpheus* was the god of dreams, named after the _____ [colors / forms] seen in dreams.

forms

■ An *anthropomorphic* god is in the _____ (*morph*) of a _____ (*anthrop*).

form

man

---

## Quiz

Write the meaning of each boldface Greek root.

1. measure
2. water
3. study
4. form
5. same

1. hydro**meter**      *m* _____
2. **hydr**ophobia      *w* _____
3. geo**logy**      *s* _____
4. iso**morph**      *f* _____
5. **homo**logous      *s* _____

---

**21. neur:** nerve.

> Derivatives: *neural, neuralgia, neurasthenia, neurocirculatory, neurogenic, neurologist, neuromotor, neuromuscular, neuron, neurosis, neurotic.*

■ A *neurotic* suffers from a _____ [speech / nervous] disorder.

nervous

■ *Neuritis* is a painful inflammation of the _____ [skin / nerves].

nerves

| | |
|---|---|
| *neur* | ■ The Greek root for *nerve* is n_____ . |
| neurosis | ■ The *neurotic* has what is called a _____ [neurosis / psychosis]. |
| neurasthenia | ■ If you develop fatigue, worries, and pains without apparent cause, your condition is called _____*nia.* |
| neurologist | ■ If you need a *nerve* specialist, go to a _____*ist.* |

**22. orth:** right; true.

Derivatives: *orthochromatic, orthodontics, orthodox, orthogenesis, orthography, orthopedics, orthopsychiatry, orthoscope.*

| | |
|---|---|
| (a) | ■ The *orthodox* religion is presumably (a) the established "true" faith, (b) a modern variation of religious faith. (    ) |
| *orth* | ■ The Greek root for *right* or *true* is o_____ . |
| orthopedist | ■ To *right* or correct skeletal deformities is the job of the _____ [orthopedist / cyclopedist]. |
| orthodontist | ■ The straightening and *trueing* of teeth is done by the _____ [neurologist / orthodontist]. |
| right | ■ *Orthography* deals with _____ [right / foreign] spelling. |
| true | ■ *Orthochromatic* film should produce _____ [altered / true] colors. |

**23. paleo:** ancient.

Derivatives: *paleobotany, Paleocene, paleography, paleolithic, paleontology, Paleozoic, paleozoology.*

| | |
|---|---|
| ancient | ■ The *Paleozoic, Paleocene,* and *paleolithic* periods belong to an _____ [ancient / recent] era. |
| *paleo* | ■ The Greek root for *ancient* is p_____ . |
| paleontology | ■ The study of *ancient* forms of plant and animal life is called _____*ology.* |

| | |
|---|---|
| paleolith | ■ An *ancient* stone tool is a _____ *lith.* |
| ancient | ■ The word *paleography* has two Greek roots, meaning _____ |
| writing | and _____ . |

---

**24. pan:** all.

> Derivatives: *panacea, Pan-American, Pan-Asiatic, panchromatic, pancreas, pandemic, pandemonium, panegyric, Panhellenic, panorama, pantheism, pantheon, pantomime.*

| | |
|---|---|
| all | ■ *Panchromatic* film is sensitive to _____ [no / all] colors. |
| all | ■ A *panacea* is a supposed cure for _____ [one / all] disease or trouble. |
| *pan* | ■ The Greek root for *all* is *p* _____ . |
| panorama | ■ A picture with a view in *all* directions is a _____ *ama.* |
| pandemic | ■ A disease that is very widespread is _____ *ic.* |
| Panhellenic | ■ A league of *all* the campus Greek-letter (Hellenic) fraternities and sororities is _____ *ic.* |
| Pantheon | ■ A temple for *all* the gods was the _____ [Colosseum / Pantheon]. |
| all | ■ *Pan* means _____ . |

---

**25. path:** disease; feeling.

> Derivatives: *antipathy, apathy, empathy, neuropathy, osteopathy, pathetic, pathologist, pathos, psychopath, sympathy, telepathy.*

| | |
|---|---|
| *path* | ■ The Greek root *p* _____ means *feeling.* |
| pathetic | ■ A *feeling* of pity is aroused by *pathos* or that which is _____ *ic.* |
| sympathy | ■ Your compassion for another person is *sym* _____ , and your complete projection of yourself into the *feelings* of another |
| empathy | person is *em* _____ . |

diseases

■ The root *path* means *feeling,* but it can also mean *disease;* thus, a *pathologist* is a specialist in _____ [paths and trails / diseases].

psychopath

■ A serious mental disorder would be found in a _____ [psychopath / bibliopole].

## Quiz

Write the meaning of each boldface Greek root.

1. right
2. nerve
3. ancient
4. feeling
5. all

1. **orth**ography     *r* _____
2. **neur**on     *n* _____
3. **paleo**botany     *a* _____
4. a**path**etic     *f* _____
5. **pan**acea     *a* _____

# REVIEW TEST

Write *True* or *False*.

_____ 1. *Cryptography* deals with secret writing.

_____ 2. *Bibliomania* refers to excessive use of alcohol.

_____ 3. *Graphite* can be used to write with.

_____ 4. *Paleontologists* are interested in fossils.

_____ 5. *Autosuggestion* requires two or more people.

_____ 6. *Orthodox* beliefs are new and daring.

_____ 7. *Homogenized* milk has its cream floating at the top.

_____ 8. *Dermatology* deals with the skin.

_____ 9. *Neurasthenia* refers to a hardening of the arteries.

_____ 10. A wristwatch is a type of *chronometer*.

---

Write the meaning of each boldface Greek root. The first letter of each answer is given.

11. an **anthrop**omorphic god            *m*_____

12. **pan**hellenic organizations          *a* _____

13. suffering from de**hydr**ation          *w* _____

14. the Dewey **dec**imal system           *t* _____

15. the **chrom**osome number              *c* _____

16. a sudden meta**morph**osis             *f* _____

17. overuse of anti**biot**ics              *l* _____

18. faith in **dem**ocracy                  *p* _____

19. the **hetero**doxies of Berkeley        *o* _____

20. a sensitive volt**meter**               *m*_____

---

Write the letter that indicates the best completion.

(    ) 21. An *asterisk* is a printing symbol that looks like (a) a number, (b) a star, (c) a slanted line, (d) a question mark.

(    ) 22. *Pathogenesis* has to do with the origin of (a) a disease, (b) a path, (c) God, (d) sin.

(    ) 23. A *dynamometer* measures (a) speed of rotation, (b) spark, (c) power, (d) sound.

**Greek Derivatives I**    121

( ) 24. The Greek root for *circle* is used in which word?—(a) cryptic, (b) cardiac, (c) encyclical, (d) eclipse.

( ) 25. The Greek root which is common to both *geology* and *proctology* means (a) earth, (b) study, (c) tunnel, (d) the end.

## Key to Review Test

Check your test answers with the following key. Deduct 4% per error from a possible 100%

| | | |
|---|---|---|
| 1. True | 10. True | 19. other |
| 2. False | 11. man | 20. measure |
| 3. True | 12. all | 21. (b) |
| 4. True | 13. water | 22. (a) |
| 5. False | 14. ten | 23. (c) |
| 6. False | 15. color | 24. (c) |
| 7. False | 16. form | 25. (b) |
| 8. True | 17. life | |
| 9. False | 18. people | |

Score: _____ %

# 9

# Greek Derivatives II

| ROOTS | | PREFIXES |
|-------|------|----------|
| 1. *phil* | 10. *therm* | 19. *kilo* |
| 2. *phon* | 11. *amphi* | 20. *meta* |
| 3. *physi* | 12. *anti* | 21. *mono* |
| 4. *pseudo* | 13. *arch* | 22. *neo* |
| 5. *psych* | 14. *dia* | 23. *peri* |
| 6. *pyr* | 15. *epi* | 24. *poly* |
| 7. *soph* | 16. *eu* | 25. *syn, sym* |
| 8. *tele* | 17. *hyper* | |
| 9. *the* | 18. *hypo* | |

Chapter 9 continues our study of Greek derivatives. Follow the same procedure as in Chapter 8.

## Roots

_____

**1. phil:** loving.

Derivatives: *Anglophile, bibliophile, Francophile, philander, philanthropy, philatelist, philharmonic, philodendron, philogynist, philology, philoprogenitive, philosophy, philter.*

*phil*

■ The Greek root for *loving* is *p* _____ .

bibliophile

■ One who *loves* books (*bibli*) is a _____ *ile.*

■ One with *love,* or charity, for man (*anthrop*) is called a

philanthropist

_____ *ist.*

philosopher

■ One who *loves* wisdom (*soph*) is a _____ *er.*

philogynist

■ One who *loves* women (*gyn*) is a _____ *ist;* but if he

philanderer

trifles with their *love* he may be called a _____ [demagogue/philanderer].

philharmonic

■ If you *love* musical harmony, you might join a _____ *ic* orchestra.

Francophile

■ If you *love* or admire the French, you are a _____ [Francophobe / Francophile].

philatelist

■ If you *love* stamps and collect them, you are a _____ [psychopath / philatelist].

_____

**2. phon:** sound.

Derivatives: *phoneme, phonetic, phonics, phonograph, phonology, phonometer, phonoscope, telephone.*

■ The word *telephone* deals with *sound,* as is suggested by its Greek

*phon*

root *p* _____ .

sound

■ *Phonetic* spelling is based on the _____ [sound / general appearance] of words.

| | |
|---|---|
| phoneme | ■ In linguistics, a specific speech *sound* is called a _____ eme. |
| phonometer | ■ An instrument which measures (*meter*) the intensity and the frequency of *sound* vibrations is a _____ [chronometer / phonometer]. |
| (b) | ■ *Phonics* deals with (a) picture transmission, (b) speech sound, especially as related to the teaching of reading and pronunciation. ( ) |
| sound | ■ *Phon* means _____ . |

---

### 3. physi: nature.

Derivatives: *physical, physician, physicist, physiocrat, physiognomy, physiography, physiology, physiotherapy.*

| | |
|---|---|
| nature | ■ A *physicist* studies the laws of _____ [poetry / nature]. |
| *physi* | ■ The Greek root for *nature* is ph_____ . |
| physiography | ■ The description of *nature* and natural phenomena is sometimes called _____ [empathy / physiography]. |
| (a) | ■ A *physiocrat* believes that the only true source of wealth is (a) the land and its products, (b) gambling. ( ) |
| nature | ■ *Physi* means _____ . |
| physiology | ■ The branch of biology that deals with the parts and the functions of the body is _____ gy. |
| physiognomy | ■ Your face is your _____ nomy. |

---

### 4. pseudo: false.

Derivatives: *pseudoaquatic, pseudoclassic, pseudomorph, pseudonym, pseudopod, pseudoscience.*

| | |
|---|---|
| pseudonym | ■ An author's fictitious or *false* name, such as *Mark Twain* or *George Eliot* or *Lewis Carroll,* is a _____ [surname / pseudonym]. |
| false | ■ *Pseudo* means f_____ . |

| | |
|---|---|
| (b) | ■ When a critic refers to a novel as "a pseudoclassic," he means that it is (a) a genuine classic, (b) not a genuine classic. (    ) |
| pseudosciences | ■ Unreliable studies such as phrenology and astrology are actually _____ [social sciences / pseudosciences]. |
| is not | ■ A *pseudoaquatic* plant _____ [is / is not] genuinely aquatic. |
| false form | ■ A *pseudomorph* is a mineral which looks like another one—for example, copper pyrites, known as "fools' gold"—and the word literally means _____ _____ . |

---

**5. psych:** mind; spirit.

Derivatives: *psyche, psychedelic, psychic, psychiatrist, psychoanalysis, psychodrama, psychograph, psychology, psychometry, psychoneurosis, psychopath, psychosis, psychosomatic, psychotherapy.*

| | |
|---|---|
| mind | ■ *Psychiatry* treats disorders of the _____ [eye / mind]. |
| psychoanalysis | ■ Freudian analysis to cure the *mind* is _____ *sis*. |
| *psych* | ■ The Greek root for *mind* is *ps* _____ . |
| psychograph | ■ A chart of one's personality traits is a _____ [psychograph / pseudomorph]. |
| mind | ■ A *psychic* shock or trauma has a permanent effect on the _____ [heart / mind]. |
| psychedelic | ■ Drugs like LSD which affect the *mind* are _____ *lic*. |

---

## Quiz

Write the meaning of each boldface Greek root.

1. false
2. nature
3. sound
4. mind
5. loving

1. **pseudo**pod    *f* _____
2. **physi**cian    *n* _____
3. **phon**ograph    *s* _____
4. **psych**osis    *m* _____
5. **phil**harmonic    *l* _____

---

**6. pyr:** fire.

Derivatives: *pyre, pyretic, Pyrex, pyrexia, pyrites, pyritology, pyrochemical, pyrogenic, pyrolysis, pyromancy, pyromaniac, pyrometry, pyrophobia, pyrosis, pyrostat, pyrotechnics.*

start fires

■ A *pyromaniac* has a compulsion to _____ [steal things / start fires].

fireworks

■ *Pyrotechnics* is the art of making and displaying _____ [advertisements / fireworks].

*pyr*

■ The Greek root for *fire* is *p*_____ .

pyre

■ Hindu widows used to be cremated on their husband's funeral _____ *e.*

Pyrex

■ American cooks use heat-resistant glassware called _____ *x.*

fever

■ A child with *pyrexia* is suffering from _____ [chills / fever].

fire

■ A *pyrostat* is an alarm device protecting against _____ [burglar / fire].

pyrophobia

■ An irrational fear of *fire* is called _____ *bia.*

unhappy

■ A *pyromaniac* and a *pyrophobe* would probably be _____ [happy / unhappy] together.

---

**7. soph:** wisdom.

Derivatives: *gymnosophist, philosophy, Sophia, sophism, sophisticated, sophistry, Sophocles, sophomore, sophomoric, theosophy.*

The word *sophomore* has two Greek roots: *soph,* which means

wise

_____ [wise / strong], and *mor* (as in *moron*), which means *foolish.* Therefore an immature person who acts like a know-it-all

sophomoric

is said to be _____ [sophomoric / heterogeneous].

Since the *sophists* were notorious for their clever but deceptive

sophistry

logic, a misleading argument is sometimes called a _____ *ry.*

sophisticated

People who are *worldly-wise* are _____ *ed.*

A rocket or electronic device that is very subtle and complicated

sophisticated

in design is also said to be _____ *ed.*

According to its Greek roots, the word *philosophy* means *the love*

wisdom

*of w* _____ .

---

**8. tele:** far.

Derivatives: *telecast, telegenic, telegraph, telekinesis, telemechanics, telemeter, telepathy, telephone, telephoto, telescope, telethermometer, telethon, teletype, television.*

The word *telephone* literally means *far + sound.* Similarly, *tele-*

far, writing

*graph* means *f* _____ + *w* _____ .

far, seeing

*Television* means _____ + _____ [advertising / seeing].

*tele*

The Greek root for *far* is *t* _____ .

A thermometer that measures temperature from *afar* is a

telethermometer

_____ *er.*

telephoto

Photos can be taken from *afar* by _____ *to.*

Mechanisms can be radio-operated from *afar* by techniques

telemechanics

of _____ *mechanics.*

Transmitting thoughts without use of the five senses is

telepathy

called _____ *pathy*

**9. the:** god.

Derivatives: *atheism, monotheism, pantheism, pantheon, polytheism, theanthropic, theism, theocentric, theocracy, theology, theosophy.*

■ *Theism* and *monotheism* generally refer to a belief in G_____ .

God

■ Belief in many *gods* is *poly*_____ .

polytheism

■ Belief in no *god* is *a*_____ .

atheism

■ The Greek root for *god* is *t*_____ .

*the*

■ Puritan New England, ruled by *God* and the church, was a _____ [democracy / theocracy].

theocracy

■ The study of *God* and religious doctrines is called _____*gy.*

theology

■ *The* means _____ .

god

■ A cultural pattern in which *God* is the center of interest is _____ [anthropocentric / theocentric].

theocentric

**10. therm:** heat.

Derivatives: *diathermy, hydrothermal, isotherm, thermal, thermocouple, thermodynamics, thermograph, thermometer, thermonuclear, thermopile, thermos, thermostat.*

■ In a *thermonuclear* blast the nuclear fission releases _____ [psychic waves / heat].

heat

■ A *thermostat* controls (a) heat, (b) water. (    )

(a)

■ The word *hydrothermal* literally means (a) electric power, (b) hot water. (    )

(b)

■ A record of temperature is made by the _____*ph.*

thermograph

■ A line on the weather map between points of equal temperature is an _____ [isotherm / isobar].

isotherm

■ The relations between *heat* and other forms of energy are dealt with in _____ *ics*.

thermodynamics

thermos

■ Coffee keeps its *heat* in a _____ *s* jug.

## Quiz

Write the meaning of each boldface Greek root.

1. god
2. fire
3. far
4. wisdom
5. heat

1. **the**osophy    *g* _____
2. **pyr**ometry    *f* _____
3. **tele**scope    *f* _____
4. **soph**omore    *w* _____
5. dia**therm**y    *h* _____

## Prefixes

**11. amphi:** around; on both sides.

    Examples: *amphibians, amphibolous, amphitheater.*

amphibians

■ Since frogs live *both* on land and in water they are _____ [bisexuals / amphibians].

amphitheater

■ An arena with spectators seated *around* it is an _____ *ter*.

amphibolous

■ A statement with two possible meanings—such as "The Duke yet lives that Henry shall depose"—is _____ [amphibolous / anthropomorphic].

**12. anti:** against.

    Examples: *antibiotic, antipathy, antithesis.*

against

■ An *antipathy* is a feeling _____ [for / against] something.

contrast

■ In *antithesis* the two parts of a sentence present a _____ [similarity / contrast].

(b)

■ A substance such as penicillin or streptomycin which works *against* certain germs and viruses is known as (a) insulin, (b) an antibiotic. (   )

---

**13. arch:** chief.

Examples: *archangel, archfiend, architect.*

chief

■ An *archangel* is a _____ [common / chief] angel.

(b)

■ In Milton's *Paradise Lost* the *archfiend* is (a) a run-of-the-mill devil, (b) Satan himself. (   )

architect

■ The *chief* worker in charge of designing a building is the _____ [stonemason / architect].

---

**14. dia:** through.

Examples: *diabetes, diameter, diathermy.*

through

■ *Diathermy* sends heat _____ [through / around] one's body.

diameter

■ The distance *through* a circle is called the _____ .

(b)

■ A disease associated with excess sugar passing *through* the body is (a) carditis, (b) diabetes. (   )

---

**15. epi:** upon; beside.

Examples: *epicenter, epidermis, epitaph.*

upon

■ The *epidermis* is the outer, nonsensitive layer that lies _____ [upon / below] the true skin.

epicenter

■ The point above and *upon* the center of an earthquake is the _____ [seismograph / epicenter].

epitaph

■ The inscription *upon* a tomb is an _____ [anagram / epitaph].

---

**16. eu:** good; well.

Examples: *eulogy, eupepsia, euphoria, euthanasia.*

well-being

■ *Euphoria* is a feeling of _____ [pain / well-being].

good

■ *Eupepsia* means _____ [good / bad] digestion.

praises

■ A *eulogy* _____ [praises / condemns].

euthanasia

■ Mercy killing is known as _____ [asphyxia / euthanasia].

**17. hyper:** excessive.

Examples: *hypercritical, hyperopia, hyperthyroidism.*

■ One who finds fault with an *excessive* number of details is

hypercritical

_____ [hypocritical / hypercritical].

■ A person whose eyes can see an *excessive* distance probably has

hyperopia

_____ [myopia / hyperopia].

■ *Hyperthyroidism,* marked by rapid pulse and sleeplessness, may be

excessive

caused by _____ [insufficient / excessive] activity of the thyroid gland.

**18. hypo:** under.

Examples: *hypocrite, hypothermia, hypothesis.*

below

■ A patient with *hypothermia* has a temperature _____ [above / below] normal.

■ An assumption which *underlies* an investigation is called a

hypothesis

_____ [hypothesis / prosthesis].

■ A person who pretends to be sincere, honest, or good but *under* it

hypocrite

all is insincere, dishonest, or evil is a _____te.

**19. kilo:** thousand.

Examples: *kilocycle, kilometer, kilowatt.*

thousand

■ A *kilocycle* equals one _____ [hundred / thousand] cycles per second.

kilometer

■ One *thousand* meters equal one _____.

one

■ Problem: One *thousand* watts of electrical energy used for sixty minutes equal _____ [one / 60,000] kilowatt-hour[s].

---

**20. meta:** change; after.

Examples: *metabolism, metamorphic, metempsychosis.*

■ Rocks such as marble which have *changed* their form under pres-

metamorphic

sure are _____ [anthropomorphic / metamorphic].

■ The body's chemical and physical *changes,* with release of energy,

metabolism

are aspects of _____ [morphology / metabolism].

■ *Metempsychosis* assumes that at one's death his soul (a) also dies,

(b)

(b) makes a change, passing into another body. (     )

---

**21. mono:** one.

Examples: *monodrama, monogamy, monomania.*

■ Being married to only one person at a time is called

monogamy

_____ [polygamy / monogamy].

monodrama

■ A play with *one* performer is a _____ [monodrama / melodrama].

■ Captain Ahab's irrational interest in *one* subject, Moby Dick,

monomania

amounts to _____ [bipolarity / monomania].

### 22. **neo:** new.

Examples: *neoclassicism, neologism, neophyte.*

new

■ A *neophyte* in a religious order is a _____ [new / elderly] member.

neologism

■ A *new* word, freshly coined, is a _____ [neologism / hyperbole].

■ A period of a *new* version, or revival, of classical literary style is

neoclassicism

known as _____ [romanticism / neoclassicism].

### 23. **peri:** around.

Examples: *perimeter, periphrasis, periscope.*

around

■ The *perimeter* of a ranch is the distance _____ [across / around] it.

(b)

■ An optical instrument used in submarines for looking *around* an obstruction is known as a (a) stereoscope, (b) periscope. (     )

(a)

■ *Periphrasis* is a *roundabout* way of phrasing, as in (a) "I did dance and Joe did shout," (b) "I danced and Joe hollered." (     )

### 24. **poly:** many.

Examples: *polygon, polysyllable, polytechnic.*

many

■ A *polytechnic* institution offers courses in _____ [one or two / many] technical fields.

polygon

■ A plane figure with *many* sides is a _____ [polygon / mastodon].

(b)

■ A *polysyllable* has *many* (at least three ) syllables, like the word (a) "logic," (b) "transcendentalism." (     )

**25. syn, sym:** together.

Examples: *synchronize, syndrome, synthesis.*

■ *Synthesis* involves (a) bringing things together, (b) taking things apart. (          )

(a)

■ Actions that are timed *together* are _____ [acclimated / synchronized].

synchronized

■ Symptoms which occur *together* and indicate a specific disease are called a _____ [syndrome / eupepsia].

syndrome

## REVIEW TEST

Write *True* or *False*.

_____ 1. The *archdeacon* has a higher rank than the deacon.

_____ 2. *Hyperacidity* refers to a lack of enough stomach acid.

_____ 3. *Metamorphic* rocks have undergone a change of form.

_____ 4. A *polytheist* believes in the oneness of God.

_____ 5. The feminine name *Sophia* originally meant "stupid."

_____ 6. An *amphibian* plane can take off from land or sea.

_____ 7. *Antipathy* is warm affection.

_____ 8. A *phonoscope* enables one to see certain characteristics of sounds.

_____ 9. *Synchronized* movements are timed together.

_____ 10. A *kilogram* weighs one thousand pounds.

---

Write the meaning of each boldface Greek root or prefix. The first letter of each answer is given.

11. a **pseudo**medieval ballad      *f* _____

12. a jutting **peri**scope      *a* _____

13. the doctor's **dia**gnosis      *t* _____

14. cooking with **Pyr**ex      *f* _____

15. the actor's **mono**cle      *o* _____

16. **neo**-impressionism in art      *n* _____

17. the gentle **phil**osopher      *l* _____

18. suffering from **hypo**glycemia      *u* _____

19. a sensitive **therm**ocouple      *h* _____

20. cutting the **epi**cardium      *u* _____

---

Write the letter that indicates the best completion.

(     ) 21. *Euphoria* refers to a feeling of (a) well-being, (b) weariness, (c) drowsiness, (d) hunger.

(     ) 22. *Physics* is the study of (a) diseases, (b) chemicals, (c) nature, (d) beauty.

( ) 23. *Psychosurgery* involves cutting into (a) the lungs, (b) the face, (c) the muscles, (d) the brain.

( ) 24. *Tele* means (a) *sound,* (b) *star,* (c) *far,* (d) *sight.*

( ) 25. The Greek root which is common to both *pantheism* and *theology* means (a) *all,* (b) *god,* (c) *study,* (d) *nature.*

## Key to Review Test

Check your test answers with the following key. Deduct 4% per error from a possible 100%

| | | |
|---|---|---|
| 1. True | 10. False | 19. heat |
| 2. False | 11. False | 20. upon |
| 3. True | 12. around | 21. (a) |
| 4. False | 13. through | 22. (c) |
| 5. False | 14. fire | 23. (d) |
| 6. True | 15. one | 24. (c) |
| 7. False | 16. new | 25. (b) |
| 8. True | 17. loving | |
| 9. True | 18. under | |

Score: _____ %

## Supplementary Exercise

One derivative of each Greek root is given. Write three more derivatives. If in doubt about a word, check its etymology in a dictionary.

| ROOT | MEANING | DERIVATIVES |
|------|---------|-------------|
| 1. *cosm* | world; order | cosmic, _____, _____, _____ |
| 2. *crac, crat* | power | plutocrat, _____, _____, _____ |
| 3. *gam* | marriage | monogamy, _____, _____, _____ |
| 4. *gen* | race; kind | genetics, _____, _____, _____ |
| 5. *geo* | earth | geometry, _____, _____, _____ |
| 6. *gon* | angle | hexagon, _____, _____, _____ |
| 7. *gyn* | woman | gynecology, _____, _____, _____ |
| 8. *iso* | same | isobar, _____, _____, _____ |
| 9. *lith* | rock | monolith, _____, _____, _____ |
| 10. *mega* | great | megaphone, _____, _____, _____ |
| 11. *micro* | small | microbe, _____, _____, _____ |
| 12. *necr* | dead | necrosis, _____, _____, _____ |
| 13. *nom* | law; order | economy, _____, _____, _____ |
| 14. *onym* | name | antonym, _____, _____, _____ |
| 15. *ped* | child | pedant, _____, _____, _____ |
| 16. *phos, phot* | light | photograph, _____, _____, _____ |
| 17. *poli* | city | police, _____, _____, _____ |
| 18. *scop* | see; watch | episcopal, _____, _____, _____ |
| 19. *techn* | art; skill | technique, _____, _____, _____ |
| 20. *zoo* | animal | zoo, _____, _____, _____ |

# 10

# Characterization Words

1. *bigot*
2. *braggart*
3. *buffoon*
4. *bungler*
5. *charlatan*
6. *colleague*
7. *connoisseur*
8. *culprit*
9. *dilettante*
10. *felon*
11. *feminist*
12. *glutton*

13. *gourmet*
14. *huckster*
15. *ingénue*
16. *luminary*
17. *magnate*
18. *martyr*
19. *nomad*
20. *oracle*
21. *pacifist*
22. *paragon*
23. *patriarch*
24. *prodigy*

25. *pundit*
26. *raconteur*
27. *recluse*
28. *ruffian*
29. *saboteur*
30. *schlemiel*
31. *skeptic*
32. *tippler*
33. *tycoon*
34. *urchin*
35. *virtuoso*
36. *zealot*

*The need to describe people arises constantly. You may write, for example, that Mr. More is a truck driver. That takes care of his occupation. But the reader may wish to know* more *about More. After all, truck drivers differ considerably in personality. One stops and changes a tire for you; another sideswipes your fender and jeers, "May I have the last dents?" The first is a* paragon; *the second is a* bungler, *a* ruffian, *or possibly—heaven forbid!—a* tippler. *Such characterization words can add a dimension to description.*

*This chapter is not about the names of jobs—architect, custodian, lion tamer—rather it puts the spotlight on terms that characterize people.*

*A further challenge? Test your skill in the exercise at the end of this chapter involving an additional twenty-five characterization words.*

COVER THIS STRIP

1. **bigot** (big′ət): a narrow-minded, prejudiced person.
2. **braggart** (brag′ərt): a very boastful person.
3. **buffoon** (bə-fōon′): somebody who is always clowning around and trying to be funny.

bigot

■ "Nobody of that racial group should ever get voted into this high-minded country club," said the *bi* _____ .

braggart

■ "I raised a hog so big that the snapshot of it weighs three pounds," said the *br* _____ .

buffoon

■ In my coat pocket was a fat frog, placed there by the class *bu* _____ .

braggart
bigot
buffoon

■ Every village has its conceited *br* _____ , its intolerant *b* _____ , and its life-of-the-party, lampshade-wearing *b* _____ .

braggart
bigot
buffoon

■ The fishing trip? "I caught barrels of sea bass," said the _____ . "I don't associate with common sailors," said the _____ . "I nailed my shorts to the top of the mast," snickered the _____ .

4. **bungler:** a clumsy, blundering fellow.
5. **charlatan** (shär′lə-tən): a quack; one who pretends to have expertise, as in medicine, that he doesn't have.
6. **colleague** (kol′ēg): a fellow worker in the same profession.

colleague

■ My professor was not in his office so I spoke to his *co* _____ .

bungler
charlatan

■ When the island "dentist" loosened the wrong tooth, I suspected he was a *bu* _____ , but when he hit my jaw with a coconut, I realized he was a *ch* _____ .

■ "Professional ethics prevent you from bad-mouthing a

colleague     co _____," I said to the surgeon, "but I'm getting a heart

colleague     transplant; and if your new *co* _____ is a diddling

charlatan, bungler     *ch* _____ or a clumsy *bu* _____, I'm coming
back to haunt you."

colleague     ■ "Mr. Swindell is a former *co* _____ of mine," confided
the lawyer, "and nobody is less qualified than that ignorant

bungler     *bu* _____. His only expertise is to stage a car accident and

charlatan     sue for five million green ones. A first-class *ch* _____!

---

7. **connoisseur** (kon′ə-sŏŏr′): an expert in a special field, generally in one of the fine arts or in matters of taste.
8. **culprit:** one who is guilty of a crime or fault.
9. **dilettante** (dil′i-tänt′): a dabbler in the arts and sciences; one
   who follows an art in a superficial way.

culprit     ■ A one-fingered pickpocket stole a ring of keys from my pocket,
but Detective Butts nabbed the *cu* _____.

connoisseur     ■ Mr. Snorkel says our champagne is "frisky but somewhat unfo-
cused." Only a *co* _____ of wine can talk like that.

dilettante     ■ Hans poses as an expert in classical music, but his inane opinions
show him to be a mere *di* _____.

connoisseur     ■ A young girl, not at all an art *co* _____, saw a splash of
ketchup on a Picasso—it had been unnoticed for several weeks—and

culprit     we are now looking for the *cu* _____.

(b)     ■ Whether this is a fake Rembrandt should be determined by (a) a
dilettante, (b) a connoisseur. ( ) If we've been sold a forgery, we

culprit     must go after the *cu* _____.

---

Write the letter that indicates the best definition.

1. (g)     ( ) 1. bigot          a. a clown type
2. (e)     ( ) 2. braggart       b. a dabbler in the arts
3. (a)     ( ) 3. buffoon        c. a clumsy fellow
4. (c)     ( ) 4. bungler        d. a fine arts expert

5. (f)
6. (i)
7. (d)
8. (h)
9. (b)

| | | | |
|---|---|---|---|
| ( | ) 5. | charlatan | e. a boaster |
| ( | ) 6. | colleague | f. a quack; a fake "healer" |
| ( | ) 7. | connoisseur | g. a highly prejudiced person |
| ( | ) 8. | culprit | h. one guilty of a prank or crime |
| ( | ) 9. | dilettante | i. a fellow worker; an associate |

**10. felon** (fel′ən): a person who has committed a serious crime such as murder or burglary.

**11. feminist:** one who advocates economic, social, and political rights for women equal to those of men.

**12. glutton:** a person who greedily eats too much, or who has a great capacity for something. "I'm a *glutton* for soap operas."

glutton

■ "Tiny" Joe, a noted *gl*_____, ate six hot dogs.

feminist

■ Gloria, who despises male chauvinism, is an outspoken *fe*_____.

glutton

■ The robber whispered, "Hand it over, gal. I'm a *gl*_____ for cash." The bank clerk replied, "Straighten your tie. You're a

felon

*fe*_____ and you're on camera."

feminist
felon
glutton

■ Everybody has a dream. The *f*_____ dreams of equal pay for equal work; the *f*_____ dreams of a pardon from the governor; the *g*_____ dreams of roast pig.

Name the character type of each speaker.

glutton

"When I eat, sparks fly from my knife and fork." _____

feminist

"Open those top jobs to women as well as men." _____

felon

"Nineteen more years in the slammer. Wait for me, honey." _____

**13. gourmet** (goor′mā): a specialist in delicacies of the table; an excellent judge of fine foods and drink.

**14. huckster:** an aggressive salesperson, possibly of vegetables, fruit, and small articles.

**15. ingénue** (an′zhi-n$\overline{oo}$′): the role in a play of the sweet, innocent, inexperienced young woman.

■ Flora is too sophisticated and matronly to be cast as the *in* _____ .

ingénue

■ "Grape tarts and mulled wine," ordered the *g* _____ .

gourmet

■ "Fish! Nice fresh fish!" cried the *h* _____ .

huckster

■ Mr. Fresser loves exotic delicacies of the table. In fact, he's a dedicated *g* _____ .

gourmet

■ A stadium *h* _____ sold me a bag of eight stale peanuts, not exactly *g* _____ food.

huckster
gourmet

■ Donna looks young, pretty, and a bit stupid—the director says she'll be a perfect *in* _____ .

ingénue

Name the character type of each speaker.

"Buy your steel radials from Smiling Sam." _____

huckster

"Only a French chef understands frog legs." _____

gourmet

"Just a li'l girl from Dingville, and—pure luck!—already I been invited to this city feller's apartment tonight to look at his picture albums." _____

ingénue

16. **luminary:** a famous person inspirational to others.
17. **magnate** (mag′nāt): a powerful or influential person in business or industry.
18. **martyr** (mär′tər): one who suffers for a cause.

■ Andrew Carnegie was an early steel *m* _____ .

magnate

■ Nathan Hale, hanged as a rebel, was a *m* _____ .

martyr

■ Among film comedians, Chaplin was a *lu* _____ .

luminary

■ Famous Americans of past years include Henry Ford, the automobile *m* _____ , Ernest Hemingway, a *l* _____ among prose writers, and Martin Luther King, a *m* _____ to the cause of civil rights.

magnate,
luminary
martyr

luminary

magnate, martyr

■ More American heroes: Thomas Edison was a *l* _____ among inventors; James Hill was a railroad builder and *m* _____ ; and many a child has been a *m* _____ to our sweat shops.

## Quiz

Write the letter that indicates the best definition.

1. (c)
2. (f)
3. (e)
4. (h)
5. (a)
6. (g)
7. (i)
8. (d)
9. (b)

(    ) 1. felon         a. a sweet, naive young woman
(    ) 2. feminist      b. one who suffers for ideals
(    ) 3. glutton       c. a criminal
(    ) 4. gourmet      d. a powerful industrial leader
(    ) 5. ingénue       e. a greety eater
(    ) 6. huckster      f. an advocate of women's rights
(    ) 7. luminary     g. a pushy salesperson or peddler
(    ) 8. magnate      h. a lover of fine foods
(    ) 9. martyr        i. a famous person in some field

**19. nomad** (nō′mad′): a wanderer without a fixed home.

**20. oracle:** one who makes wise or prophetic statements.

**21. pacifist:** one who is opposed to war and violence or who, as a matter of conscience, resists the draft.

nomad

■ Hobo Hank travels everywhere. He's a *no* _____ .

oracle

■ How prophetic! Linda is a true *or* _____ .

pacifist

■ "In war, everybody loses," says the *pa* _____ .

oracle

■ More rain? Let's consult the weather *o* _____ .

nomad

■ Abou, a desert *n* _____ , claims that a camel is really a horse put together by a committee.

Name the character type of each speaker.

nomad

"My tribe will wander the Sahara forever." _____

pacifist

"There never was a good war or a bad peace." _____

oracle

"I foresee a day when men will be judged only by their merit." _____

22. **paragon** (par′ə-gon′):  one who is a model of excellence.
23. **patriarch** (pā′trē-ärk′):  the aging father or ruler of a family or tribe.
24. **prodigy** (prod′i-jē):  a remarkably talented child or person; a marvel.

patriarch

■ The tribe was led by its white-haired *pat*_____ .

prodigy

■ The five-year-old chess *pr*_____ blitzed me.

paragon

■ Jeeves, a *par*_____ among butlers, handled every detail.

prodigy

■ The Vesuvius eruption, burying Pompeii, was a tragic *pr*_____ of nature.

patriarch

paragon

■ The priest eulogized the aged _____ of the clan, calling him a *par*_____ of virtue.

Name the character type that is being described.

prodigy

Little Wolfgang will play the five concertos by memory. _____

patriarch

Sixty-two grandchildren danced at the picnic in his honor. _____

paragon

Helpful, talented, loving—the perfect spouse! _____

25. **pundit:**  a very learned person.
26. **raconteur** (rak′on-tûr′):  a skilled teller of anecdotes.
27. **recluse** (rek′lōōs):  one who lives alone; a hermit.

raconteur

■ Salty stories poured out of the *ra*_____ like sewage from a broken main.

pundit

■ We were dizzied by the philosophical lecture of the Harvard *pu*_____ .

recluse

■ Fear of crime turned Fred into a lonely *r*_____ .

(a)

■ Depth of learning is the mark of the (a) pundit, (b) recluse, (c) raconteur. (     )

recluse

raconteur

■ The holy cave-dweller, a genuine *rec*_____ , nearly fainted at the racy jokes of the *ra*_____ .

Name the character type of each speaker.

pundit

"This is my third book on medieval culture." _____

recluse

"I like living alone. People turn me off." _____

raconteur

"Did you hear the one about the old lady and the broccoli?" _____

---

## Quiz

Write the letter that indicates the best definition.

1. (f)
2. (d)
3. (a)
4. (h)
5. (g)
6. (c)
7. (i)
8. (e)
9. (b)

(   ) 1. nomad      a. one who is opposed to war
(   ) 2. oracle      b. a hermit
(   ) 3. pacifist      c. an extremely gifted child
(   ) 4. paragon      d. one who is prophetic and wise
(   ) 5. patriarch      e. one who tells anecdotes
(   ) 6. prodigy      f. a wanderer
(   ) 7. pundit      g. the old ruler of a tribe
(   ) 8. raconteur      h. a model of excellence
(   ) 9. recluse      i. a very scholarly person

---

28. **ruffian** (ruf′yən): a brutal, lawless person; a hoodlum.
29. **saboteur** (sab′ə-tûr′): one who deliberately damages machines or materials in time of war or labor disputes.
30. **schlemiel** (shlə-mēl′): *Slang.* an awkward unlucky person, easily victimized; a born loser.

saboteur

■ We caught the *sab*_____ just as he was pouring mucilage into the fludbunnies.

schlemiel

■ Tore his pants on the piano? What a *sc*_____!

■ The Good Humor man was brutally beaten by a bad-humored

ruffian

*ruf*_____ .

saboteur

■ The factory explosion was not caused by a *sa*_____, but

schlemiel

by a *sc*_____ who stumbled and dropped a torpedo.

ruffian

■ In the alley I met a *ru*_____ who had knifed more people than a surgeon.

Name the character type of each speaker.

saboteur

"I fixed the guns so they shoot backwards." _____

ruffian

"Let's beat up on them little guys. . . ." _____

schlemiel

"I fell on my back and broke my nose." _____

**31. skeptic:** one with a doubting attitude toward matters that most people accept.

**32. tippler:** one who habitually drinks small quantities of alcoholic beverages.

**33. tycoon** (tī-kōōn'): a wealthy and powerful industrialist or businessperson.

skeptic

■ A flat earth? Columbus was a *sk*_____ about that.

tippler

■ My uncle, a chronic *ti*_____, drinks to calm himself. Sometimes he gets so calm he can't move.

skeptic

■ Oswald Spengler, in *The Decline of the West,* is a *sk*_____ about our future.

tycoon

■ Jason's career as an industrial *ty*_____ was ruined when

tippler

he became a *ti*_____. "I took a snort only at odd hours—one, three, five. . . ."

Name the character type of each speaker.

skeptic

"What good is space travel? It's for the birds." _____

tycoon

"Our Cadillac franchises really paid off." _____

tippler

"I'm not so think as I drunk I am." _____

**34. urchin:** a small mischievous boy; any youngster.

**35. virtuoso** (vûr'chōō-ō'sō): a person with a dazzling technique in an art such as music.

**36. zealot** (zel'ət): one who is extremely devoted to a cause; a fanatic.

virtuoso

■ Paganini was a noted violin *vi*_____.

urchin

■ I chased the *ur*_____ who'd let the air out of our tires.

zealot

virtuoso

zealot

urchin

zealot

urchin

virtuoso

■ "Home run!" The Dodger z_____ behind me pounded my back.

■ Hoping to become a flute v_____, I asked the maestro about my execution. He favored it.

■ I'm an anti-violence z_____, but if I ever catch the ur_____ who dumped manure into my swimming pool, I'll kick him into orbit.

Name the character type that is described.

Velma is passionately involved in the anti-vivisection crusade.

_____

Please excuse Jimmy for being tardy yesterday. He was playing marbles. _____

The cellist gave a brilliant interpretation of Shnook's intricate "Sonata in Six Flats and a Basement." _____

## Quiz

Write the letter that indicates the best definition.

(   ) 1. ruffian      a. a mischievous child
(   ) 2. saboteur      b. a hoodlum
(   ) 3. schlemiel      c. a fanatic for a cause
(   ) 4. skeptic      d. a wealthy captain of industry
(   ) 5. tippler      e. a war machine wrecker
(   ) 6. tycoon      f. a clumsy, unlucky person
(   ) 7. virtuoso      g. one who hits the bottle
(   ) 8. urchin      h. a doubter; a nonbeliever
(   ) 9. zealot      i. a brilliant instrumentalist

Write the word studied in this chapter that will complete the sentence.

1. Only six and she studies calculus? A child *pr*_____!

2. Ingersoll doubted miracles and became a religious *sk*_____.

3. Joan of Arc died at the stake, a *ma*_____ to her faith.

4. To foresee the future, the Greeks consulted an *or*_____.

5. "Thou shalt not exploit women"—thus saith the *fem*_____.

6. Hank crowed that he would make four touchdowns, but the *br*_____ lost yardage.

7. "Popcorn! Buy your popcorn here," wheedled the *hu*_____.

8. In "My Sister Eileen" she starred as the innocent, lovable young woman—the *in*_____.

9. Should this mother of twelve bring yet another *ur*_____ into this inhospitable world?

10. Extremely knowledgeable, Samuel Johnson was the *pu*_____ of his era.

11. If he claims his medicine cures cancer, he's probably a *ch*_____.

12. The venerable *ra*_____ pelted us with a stream of baseball anecdotes.

Write *True* or *False*.

_____ 13. A business *tycoon* is a *magnate*.

_____ 14. A *pacifist* is a *ruffian*.

_____ 15. A *schlemiel* is a *bungler*.

_____ 16. A *gourmet* is a *connoisseur*.

_____ 17. A *dilettante* is a *virtuoso*.

_____ 18. A *recluse* is a *nomad*.

_____ 19. In time of war, a *saboteur* is a *felon*.

_____ 20. Both the *tippler* and the *glutton* consume too much.

Matching. Write the letter that indicates the best definition.

(     ) 21. bigot                a. a fanatic

(     ) 22. buffoon          b. a hunter of jungle animals

(     ) 23. culprit             c. a big industrial leader

(     ) 24. paragon         d. a prejudiced person

(     ) 25. zealot             e. one guilty of a crime or offense

                                           f. an insane person

                                           g. one given to pranks and clowning

                                           h. a flawless person; a role model

## Key to Review Test

Check your test answers with the following key. Deduct 4% per error from a possible 100%.

| | | |
|---|---|---|
| 1. prodigy | 10. pundit | 19. True |
| 2. skeptic | 11. charlatan | 20. True |
| 3. martyr | 12. raconteur | 21. (d) |
| 4. oracle | 13. True | 22. (g) |
| 5. feminist | 14. False | 23. (e) |
| 6. braggart | 15. True | 24. (h) |
| 7. huckster | 16. True | 25. (a) |
| 8. ingénue | 17. False | |
| 9. urchin | 18. False | |

Score: _____ %

## SUPPLEMENTARY EXERCISE

Fill in the blanks at the left with the characterization words that fit the definitions. Although these words were not defined in this chapter, you should recognize most of them. Check your answers with the key at the end of the exercise. Use your dictionary to study any unknown words.

■ antagonist, apostate, aristocrat, avenger, cherub

1. _____ one who punishes to get even
2. _____ one who has deserted his or her faith
3. _____ an angelic child
4. _____ an opponent; an adversary
5. _____ a member of a proud, privileged class

■ clodhopper, confidant, conniver, disciple, dowager

6. _____ an elderly woman of dignity and wealth
7. _____ *Informal.* A country hick
8. _____ one who cooperates with evildoers
9. _____ a person entrusted with secrets
10. _____ a follower of a teacher or doctrine

■ factotum, jingoist, mendicant, orphan, pagan

11. _____ somebody hired to do all sorts of work
12. _____ a child without parents; a cast-off
13. _____ one who favors a warlike foreign policy
14. _____ a heathen
15. _____ a beggar

■ paraplegic, parasite, parvenu, reactionary, scavenger

16. _____ an extreme conservative in politics
17. _____ one who searches through rubbish
18. _____ one who lives at the expense of another
19. _____ a paralyzed person
20. _____ one who is newly rich; an upstart

■ sycophant, tenant, thespian, truant, turncoat

21. _____ a traitor
22. _____ a student who skips school

**Characterization Words    151**

23. _____ a self-serving flatterer

24. _____ one who occupies some property

25. _____ an actor or actress

## Key to Supplementary Exercise

Check your test answers with the following key. Deduct 4% per error from a possible 100%.

| | | |
|---|---|---|
| 1. avenger | 10. disciple | 19. paraplegic |
| 2. apostate | 11. factotum | 20. parvenu |
| 3. cherub | 12. orphan | 21. turncoat |
| 4. antagonist | 13. jingoist | 22. truant |
| 5. aristocrat | 14. pagan | 23. sycophant |
| 6. dowager | 15. mendicant | 24. tenant |
| 7. clodhopper | 16. reactionary | 25. thespian |
| 8. conniver | 17. scavenger | |
| 9. confidant | 18. parasite | |

Score: _____ %

# 11

# Descriptive Words I

| | | |
|---|---|---|
| 1. affable | 13. cadaverous | 25. dubious |
| 2. altruistic | 14. candid | 26. eccentric |
| 3. ambidextrous | 15. craven | 27. enigmatic |
| 4. aromatic | 16. dastardly | 28. erotic |
| 5. asinine | 17. deft | 29. exorbitant |
| 6. astute | 18. defunct | 30. feasible |
| 7. bawdy | 19. destitute | 31. fluent |
| 8. bellicose | 20. diabolic | 32. frugal |
| 9. berserk | 21. discreet | 33. furtive |
| 10. bizarre | 22. disenchanted | 34. gullible |
| 11. buoyant | 23. dogmatic | 35. impeccable |
| 12. buxom | 24. droll | 36. impromptu |

*The right descriptive word can be worth diamonds in a composition. Of course, as Mark Twain said, it must be the right word, not its second cousin. Naturally, if you know thirty ways to describe a man or a voice or a smile instead of only five ways, you have a wider selection and your chances of picking an effective word are much improved.*

*Chapters 11 and 12 present descriptive words that should be part of the stock in trade of any writer of themes or reader of literature. Study carefully the definitions at the beginning of each frame. Then fill in the blanks with words defined in that frame, unless other choices are offered.*

## EXERCISES

COVER THIS STRIP

1. **affable** (af′ə-bəl): easy to talk to; amiable.
2. **altruistic** (al′trōō-is′tik): unselfish; concerned for the welfare of others.

(b)

■ An *affable* professor is (a) hostile, (b) friendly. (    )

(a)

■ An *altruistic* woman is one who sacrifices to help (a) others, b) only herself. (    )

affable

■ We found Homer in a friendly, talkative mood, in fact, quite *af_____* .

altruistic

■ Devoted to public charities, Straus was certainly *al_____* .

affable

■ In *A Tale of Two Cities,* the executioner stands grim and silent, hardly an *af_____* fellow. Then Sydney Carton gives his life—loses his head, in fact—to save a friend. What an

altruistic

*al_____* deed!

3. **ambidextrous** (am′bə-dek′strəs): able to use both hands with equal ease.
4. **aromatic** (ar′ə-mat′ik): fragrant; spicy; sweet-smelling.

(b)

■ *Aromatic* plants are (a) odorless, (b) pleasantly scented. (    )

ambidextrous

■ A basketball player who shoots baskets with either hand is _____ [ambidextrous / paraplegic].

ambidextrous

■ Wilma bats the baseball equally well from either side of the plate because she is *am_____* .

aromatic

■ Her boudoir was *ar_____* with subtle perfumes and incense.

aromatic
ambidextrous

■ At harvest these orchards are *ar_____* , and the owner hires a few fast, cheap, *amb_____* pickers.

**5. asinine** (as′ə-nīn′): stupid; silly; ass-like.

**6. astute** (ə-stŌŌt′): shrewd; keen in judgment; cunning.

■ The baseball fan's *asinine* comments made it clear that he was (a) a knucklehead, (b) a deep thinker. (   )

(a)

astute

■ Our nation needs _____ [astute / asinine] diplomats.

astute

■ Not everyone is shrewd enough to make *as*_____ investments.

■ Trusting the strange door-to-door salesman with all my savings

asinine

was an *as*_____ thing to do.

astute

■ Even the most *ast*_____ student can make a mistake, but

asinine

to keep repeating the same mistakes is *as*_____.

---

### Quiz

Write the letter that indicates the best definition.

1. (e)
2. (c)
3. (b)
4. (f)
5. (a)
6. (d)

| | | |
|---|---|---|
| (   ) 1. affable | a. very stupid | |
| (   ) 2. altruistic | b. using both hands equally well | |
| (   ) 3. ambidextrous | c. completely unselfish | |
| (   ) 4. aromatic | d. keenly intelligent | |
| (   ) 5. asinine | e. warm and friendly | |
| (   ) 6. astute | f. sweet-scented | |

---

**7. bawdy** (bô′dē): indecent; obscene.

**8. bellicose** (bel′ə-kōs′): hostile; eager to fight; warlike.

■ *Bawdy* shows can be expected at (a) Sunday schools, (b) Las

(b)

Vegas. (   )

■ World tension is increased when national leaders exchange

bellicose

_____ [affable / bellicose] remarks.

bellicose

■ Bouncing his knuckles off my nose seemed to me a *be*_____ gesture.

bawdy

■ The minister's daughter blushed at the *ba*_____ anecdote.

| | |
|---|---|
| bawdy | ■ When I tried to hush the drunken stranger who was singing a vulgar, *ba*_____ song in our church, he became quite |
| bellicose | *be*_____. |

**9. berserk** (bər-sûrk′): crazed; in a destructive frenzy.

**10. bizarre** (bi-zär′): odd in appearance; grotesque; queer. (Don't confuse with *bazaar*—a market or sale.)

| | |
|---|---|
| bizarre | ■ Halloween masks are usually _____ [bazaar / bizarre]. |
| (a) | ■ People who go *berserk* belong in (a) asylums, (b) crowded buses. ( ) |
| berserk | ■ The brand-new straitjacket looks stylish on the man who went *ber*_____. |
| bizarre | ■ The green wig gave my aunt a *bi*_____ appearance. |
| bizarre berserk | ■ The painting was so *bi*_____ that Twain thought it depicted a cat going _____ in a platter of tomatoes. |

**11. buoyant** (boi′ənt): tending to float; light of spirit; cheerful.

**12. buxom** (buk′səm): healthily plump; full-bosomed; attractive.

| | |
|---|---|
| (a) | ■ When drowning, grab a *buoyant* material, like (a) cork, (b) a lead pipe. ( ) |
| buxom | ■ The Flemish women painted by Rubens tend to be fleshy—that is, _____ [buxom / buoyant]. |
| buxom buoyant | ■ After a week at the health spa, Amy lost her _____*m* figure, and her step became _____*nt*. |
| buoyant | ■ The balloonist said that hydrogen was lighter and more _____*nt* than helium, and that he got a bigger bang out of using it. |
| buxom buoyant | ■ The astronauts looked _____*m* in their space suits, and they floated about in _____*nt* weightlessness. |

Write the letter that indicates the best definition.

| | | |
|---|---|---|
| 1. (b) | ( ) 1. bawdy | a. tending to float; cheerful |
| 2. (d) | ( ) 2. bellicose | b. off-color; indecent |
| 3. (f) | ( ) 3. berserk | c. attractively plump |
| 4. (e) | ( ) 4. bizarre | d. warlike; pugnacious |
| 5. (a) | ( ) 5. buoyant | e. peculiar in appearance |
| 6. (c) | ( ) 6. buxom | f. destructively enraged |

---

**13. cadaverous** (kə-dav′ər-əs): gaunt; haggard; corpse-like.

**14. candid:** frank; unprejudiced; outspoken.

(b)

■ A *cadaverous* person should probably (a) reduce, (b) put on weight. ( )

candid

■ I want the unvarnished truth, so give me a _____ [candid / candied] report.

candid

■ The editor said that my poems stank. He was quite _____ d.

cadaverous

■ After forty days of fasting, Maximilian looked pale and *cad* _____ .

cadaverous

candid

■ The sick hermit was so wasted and _____ that, to be *can* _____ , the doctor hardly knew whether to feed him or bury him.

---

**15. craven:** cowardly; timid; chicken-hearted.

**16. dastardly:** sneaky and mean; brutal.

(b)

■ It was *dastardly* of Punky Jones to (a) chase the cattle rustlers, (b) trip and rob the blind man. ( )

(a)

■ It was *craven* of me (a) to flee from the dachshund, (b) to challenge the bully. ( )

craven

■ Amid flying bullets one tends to develop a timid, even a *cr* _____ spirit.

dastardly

■ Beating his infants was *das* _____ , even if they did pour syrup on his stamp collection.

dastardly, craven

■ Who painted the captain's horse blue? Private Jubbs did the d_____ deed, but he was too *cr*_____ to admit it.

---

**17. deft:** skilled and neat in action; adroit; dexterous.

**18. defunct** (di-fungkt′): dead; deceased; no longer existing.

(a)

■ One must be particularly *deft* to (a) do needlework, (b) ride escalators. (    )

(a)

■ A *defunct* enterprise belongs to (a) the past, (b) the future. (       )

deft

■ I found that to play Chopin's "Minute Waltz" in less than five minutes requires quick, *d*_____ fingers.

defunct

■ Alas, poor Yorick, whose skull I hold—he is _____*ct*.

deft, defunct

■ To walk across this boulevard of speeding cars, you must be _____ or soon you'll be _____.

---

## Quiz

Write the letter that indicates the best definition.

1. (f)
2. (b)
3. (d)
4. (e)
5. (c)
6. (a)

(    ) 1. cadaverous      a. dead; functioning no more
(    ) 2. candid          b. frank; open and sincere
(    ) 3. craven          c. skillful
(    ) 4. dastardly       d. cowardly; timid
(    ) 5. deft            e. mean; villainous
(    ) 6. defunct         f. haggard; like a corpse

---

**19. destitute** (des′ti-tōōt′): extremely poor; lacking the necessities of life.

**20. diabolic** (dī′ə-bol′ik): devilish, fiendish.

(a)

■ His *diabolic* ambition was to destroy (a) mankind, (b) disease. (    )

(b)

■ The *destitute* have more than their share of (a) money, (b) poverty. (    )

destitute

■ Her husband died three days after his insurance lapsed, and she was left *des*_____.

diabolic

■ King Edward IV plotted to have his brother Clarence stabbed and drowned in a barrel of wine. How *dia*_____!

destitute, diabolic

■ The melodrama dealt with a penniless old couple—absolutely *des*_____—the victims of a _____ villain who foreclosed on the mortgage.

---

**21. discreet:** prudent; tactful; careful not to talk or act unwisely.
**22. disenchanted:** set free from one's rosy illusions.

disenchanted

■ Those who expected to find fat gold nuggets lying on the Yukon snowbanks were quickly _____ [vindicated / disenchanted].

(a)

■ A *discreet* roommate (a) keeps a secret, (b) blabs about confidential matters. (   )

discreet

■ This juicy story should not be publicized, fellows, so please be *dis*_____.

disenchanted

■ Those who trusted Stalin's promises were soon *dis*_____.

discreet

disenchanted

■ After marriage William was less *dis*_____ in his drinking; and his bride, stumbling among his bottles, was _____*ed.*

---

**23. dogmatic** (dog-mat′ik): asserting opinions in a dictatorial way; positive; strongly opinionated.
**24. droll** (drōl): comical; quaintly amusing.

(b)

■ A *droll* fellow at the circus is (a) the tiger, (b) the clown. (   )

(b)

■ Highly *dogmatic* conversationalists are usually (a) popular, (b) obnoxious. (   )

droll

■ The audience laughed at Will Rogers' *dr*_____ remarks.

dogmatic

■ Military men often become opinionated and *dog*_____.

dogmatic

droll

■ Our landlord kept ordering us in *do*_____ fashion to clean our rooms; nor did he smile at Bill's *dr*_____ remark that the garbage disposal must have backfired.

Write the letter that indicates the best definition.

1. (f)
2. (c)
3. (b)
4. (a)
5. (e)
6. (d)

(     ) 1. destitute     a. losing one's romantic beliefs
(     ) 2. diabolic     b. prudent in speech and conduct
(     ) 3. discreet     c. fiendish; outrageously wicked
(     ) 4. disenchanted     d. comical; whimsically amusing
(     ) 5. dogmatic     e. opinionated; dictatorial
(     ) 6. droll     f. needy; penniless

---

**25. dubious** (dōō'bi-əs): doubtful; vague; skeptical; questionable.

**26. eccentric** (ik-sen'trik): odd; peculiar; unconventional; off-center.

■ The bearded gentleman skating around in the drugstore is thought
to be rather _____ [eccentric / conventional].

eccentric

■ Although madman Columbus said the world was round, his listeners could see it was flat, and so they were naturally _____
[dubious / delusive].

dubious

■ Mrs. Doodle often takes her Flemish rabbit for a walk on a leash—
another one of her *ec*_____ habits.

eccentric

■ The drug addict claimed he could fly from the hotel roof, but the
police officers were *dub*_____ .

dubious

■ The farmer decided that the nudists were either crazy or highly
*ec*_____ ; he was *du*_____ about them.

eccentric, dubious

---

**27. enigmatic** (en'ig-mat'ik): puzzling; perplexing; mysterious.

**28. erotic** (i-rot'ik): pertaining to sexual love; amatory.

■ "Adult movies" are usually more _____ [prudish /
erotic] than "family movies."

erotic

■ We refer to Mona Lisa's smile as *enigmatic* because it is (a) dazzling, (b) puzzling. (     )

(b)

■ I was mystified by the *en*_____ warning.

enigmatic

erotic

■ The sexy passages in *Tropic of Cancer* were so *er*_____ that they gave off blue smoke.

erotic

■ If you cut all the *er*_____ passages from Noodle's last novel, the book would disappear. When asked why he wrote it,

enigmatic

Noodle winked in *en*_____ fashion.

---

**29. exorbitant** (ig-zôr'bə-tənt): extravagant; excessive in price; unreasonable.

**30. feasible** (fē'zə-bəl): capable of being done; practicable; suitable.

exorbitant

■ Five dollars an egg, as paid by those early miners, would ordinarily seem _____ [cheap / exorbitant].

not feasible

■ To build a bridge across the Pacific is at present _____ [feasible / not feasible].

feasible

■ Your plan to feed the whole world is charitable, but is it *fea*_____?

exorbitant

■ "Twenty dollars to clip my dog is an *ex*_____ fee— you've clipped me, too!"

exorbitant

feasible

■ Gasoline prices rose to *ex*_____ levels, and Archy decided that riding a skateboard might be *fe*_____.

---

### Quiz

Write the letter that indicates the best definition.

1. (e)
2. (d)
3. (a)
4. (f)
5. (b)
6. (c)

( ) 1. dubious      a. mysterious
( ) 2. eccentric     b. too high-priced
( ) 3. enigmatic    c. practicable; reasonable
( ) 4. erotic        d. peculiar; having odd traits
( ) 5. exorbitant   e. doubtful; skeptical
( ) 6. feasible     f. having to do with sexual desire

---

**31. fluent** (floo'ənt): able to speak or write readily; flowing smoothly.

**32. frugal** (froo'gəl): costing little; spending little; meager; scanty.

(b)

■ A tongue-tied immigrant who learned English from a book will probably (a) be fluent, (b) not be fluent. (    )

(a)

■ A *frugal* meal (a) is cheap and plain, (b) contains fruit. (    )

frugal

■ On his tiny pension Mr. Snurd eked out a *fru*_____ existence.

fluent

■ To make the debate squad you should be a *fl*_____ speaker.

frugal

fluent

■ For thirty years the woman saved, suffered, lived a *fr*_____ life, for her dream was to become a lawyer and to deliver *fl*_____ speeches in court.

---

**33. furtive:** stealthy; sly; done in secret; clandestine.

**34. gullible** (gul′ə-bəl): easily cheated or tricked; credulous.

gullible

■ Brooklyn Bridge has often been sold to the _____ [gullible / sophisticated] visitor.

furtive

■ A stealthy gesture is said to be _____ [ambidextrous / furtive].

furtive

■ Mike stole a *fur*_____ glance at the blonde.

gullible

■ The con man got rich selling swampland to *gul*_____ investors.

gullible

furtive

■ Nancy believed the handsome stranger's promises, for she was innocent and *g*_____; and she gave his hand a *f*_____ sqeeze.

---

**35. impeccable** (im-pek′ə-bəl): faultless; without sin or error.

**36. impromptu** (im-promp′to͞o): done on the spur of the moment; offhand.

impeccable

■ Banks should hire employees of _____ [dubious / impeccable] honesty.

(a)

■ *Impromptu* remarks are (a) spontaneous, (b) planned in advance. (    )

impromptu

■ Called on unexpectedly, Daniel Webster delivered a brilliant _____ *tu* talk.

impeccable

■ Our eminent minister was presumably of *imp*_____ moral character.

impromptu

■ College freshmen must often quickly scribble an _____ *tu* theme in class; and naturally the professor feels insulted if the pro-

impeccable

duction is not brilliant and _____ *able.*

## Quiz

Write the letter that indicates the best definition.

1. (c)
2. (e)
3. (a)
4. (d)
5. (f)
6. (b)

(    ) 1. fluent        a. sly; stealthy
(    ) 2. frugal        b. improvised; spur of the moment
(    ) 3. furtive        c. smooth flowing in speech
(    ) 4. gullible        d. easily swindled
(    ) 5. impeccable        e. meager and costing little
(    ) 6. impromptu        f. flawless

Write the word studied in this chapter that will complete the sentence.

_____  1. The waiter screamed and threw soup at us. He'd gone [ber-].

_____  2. My hungry uncle found his false teeth just as the banquet began, and his spirits were now [bu-].

_____  3. The widow distrusted Mr. Finn because of his [du-] reputation.

_____  4. Those who expected modern plumbing in Morocco were soon [dis-].

_____  5. Our lease had expired. It was as [def-] as Benedict Arnold.

_____  6. Nine dollars for a dish of prunes? Isn't that a bit [ex-]?

_____  7. The swindler had been talkative and friendly, an [af-] fellow.

_____  8. Discuss this untidy affair with no one. Try to be [dis-].

_____  9. Uncle Phil was an oddball; in fact, he was downright [ec-].

_____  10. He slipped into the vat of cologne and smelled quite [ar-].

_____  11. Was that an [imp-] speech, or had you rehearsed it for a week?

_____  12. Please be frank. I want your [ca-] opinion.

_____  13. The taxi driver swore and raised his fists in [bel-] fashion.

_____  14. She donated a kidney to save her sister. An [alt-] act!

_____  15. Don't stammer. With self-confidence you can be smooth and [fl-].

_____  16. The fire and flood left the old widow [des-].

_____  17. Tripping and robbing that feeble man was a [das-] act.

_____  18. Knute likes sexy soap operas, the more [er-] the better.

Matching. Write the letter that indicates the best definition.

(    ) 19. asinine       a. capable of being done

(    ) 20. deft       b. birdlike

(    ) 21. bizarre       c. stupid as a donkey

(    ) 22. diabolic       d. pertaining to washing canines

(    ) 23. gullible       e. dextrous; skillful in action

(    ) 24. dogmatic       f. a church money-raiser sale

(    ) 25. feasible       g. easily fooled

h. opinionated

i. odd in appearance

j. devilishly wicked

## Key to Review Test

Check your test answers with the following key. Deduct 4% per error from a possible 100%.

| | | |
|---|---|---|
| 1. berserk | 10. aromatic | 19. (c) |
| 2. buoyant | 11. impromptu | 20. (e) |
| 3. dubious | 12. candid | 21. (i) |
| 4. disenchanted | 13. bellicose | 22. (j) |
| 5. defunct | 14. altruistic | 23. (g) |
| 6. exorbitant | 15. fluent | 24. (h) |
| 7. affable | 16. destitute | 25. (a) |
| 8. discreet | 17. dastardly | |
| 9. eccentric | 18. erotic | |

Score: _____ %

## SUPPLEMENTARY EXERCISE

Fill in the blank with the descriptive word that fits the definition. Although these words were not defined in Chapter 11, you should recognize most of them. Check your answers with the key at the end of the exercise. Use your dictionary to study any unknown words.

■ abstemious, articulate, astute, auspicious, bland

1. _____ mild; nonstimulating; insipid
2. _____ shrewd; clever; cunning
3. _____ temperate; eating and drinking sparingly
4. _____ favorable; propitious; of good omen
5. _____ able to express oneself well; clearly presented

■ caustic, compatible, copious, culpable, deferential

6. _____ able to get along well together
7. _____ very respectful; courteous
8. _____ at fault; deserving blame
9. _____ corrosive; stinging; sarcastic
10. _____ very plentiful; abundant

■ delectable, delusive, derisive, disgruntled, disoriented

11. _____ ridiculing; mocking
12. _____ disappointed; displeased; sulky
13. _____ misleading; false; deceptive
14. _____ delightful; enjoyable
15. _____ confused; out of adjustment to one's environment

■ dissident, dormant, dyspeptic, erudite, exotic

16. _____ strangely beautiful; foreign and fascinating
17. _____ grouchy and gloomy because of indigestion
18. _____ as if asleep; inactive
19. _____ not agreeing; differing; dissenting
20. _____ learned; scholarly

■ heinous, illicit, immaculate, imperturbable, impotent

21. _____ pure; flawless; completely clean

22. _____ atrocious; extremely wicked

23. _____ powerless; helpless; without virility

24. _____ calm; unruffled

25. _____ unlawful; improper

## Key to Supplementary Exercise

1. bland
2. astute
3. abstemious
4. auspicious
5. articulate
6. compatible
7. deferential
8. culpable
9. caustic.

10. copious
11. derisive
12. disgruntled
13. delusive
14. delectable
15. disoriented
16. exotic
17. dyspeptic
18. dormant

19. dissident
20. erudite
21. immaculate
22. heinous
23. impotent
24. imperturbable
25. illicit

Score: _____ %

# 12

# Descriptive Words II

1. *indomitable*
2. *inept*
3. *innate*
4. *inscrutable*
5. *insidious*
6. *intrepid*
7. *lethal*
8. *lethargic*
9. *lucid*
10. *lunar*
11. *myopic*
12. *naive*
13. *nebulous*
14. *nostalgic*
15. *occult*
16. *ominous*
17. *opaque*
18. *ostentatious*
19. *picayune*
20. *prolific*
21. *pusillanimous*
22. *raucous*
23. *sagacious*
24. *sedentary*
25. *senile*
26. *sinister*
27. *stoical*
28. *succinct*
29. *taciturn*
30. *toxic*
31. *venerable*
32. *verbose*
33. *verdant*
34. *vicarious*
35. *vindictive*
36. *zealous*

*Chapter 12 continues our study of descriptive words. Follow the same procedure as in Chapter 11.*

COVER THIS STRIP

1. **indomitable** (in-dom′i-tə-bəl):  unconquerable; unyielding.

2. **inept:**  clumsy; incompetent; not suitable.

(a)

■ An *indomitable* fighter (a) fights on and on, (b) quits. (     )

inept

■ A pianist wearing mittens would probably be _____ [impeccable / inept].

indomitable

■ Every nation speaks of its soldiers' *ind*_____ courage.

■ The Dodgers made five errors in the field and were just as

inept

_____*pt* at the plate.

indomitable

■ Wanda climbed to the peak, for her spirit was _____*ble;*

inept

but I slipped off a boulder, for I was _____*pt.*

3. **innate** (i-nāt′):  inborn; natural, not acquired.

4. **inscrutable** (in-skr$\overline{oo}$′tə-bəl):  mysterious; not able to be under-stood.

not innate

■ One's political beliefs are _____ [innate / not innate].

cannot

■ When we speak of *"inscrutable fate,"* we mean that we _____ [can / cannot] easily foresee the future.

■ At one time no mystery melodrama was complete without its slink-

inscrutable

ing and *ins*_____ foreign butler.

innate

■ Ducklings seem to have an *inn*_____ attraction to water.

innate

■ At age five Capablanca had already shown an *inn*_____ talent for chess; and his face over the tournament board was tight-

inscrutable

lipped and *ins*_____ .

5. **insidious** (in-sid′ē-əs):  treacherous; crafty; more dangerous than is apparent.

6. **intrepid** (in-trep′id):  very brave; dauntless; bold.

insidious

intrepid

intrepid

insidious

intrepid

insidious

■ Traitors who bore from within are _____ [innate / insidious].

■ Courageous aviators are said to be _____ [intrepid / craven].

■ Only hardy and *int*_____ men could reach the North Pole.

■ Socrates was accused of corrupting the Athenian youths with *ins*_____ doctrines.

■ Sam danced into the lion's cage to prove how _____ *id* he was, but some *ins*_____ fellow had left a banana peel on the floor.

## Quiz

Write the letter that indicates the best definition.

1. (f)
2. (d)
3. (b)
4. (c)
5. (a)
6. (e)

(   ) 1. indomitable    a. stealthily treacherous
(   ) 2. inept    b. inborn
(   ) 3. innate    c. mysterious; beyond understanding
(   ) 4. inscrutable    d. awkward; clumsy
(   ) 5. insidious    e. fearless; brave
(   ) 6. intrepid    f. unable to be defeated

**7. lethal** (lē′thəl): causing death; deadly; fatal.

**8. lethargic** (li-thär′jik): sluggish; dull; drowsy.

chlorine

lethal

lethargic

lethargic

lethargic

lethal

■ A *lethal* gas used in the first World War was _____ [oxygen / chlorine].

■ A gun, a knife, an automobile—any of these may be considered a _____ *al* weapon in a court case.

■ Basketball coaches don't want _____ [ambidextrous / lethargic] athletes.

■ Having swallowed the pig, the snake became *le*_____ and sleepy.

■ This heavy smog has slowed me up, and I feel _____; I hope the stuff is not _____ *al*.

**9. lucid** (lo͞o′sid): clear; easily understood; mentally sound.

**10. lunar** (lo͞o′nər): pertaining to the moon.

(b)

■ A *lunar* eclipse blots out (a) the sun, (b) the moon. (     )

lucid

■ Technical directions ought to be _____ [enigmatic / lucid].

lunar

■ On the moon the astronauts conducted certain _____ *ar* experiments.

lucid

■ Velma says her friend is crazy but that he has his _____ *id* moments.

lucid

lunar

■ The friendly astronomer gave us a _____ *d* description of the _____ *r* landscape.

**11. myopic** (mī-op′ik): nearsighted.

**12. naive** (na-ēv′): childlike; artless; lacking in worldly wisdom.

myopic

■ Nearsighted people are _____ [myopic / hyperopic].

naive

■ Anyone who thinks that concert artists don't have to practice is pretty _____ [naive / astute].

myopic

■ Benny sat in the front row and strained to see the movie. He was quite *my* _____ .

naive

■ College freshmen range from the very sophisticated to the very *na* _____ .

### Quiz

Write the letter that indicates the best definition.

1. (f)
2. (b)
3. (c)
4. (e)
5. (a)
6. (d)

(     ) 1. lethal     a. nearsighted
(     ) 2. lethargic     b. slow-moving; sluggish
(     ) 3. lucid     c. easy to understand; clear
(     ) 4. lunar     d. childlike; unsophisticated
(     ) 5. myopic     e. of the moon
(     ) 6. naive     f. deadly

13. **nebulous** (neb′yoo-ləs):   cloudy; vague; indefinite.
14. **nostalgic** (nos-tal′jik):   homesick; yearning for what is past or far away.

(b)

■ *Nebulous* plans are (a) clearly detailed, (b) vague. (     )

(b)

■ A *nostalgic* line is (a) "Brevity is the soul of wit," (b) "Gone, gone, are the lovely lasses of yesteryear." (     )

nostalgic

■ Recalling his three happy years in the fifth grade, Grandpa became *no* _____ .

nebulous

■ Through the Los Angeles smog we could make out the *neb* _____ outline of the city hall.

nostalgic

nebulous

■ Dad sings "When You and I Were Young, Maggie" and other *no* _____ songs; meanwhile his prospects for finding a job are *ne* _____ .

---

15. **occult** (ə-kult′):   beyond human understanding; mysterious.
16. **ominous** (om′ə-nəs):   threatening; menacing.

(b)

■ *Occult* subjects include (a) geometry, (b) astrology. (     )

occult

■ Telepathy and reincarnation belong to those puzzling areas known as the *oc* _____ .

(b)

■ An *ominous* gesture is (a) friendly, (b) threatening. (     )

ominous

■ Over the ball park hung dark and *om* _____ clouds.

occult

ominous

■ A spiritualist with *oc* _____ powers evoked a baritone ghost—it made *om* _____ predictions that curled our hair.

---

17. **opaque** (ō-pāk′):   not letting light through; obscure; unintelligent.
18. **ostentatious** (os′tən-tā′shəs):   showy and pretentious so as to attract attention.

(a)

■ *Opaque* glass is sometimes used in (a) bathrooms, (b) automobile windshields. (     )

(b)

■ An *ostentatious* living room seems to say, (a) "I'm simple and comfortable," (b) "Look, look—see how grand and expensive I am!" (     )

Descriptive Words II     173

ostentatious

(a)

opaque

opaque

ostentatious

■ It was a bit *ost*_____ of Mrs. Schmaltz to go shopping for groceries (a) in her pink Cadillac with chauffeur, (b) on her Schwinn bicycle. (     )

■ Such a dolt! His mind is absolutely *op*_____.

■ My dusty glasses were practically *op*_____, yet I saw that Diamond Jim was wearing six or eight sparkling rings. Hmm, somewhat *ost*_____, I thought.

## Quiz

Write the letter that indicates the best definition.

1. (f)
2. (a)
3. (b)
4. (c)
5. (d)
6. (e)

(     ) 1. nebulous         a. sentimental about the past
(     ) 2. nostalgic        b. supernatural; beyond understanding
(     ) 3. occult           c. threatening
(     ) 4. ominous          d. not transparent
(     ) 5. opaque           e. showy to attract attention
(     ) 6. ostentatious     f. vague; misty

**19. picayune** (pik´ē-yoon´):  petty; trivial; contemptible.
**20. prolific** (prō-lif´ik):  fruitful; fecund; producing many works.

prolific

■ Agatha Christie, who wrote mystery novels by the dozen, was obviously very _____ [phlegmatic / prolific].

picayune

■ Charging extra for toothpicks in a restaurant is pretty _____ [picayune / petulant].

prolific

■ Rats multiply fast. They are *pr*_____.

picayune

■ The holdup netted sixty cents, or some such *pi*_____ amount.

prolific

picayune

■ Your fat batch of poems proves that you are *pr*_____, and my criticism of the spelling in your inspired poetry will seem *p*_____.

**21. pusillanimous** (pū´sə-lan´ə-məs):  cowardly; fainthearted.
**22. raucous** (rô´kəs):  rough-sounding; hoarse; boisterous.

The foghorn that awakened me was merely the sergeant's
_____ [pusillanimous / raucous] voice.

raucous

On the battlefield the braggart Falstaff was actually timid—in
fact, (a) pusillanimous, (b) raucous. (    )

(a)

Pancho is shy. He wants to marry Rosa but he is too
*pus*_____ to pop the question.

pusillanimous

One distrusts car salespeople who are pushy and *ra*_____.

raucous

A bumblebee chased me out of the park, and I heard
*r*_____ laughter from those who thought me
*pu*_____ .

raucous
pusillanimous

---

**23. sagacious** (sə-gā′shəs):  shrewd; sound in judgment.
**24. sedentary** (sed′ən-ter′i):  involving sitting; physically inactive.

A *sagacious* decision is (a) wise, (b) stupid. (    )

(a)

*Sedentary* work is done by (a) bookkeepers, (b) bricklayers.
(    )

(a)

Advertising your umbrellas for sale just before the rainy weekend
was *sag*_____ .

sagacious

The cowboy did not want office work or any other
*sed*_____ job.

sedentary

Old folks are not necessarily *sag*_____; some are just
*sed*_____ . Some are wise and some otherwise.

sagacious
sedentary

---

### Quiz

Write the letter that indicates the best definition.

| | | |
|---|---|---|
| (  ) 1. picayune | a. producing in abundance |
| (  ) 2. prolific | b. having sound judgment |
| (  ) 3. pusillanimous | c. petty; trivial |
| (  ) 4. raucous | d. involving sitting |
| (  ) 5. sagacious | e. harsh; rough-sounding |
| (  ) 6. sedentary | f. timid; cowardly |

1. (c)
2. (a)
3. (f)
4. (e)
5. (b)
6. (d)

**25. senile** (sē′nīl): aged and infirm; showing the mental and bodily weaknesses of old age.

**26. sinister** (sin′is-tər): hinting of imminent danger; threatening harm.

(a)

senile

■ *Senile* people are often cared for in a home for (a) the aged, (b) wayward girls. (    )

■ The day our old neighbor wandered away from home in his night-gown we felt he was getting *sen* _____ .

(b)

sinister

■ If you were confronted by *sinister* strangers, you would probably be (a) amused, (b) worried. (    )

■ The conspirators hatched a *si* _____ plot.

senile

sinister

■ The druggist, who was old and *se* _____ , saw nothing *si* _____ in Beulah's purchase of a quart of arsenic.

---

**27. stoical** (stō′i-kəl): indifferent to pain or pleasure.

**28. succinct** (sək-singkt′): concise; terse; brief and meaningful.

succinct

■ Cablegrams at three dollars a word should be _____ [succinct / redundant].

succinct

■ Wordiness is boring, so be *suc* _____ .

(a)

■ Even during childbirth she was *stoical:* in other words, she was (a) calm and uncomplaining, (b) screaming her head off. (    )

stoical

■ The captured warrior endured the ritual of torture with *st* _____ calm.

stoical

succinct

■ Mr. Koltz sat quiet and *st* _____ during most of Buster's birthday party, but finally he made a *su* _____ announcement: "Shut up!"

---

**29. taciturn** (tas′i-tûrn′): not inclined to talk; uncommunicative.

**30. toxic** (tok′sik): poisonous.

(a)

■ *Taciturn* people tend to (a) be silent, (b) talk your arm off. (    )

toxic

■ Pesticides are usually _____ [toxic / nutritious].

toxic

taciturn

toxic

taciturn

■ Wilbur said he wasn't afraid of *to*_____ fumes. We bury him on Tuesday.

■ Chess players are inclined to be reflective and *ta*_____ .

■ "I filled my tires with smoggy, *to*_____ New Jersey air," I explained, "and they died." Replied the *ta*_____ Vermont mechanic: "Hm-m-m-mp."

---

## Quiz

Write the letter that indicates the best definition.

1. (e)
2. (d)
3. (f)
4. (a)
5. (c)
6. (b)

(    ) 1. senile      a. concise; brief
(    ) 2. sinister      b. poisonous
(    ) 3. stoical      c. not talkative
(    ) 4. succinct      d. ominous; threatening
(    ) 5. taciturn      e. old and feeble
(    ) 6. toxic      f. showing no emotions

---

**31. venerable** (ven′ər-ə-bəl): aged and worthy of reverence.

**32. verbose** (vər-bōs′): wordy; long-winded.

venerable

(b)

verbose

venerable

venerable
verbose

■ Ulysses was a wise and _____ [venerable / venereal] warrior.

■ *Verbose* statements contain too many (a) ideas, (b) words. (    )

■ Trim your theme; it is *ver*_____ .

■ We gazed at the *ven*_____ statue of Abraham Lincoln.

■ Every evening my white-haired and *ven*_____ military friend gave me a _____*ose* account of how he won the war.

---

**33. verdant** (vûr′dənt): green; covered with grass; unsophisticated.

**34. vicarious** (vī-kâr′i-əs): participating by imagination in another's experience.

(a)

vicarious

■ *Verdant* fields are (a) grassy, (b) covered with boulders. (    )

■ By identifying yourself with your movie hero you have _____ [venerable / vicarious] pleasure.

**Descriptive Words II**      177

verdant

■ William Wordsworth trod these *ver*_____ meadows.

vicarious

■ From the adventures of D'Artagnan, Jane Eyre, and Martin Arrowsmith we derive a *vi*_____ thrill.

verdant

vicarious

■ Novels take us from foamy seas to *ver*_____ hills; they let us live a thousand *vi*_____ lives.

---

**35. vindictive** (vin-dik′tiv): revengeful; spiteful.

**36. zealous** (zel′əs): ardently devoted to a cause; enthusiastic.

vindictive

■ To spite me, Bart bored a hole in my rowboat. It was a _____ [vindictive / venerable] act.

vindictive

■ The boy who burned your garage to get even with you has a *vin*_____ nature.

(b)

■ A *zealous* reader reads with (a) reluctance, (b) enthusiasm. (    )

zealous

■ A town orchestra or museum often exists because of a few *ze*_____ supporters.

zealous

vindictive

■ My roommate, a *ze*_____ musician, played his violin all night until a *vi*_____ neighbor threw a can of beans through our window.

---

### Quiz

Write the letter that indicates the best definition.

1. (e)
2. (d)
3. (b)
4. (f)
5. (a)
6. (c)

( ) 1. venerable     a. inclined to revenge; spiteful
( ) 2. verbose       b. green with vegetation
( ) 3. verdant       c. fervent; ardently active
( ) 4. vicarious     d. wordy; talkative
( ) 5. vindictive    e. commanding respect because of age
( ) 6. zealous       f. sharing the feelings of others

---

# REVIEW TEST

Write the word studied in this chapter that will complete the sentence.

_____ 1. Last night Moe kissed Flo during the [lu-] eclipse.

_____ 2. I buy two-trouser suits because of my [sed-] occupation.

_____ 3. The astronauts reached the moon. What an [int-p-] crew!

_____ 4. The condemned man showed no emotion. He was [sto-].

_____ 5. The coalminer dreamed of trees and [ver-] meadows.

_____ 6. I'm losing my shingles. I'm old, feeble, and [sen-].

_____ 7. Cables are expensive. Keep the message [suc-].

_____ 8. Hold the book closer. I'm [my-].

_____ 9. The storm clouds looked black and [om-].

_____ 10. Thirty errors! Our ball team was incredibly [in-p-].

_____ 11. What a wise choice! You are quite [sag-].

_____ 12. Five pages for a simple message? Joe is too [v-b-s-].

_____ 13. Astrologers are steeped in supernaturalism and the [occ-].

_____ 14. The bloody fight was for a jellybean or other [pic-] item.

_____ 15. Her mink coat and flashy jewelry are a bit [ost-].

_____ 16. Junior thinks babies grow under rocks. How [n-v-]!

_____ 17. Schubert wrote hundreds of songs. He was [pro-].

_____ 18. The old man wallowed in sweet [nost-] memories of college.

Matching. Write the letter that indicates the best definition.

( ) 19. lethal      a. an unmarried woman

( ) 20. lucid      b. stony; mountainous

( ) 21. pusillanimous      c. deadly

( ) 22. raucous      d. harsh-sounding

( ) 23. sinister      e. like a smelly animal

( ) 24. venerable      f. enthusiastic; dedicated to a cause

( ) 25. zealous      g. cowardly

                             h. easy to understand; clear

                             i. old and highly respected

                             j. threatening danger

**Key to Review Test**

Check your test answers with the following key. Deduct 4% per error from a possible 100%.

| | | |
|---|---|---|
| 1. lunar | 10. inept | 19. (c) |
| 2. sedentary | 11. sagacious | 20. (h) |
| 3. intrepid | 12. verbose | 21. (g) |
| 4. stoical | 13. occult | 22. (d) |
| 5. verdant | 14. picayune | 23. (j) |
| 6. senile | 15. ostentatious | 24. (i) |
| 7. succinct | 16. naive | 25. (f) |
| 8. myopic | 17. prolific | |
| 9. ominous | 18. nostalgic | |

Score: _____ %

## SUPPLEMENTARY EXERCISE

Fill in the blank with the descriptive word that fits the definition. Although these words were not defined in Chapter 12, you should recognize most of them. Check your answers with the key at the end of the exercise. Use your dictionary to study any unknown words.

■ inclement, indolent, indefatigable, insipid, luminous

1. _____ without flavor; tasteless; dull

2. _____ stormy; without leniency

3. _____ shining; clear; bright

4. _____ tireless

5. _____ lazy; idle

■ morbid, oblivious, ornate, precocious, ruthless

6. _____ overdecorated; flowery

7. _____ unaware of; unmindful; forgetful

8. _____ cruel; pitiless

9. _____ maturing early; bright for its age

10. _____ excessively interested in gruesome matters

■ salutary, scurrilous, skeptical, spasmodic, squalid

11. _____ doubting; questioning; not easily convinced

12. _____ occurring now and then; fitful

13. _____ wretched; poverty-stricken in appearance

14. _____ foul-mouthed; grossly abusive

15. _____ beneficial; having a good effect

■ squeamish; staid, stalwart, suave, subtle

16. _____ strong; valiant; unyielding

17. _____ smoothly pleasant and polite, urbane

18. _____ oversensitive; prudish, easily disgusted

19. _____ cunning, crafty; delicately skillful

20. _____ sedate and settled

■ sullen, surreptitious, tepid, terse, voracious

21. _____ secret; stealthy; sneaky

22. _____ gloomy and resentful; glum; morose

23. _____ concise; to the point

24. _____ greedy; gluttonous; insatiable

25. _____ lukewarm

## Key to Supplementary Exercise

1. insipid
2. inclement
3. luminous
4. indefatigable
5. indolent
6. ornate
7. oblivious
8. ruthless
9. precocious

10. morbid
11. skeptical
12. spasmodic
13. squalid
14. scurrilous
15. salutary
16. stalwart
17. suave
18. squeamish

19. subtle
20. staid
21. surreptitious
22. sullen
23. terse
24. voracious
25. tepid

Score: _____ %

# 13

# Action Words

| | | |
|---|---|---|
| 1. *abscond* | 13. *disconcert* | 25. *orient* |
| 2. *acquit* | 14. *disparage* | 26. *ostracize* |
| 3. *adulterate* | 15. *disseminate* | 27. *pander* |
| 4. *alienate* | 16. *elucidate* | 28. *procrastinate* |
| 5. *blaspheme* | 17. *expurgate* | 29. *prognosticate* |
| 6. *bungle* | 18. *extradite* | 30. *rant* |
| 7. *canonize* | 19. *haggle* | 31. *raze* |
| 8. *canvass* | 20. *heckle* | 32. *recant* |
| 9. *cauterize* | 21. *immobilize* | 33. *simulate* |
| 10. *condone* | 22. *impeach* | 34. *slander* |
| 11. *decimate* | 23. *intimidate* | 35. *smirk* |
| 12. *deify* | 24. *laud* | 36. *supersede* |

*The verb is the beating heart of the sentence. A strong, meaningful verb often lets you cut out prepositional phrases that clutter and suffocate a sentence. One student writes, "The temperatures were now at a much lower level than during the previous period." Another writes, "The temperatures plunged." The good writer gets considerable mileage from vigorous, well-selected action words (verbs).*

*Chapter 13 focuses on action words. The drill technique is the same as in Chapters 11 and 12. Study carefully the words and definitions at the top of each frame, then fill in the blanks without looking back unless necessary.*

COVER THIS STRIP

---

**1. abscond** (ab-skond′):  to depart hastily and secretly, especially to escape the law.

**2. acquit** (ə-kwit′):  to declare innocent; to absolve.

(b)

■ If *acquitted* of a crime you are legally (a) guilty, (b) innocent. (    )

acquit

■ The prisoner was so pretty that the Yukon jury voted unanimously to *ac* _____ her.

absconded

■ A company clerk known as Honest Jim has _____ [absconded / abdicated] with our money.

absconded

■ Our bank teller, who was five feet tall and ten thousand dollars short, has _____ *ed*.

abscond

acquitted

■ Although the treasurer did *ab* _____ one night with the union funds, his lawyer managed later to get him _____ *ed*.

---

**3. adulterate** (ə-dul′tə-rāt′):  to cheapen by adding inferior ingredients; to corrupt.

**4. alienate** (āl′yə-nāt′):  to make unfriendly; to estrange.

adulterates

■ Adding sawdust to sausage meat _____ [fortifies / adulterates] it.

alienate

■ Insulting your friends in public is usually a good way to _____ [alienate / captivate] them.

alienate

■ If Linus flirts with everybody, he'll soon *al* _____ his girl friend.

adulterate

■ Chemical additives often *ad* _____ our food.

adulterate

■ Many bakeries add generous amounts of artificial preservative to their bread and thus *ad* _____ it; such practices

alienate

*al* _____ health-minded customers.

---

**5. blaspheme** (blas-fēm′): to speak profanely of God or sacred things; to curse.

**6. bungle:** to botch; to perform clumsily.

bungled

■ If her surgeon had been sober, he would not have _____ [bungled / misfired] that operation.

(a)

■ Those who *blaspheme* are (a) cursing, (b) praying. ( )

blaspheme

■ The priest shuddered to hear the atheist *bl*_____ near the cathedral.

bungle

■ If you *bu*_____ your baking, the upside-down cake may come out rightside-up.

■ Although the clumsy carpenter had to cut only one board, he man-

bungle, blaspheme

aged to *b*_____ the job; then he began to *bl*_____ .

---

### Quiz

Write the letter that indicates the best definition.

| | | |
|---|---|---|
| 1. (b) | ( ) 1. abscond | a. to add inferior ingredients |
| 2. (e) | ( ) 2. acquit | b. to flee from the law |
| 3. (a) | ( ) 3. adulterate | c. to do imperfectly |
| 4. (f) | ( ) 4. alienate | d. to use profanity |
| 5. (d) | ( ) 5. blaspheme | e. to declare not guilty |
| 6. (c) | ( ) 6. bungle | f. to make hostile |

---

**7. canonize** (kan′ə-nīz′): to declare a dead person to be a saint.

**8. canvass** (kan′vəs): to go through a district asking for votes, opinions, or orders.

canvass

■ We'll get Dooley elected even if we have to _____ [canvas / canvass] the whole town.

(b)

■ The Catholic Church has *canonized* (a) Columbus, (b) Saint Joan of Arc. ( )

canonize

■ Live like a saint and maybe the church will *can*_____ you.

canvass

■ "To sell tickets for—pardon the expression—*Gotterdammerung*," said Silas, "we had to *can*_____ the county."

canvass

canonize

■ When Bobo hit that grand slam home run, he became an instant saint; you didn't have to _____ss the crowd to know they would practically _____ze him.

---

**9. cauterize** (ko′tə-rīz′): to sear with a hot iron, as to cure wounds.
**10. condone** (kən-dōn′): to pardon or overlook a fault.

(a)

■ Infected wounds can be *cauterized* by (a) burning, (b) ice cubes. (   )

condone

■ When a father shrugs off his son's vandalism, he is said to _____ [condone / canonize] it.

cauterize

■ A white-hot needle was used to *cau*_____ the ugly scratch.

condone

■ Though Gauguin was an inspired artist, many cannot *con*_____ his desertion of his family.

cauterize

condoned

■ The army surgeon's failure to *c*_____ Fenwick's bullet wound cannot be _____*ed*.

---

**11. decimate** (des′ə-māt′): to kill many of.
**12. deify** (dē′ə-fī′): to make a god of; to exalt and idealize.

deify

■ We tend to _____ [decimate / deify] our top athletes.

deify

■ A heavyweight champion is not a god, and we should not *d*_____ him.

decimate

■ With the hydrogen bomb any two nations can _____ [decimate / deify] each other more efficiently.

decimate

■ We gave the South Sea natives the benefits of our modern "syphilization," and managed to *dec*_____ them.

deify

decimate

■ It was the habit of the ancient Greeks to *de*_____ the sun, the moon, and the winds; it was also their habit to *dec*_____ their enemies.

---

Write the letter that indicates the best definition.

1. (d)
2. (b)
3. (e)
4. (a)
5. (c)
6. (f)

(    ) 1. canonize      a. to shrug off a fault
(    ) 2. canvass      b. to check opinions of an area
(    ) 3. cauterize      c. to slay large numbers
(    ) 4. condone      d. to raise to sainthood
(    ) 5. decimate      e. to sear a wound
(    ) 6. deify      f. to treat as a god

---

**13. disconcert** (dis′kən-sûrt′): to embarrass; to confuse; to upset.

**14. disparage** (dis-par′ij): to belittle; to speak of with contempt.

disparage

■ To belittle an effort is to _____ [condone / disparage] it.

disconcert

■ Jeering at a speaker tends to _____ [deify / disconcert] him.

disconcert

■ Finding half a worm in my apple was enough to *dis*_____ me.

disparage

■ Don't *dis*_____ the restaurant coffee—it's quite good compared to the doughnut.

disparage, disconcert

■ The clarinet duet sounded like cats fighting, but let's not _____ *ge* it or we may_____ *ert* the young artists.

---

**15. disseminate** (di-sem′ə-nāt′): to scatter everywhere; to spread, as if sowing.

**16. elucidate** (i-lōō′si-dāt′): to make clear; to explain.

(b)

■ To *elucidate* a literary passage is (a) to disparage it, (b) to clarify its meaning. (    )

(b)

■ To *disseminate* propaganda is (a) to stifle it, (b) to spread it. (    )

elucidate

■ This poem sounds like jabberwocky. Please *el*_____ it, Sheldon.

disseminate

■ A helicopter was used to drop and *dis*_____ circulars advertising Anti-Litter Week.

disseminate

elucidate

■ The Internal Revenue Service loved to *dis*_____ among common citizens a tax form that only a genius could *el*_____ .

---

**17. expurgate** (ek′spər-gāt′): to remove obscene or objectionable matter; to purge.

**18. extradite** (ek′strə-dīt′): to return a fugitive to another state or nation.

■ The PTA members *expurgated* our class play. In other words, they (a) cleaned it up, (b) added a few dirty words. (    )

(a)

■ France promised to *extradite* Killer McGee. This means he will be (a) executed there, (b) shipped back to us. (    )

(b)

extradite

■ Argentina was requested by Israel to *ex*_____ a Nazi war criminal.

expurgate

■ Censors used a blue pencil to *ex*_____ the naughty lines.

extradite

expurgate

■ Some countries refuse to *ex*_____ political refugees; some show Hollywood films but will *ex*_____ the kissing scenes.

---

**Quiz**

Write the letter that indicates the best definition.

1. (f)
2. (c)
3. (b)
4. (d)
5. (e)
6. (a)

(    ) 1. disconcert    a. to return a fugitive across borders
(    ) 2. disparage    b. to spread everywhere
(    ) 3. disseminate    c. to speak slightingly of
(    ) 4. elucidate    d. to clarify
(    ) 5. expurgate    e. to eliminate objectionable passages
(    ) 6. extradite    f. to embarrass

---

**19. haggle:** to argue in petty fashion about terms and prices.
**20. heckle:** to harass with questions and sarcastic remarks.

■ Those who *haggle* at a garage sale are probably discussing (a) politics, (b) prices. (    )

(b)

■ To *heckle* the chairman is to shower him with words of (a) sarcasm, (b) praise. (     )

(a)

haggle

■ Natives in the marketplace would *hag* _____ ten minutes over the price of a fish.

■ Spectators in Hyde Park who disagree with speakers will mercilessly *hec* _____ them.

heckle

heckle

haggle

■ The crowd began to *h* _____ the orator; meanwhile, the peddler and the hippie continued to *h* _____ for the overripe cantaloupe.

---

**21. immobilize** (i-mō′bə-līz′): to make unable to move; to fix in place.

**22. impeach:** to accuse an official of wrongdoing.

■ President Andrew Johnson was *impeached;* this means that he was (a) guilty, (b) accused. (     )

(b)

impeach

■ If the governor has misused the funds, we should *imp* _____ him.

■ To *immobilize* a broken leg is (a) to exercise it, (b) to keep it from moving. (     )

(b)

immobilize

■ The policeman pulled Nick's arms back so as to *imm* _____ him.

impeach

■ One columnist predicts that we will *imp* _____ Senator Swindle, convict him, and send him to a prison cell to

immobilize

*imm* _____ him.

---

**23. intimidate** (in-tim′i-dāt′): to make timid; to control action by inducing fear.

**24. laud** (lôd): to praise.

intimidate

■ Bugsy's scowl and brass knuckles were enough to _____ [intimate / intimidate] me.

■ If a critics *laud* your performance, they are (a) praising it, (b) knocking it. (     )

(a)

laud

■ Some artists have to die before anyone will *l*_____ them for their accomplishments.

■ Drive a compact car in heavy traffic and the huge trucks will

intimidate

*int*_____ you.

■ Belinda saved the hikers' lives, and our newspapers all

laud

*l*_____ her bravery. She did not let the grizzly bears

intimidate

*int*_____ her.

## Quiz

Write the letter that indicates the best definition.

1. (a)
2. (c)
3. (f)
4. (e)
5. (b)
6. (d)

|     |                |     |                                  |
| --- | -------------- | --- | -------------------------------- |
| ( ) 1. | haggle     | a.  | to quibble about prices          |
| ( ) 2. | heckle     | b.  | to control by fear               |
| ( ) 3. | immobilize | c.  | to annoy with sarcastic remarks  |
| ( ) 4. | impeach    | d.  | to heap praises on               |
| ( ) 5. | intimidate | e.  | to accuse of misconduct          |
| ( ) 6. | laud       | f.  | to eliminate movement            |

**25. orient** (ôr′ē-ənt): to adjust to a situation.
**26. ostracize** (os′trə-sīz′): to exclude from society; to banish.

ostracized

■ When a person is shunned by others, he is said to be _____ [extradited / ostracized].

■ In your first days of work at the stock exchange, you will try

orient

to _____ [alienate / orient] yourself.

■ The new clerk at the department store didn't know a lace curtain

oriented

from a lace panty. He was not yet _____ *ed.*

■ Jasper was a sneak and a tattletale, so his fellow workers began to

ostracize

*os*_____ him.

orient

■ Every year this college must *or*_____ a new class of freshman and must hope that each newcomer will be accepted,

ostracized

not _____ *ed,* by campus groups.

**27. pander:** to help satisfy the base desires of others.

**28. procrastinate** (prō-kras'tə-nāt'): to delay, to postpone action.

pander

■ Dope pushers, bootleggers, and prostitutes _____ [pander / don't pander] to the vices of others.

pander

■ No lust or desire is so low but that someone will *pa* _____ to it.

(b)

■ Elmer *procrastinates,* repeating, (a) "Let's do it now," (b) "Let's wait." (   )

procrastinate

■ Huge term reports are due soon, so don't *pro* _____ .

procrastinate

■ Our town drunkard gets up early; he does not *pr* _____ .

pander

By nine a.m. he has found a bartender to *pa* _____ to his thirst.

---

**29. prognosticate** (prog-nos'tə-kāt'): to predict; to foretell.

**30. rant:** to speak wildly; to rave.

(a)

■ Every day the newspaper *prognosticates* (a) the weather, (b) accidents and crimes. (    )

(b)

■ To *rant* is to speak (a) logically, (b) loudly and wildly. (    )

rant

■ Julius mounted the soapbox and began to fling his arms around and *ra* _____ .

prognosticate

■ Madame Zaza used a crystal ball to *pro* _____ the misfortunes ahead.

rant

■ Professor Schluck would glare at us and *r* _____ about

prognosticate

our lack of discipline; then he would *pro* _____ our final reward—on the gallows.

---

### Quiz

Write the letter that indicates the best definition.

1. (c)
2. (f)
3. (a)

(    ) 1. orient          a. to serve the low desires of others
(    ) 2. ostracize       b. to put off taking action
(    ) 3. pander          c. to adjust to surroundings

4. (b)
5. (e)
6. (d)

| | | |
|---|---|---|
| (   ) 4. procrastinate | d. | to talk wildly and noisily |
| (   ) 5. prognosticate | e. | to predict future events |
| (   ) 6. rant | f. | to shut out from society |

---

**31. raze** (rāz): to tear to the ground; to demolish.

**32. recant** (ri-kant'): to renounce formally one's previous statements.

(b)

■ To *recant* is (a) to add overwhelming evidence, (b) to take back one's words. (   )

raze

■ To improve our city we should first _____ [raise / raze] more condemned tenements.

recant

■ Galileo asserted that the earth revolved around the sun, but he was forced by the church to *re* _____ .

raze

■ Let's *ra* _____ the old barn, Hiram, and build a new-fangled garage.

raze

■ Mayor Gronk promised to *ra* _____ all unsafe buildings, but when his own hotel was condemned, he decided to

recant

*re* _____ .

---

**33. simulate** (sim'yoo-lāt'): to pretend; to imitate; to counterfeit.

**34. slander:** to utter falsehoods injuring someone's reputation.

(b)

■ "Real simulated pearls," recently advertised for $15.95, are (a) genuine pearls, (b) imitations. (   )

simulate

■ Death and agony, says Emily Dickinson, are genuine and not easy to *sim* _____ .

slander

■ To print damaging lies about somebody is to libel; to speak such lies is to *sla* _____ .

slander

■ Call the tax assessor a "bribe-happy reptile" and he'll sue you for *sl* _____ .

simulate

slander

■ Thomas Paine had many enemies, and when he died a few tried to *sim* _____ grief and others continued to *sl* _____ him.

---

**35. smirk:** to smile in a conceited or affected manner.

**36. supersede** (soo′pər-sēd′): to take the place of; to replace; to supplant.

(b)

■ As a news reporter you would be insulting the guest of honor if you wrote that he (a) smiled, (b) smirked. (    )

(b)

■ If Plan X *supersedes* Plan W, then (a) both plans are in effect, (b) only Plan X is in effect. (    )

supersede

■ Yesterday's orders are void because today's orders *sup* _____ them.

smirk

■ Posing for the camera, most tourists will stand in front of a museum and *sm* _____ .

supersede

smirk

■ When Dora told Moose, the big fullback, that he was going to *su* _____ everybody else in her affections, he could only scratch his ear and *sm* _____ .

## Quiz

Write the letter that indicates the best definition.

1. (b)
2. (c)
3. (d)
4. (f)
5. (e)
6. (a)

(    ) 1. raze      a. to take the place of
(    ) 2. recant      b. to tear down
(    ) 3. simulate      c. to take back what was said
(    ) 4. slander      d. to imitate
(    ) 5. smirk      e. to smile in a silly way
(    ) 6. supersede      f. to utter defamatory remarks

## REVIEW TEST

Write the word studied in this chapter that will complete the sentence.

_____  1.  Heat the iron! We must [ca-t-z-] the wound.

_____  2.  This passage in Homer is Greek to me. Please [el-d-t-].

_____  3.  Adding chicory will merely [ad-lt-] this pure coffee.

_____  4.  Calling him a dirty thief is [sl-d-].

_____  5.  My term paper is due. Oh, why did I [pr-c-t-]?

_____  6.  Our governor is corrupt. We must [imp-] him.

_____  7.  We ignore the live artist. He dies and we [l-d] his works.

_____  8.  In Morocco one is expected to [h-gl-] over rug prices.

_____  9.  I want a candid camera shot. Please don't [sm-k].

_____  10.  Sally sprayed the ants and managed to [dec-] them.

_____  11.  He'd become St. Buster if the church would [can-] him.

_____  12.  Your leg is broken. We'll use splints to [im-b-z-] it.

_____  13.  Praise your spouse in public. Never [dis-ge] her.

_____  14.  What a mimic! She can [sim-t-] the sound of a dog-cat fight.

_____  15.  "Trigger" Sloan is a killer. Why did the jury [a-q-t] him?

_____  16.  Ohio wants the fugitive and has asked Utah to [ex-d-] him.

_____  17.  At a new school you need a week to [or-t] yourself.

_____  18.  Never have so many economists tried to [prog-] future economic trends. We need an excess prophets' tax.

Matching. Write the letter that indicates the best definition.

( ) 19. blaspheme       a. to taunt and annoy a speaker

( ) 20. canvass         b. to put up a tent

( ) 21. condone         c. to meditate

( ) 22. heckle          d. to excuse a fault

( ) 23. ostracize       e. to satisfy vulgar desires of others

( ) 24. pander          f. to swear profanely

( ) 25. rant            g. to lease to a tenant

                        h. to check district opinions

                        i. to shun socially

                        j. to speak wildly

## Key to Review Test

Check your test answers with the following key. Deduct 4% per error from a possible 100%.

| | | |
|---|---|---|
| 1. cauterize | 10. decimate | 19. (f) |
| 2. elucidate | 11. canonize | 20. (h) |
| 3. adulterate | 12. immobilize | 21. (d) |
| 4. slander | 13. disparage | 22. (a) |
| 5. procrastinate | 14. simulate | 23. (i) |
| 6. impeach | 15. acquit | 24. (e) |
| 7. laud | 16. extradite | 25. (j) |
| 8. haggle | 17. orient | |
| 9. smirk | 18. prognosticate | |

Score: _____ %

## SUPPLEMENTARY EXERCISE

Fill in the blank with the verb that fits the definition. Although these verbs were not defined in Chapter 13, you should recognize most of them. Check your answers with the key at the end of the exercise. Use your dictionary to study any unknown words.

■ atrophy, belie, browbeat, corroborate, covet

1. _____ to bully; to intimidate
2. _____ to confirm; to make more certain
3. _____ to prove false
4. _____ to desire what belongs to another
5. _____ to wither; to waste away

■ decry, deploy, dismantle, edify, emulate

6. _____ to instruct; to enlighten spiritually
7. _____ to imitate so as to equal or excel
8. _____ to spread out forces according to plan
9. _____ to denounce; to condemn; to disparage
10. _____ to strip of equipment; to disassemble

■ epitomize, equivocate, implicate, impoverish, jettison

11. _____ to represent the essence of
12. _____ to be ambiguous purposely; to hedge; to mislead
13. _____ to make poor; to reduce to poverty
14. _____ to throw cargo overboard in an emergency
15. _____ to show to be involved; to entangle

■ mollify, osculate, rankle, retaliate, retrench

16. _____ to kiss
17. _____ to cause resentment; to fester; to irritate
18. _____ to pay back injury for injury; to revenge
19. _____ to make less angry; to soothe; to appease
20. _____ to cut expenses; to economize

■ scrutinize, skulk, swelter, thwart, verify

21. _____ to prevent from accomplishing a purpose; to hinder
22. _____ to prove that something is true

23. _____ to move about furtively; to lurk; to shirk

24. _____ to examine carefully; to look at closely

25. _____ to suffer or perspire from oppressive heat

## Key to Supplementary Exercise

1. browbeat
2. corroborate
3. belie
4. covet
5. atrophy
6. edify
7. emulate
8. deploy
9. decry

10. dismantle
11. epitomize
12. equivocate
13. impoverish
14. jettison
15. implicate
16. osculate
17. rankle
18. retaliate

19. mollify
20. retrench
21. thwart
22. verify
23. skulk
24. scrutinize
25. swelter

Score: _____ %

# PART TWO

# 14

# Rhetoric

*When you write English, you are a soldier crawling through a mined field. You have to recognize and avoid the traps and snares—clichés, redundancy, plagiarism, logical fallacies. You have to know and use the helpful devices, too—concreteness, analogy, parallelism, ellipsis, idioms. As a resourceful writer you study your craft to survive.*

*Chapter 14 defines terms that deal with writing. Most frames present two definitions and the usual choices and completions. As in previous chapters, choose the right words to fill the blanks. But you can do more than learn word meanings. You can, perhaps—without damage to your creativity—apply some concepts behind these terms to your own writing.*

## EXERCISES

1. **rhetoric** (ret′ə-rik): the art of using words persuasively and effectively in writing and speaking. *Rhetoric* involves grammar, logic, style, and figures of speech.

2. **redundancy** (ri-dun′dən-sē): wordiness; needless repetition; tautology. Example: "Big in size," "in my opinion, I think," "at this point in time," "Jewish rabbi." For further examples, see Chapter 15.

rhetoric

■ The art of composition is called _____ [rhetoric / redundancy].

redundancy

■ Padded phrases like "red in color" are examples of *re_____*.

redundancy

rhetoric

■ The phrase "necessary essentials" also illustrates _____ and is poor *rh_____*.

(a)

■ Mere *rhetoric* without sound ideas usually results in (a) empty eloquence, (b) a literary masterpiece. (     )

■ Terms like *tautology, pleonasm, verbiage, verbosity, circumlocution, diffuseness, periphrasis,* and *prolixity* refer to various aspects of wordi-

redundancy

ness, or *re_____*.

rhetoric

(b)

■ The master of effective writing, or *rh_____*, avoids *redundant* phrases such as (a) "a hot pastrami sandwich," (b) "edible food to eat." (     )

3. **malapropism** (mal′ə-prop-iz′əm): ridiculous misuse of a word for another one that sounds like it. Mrs. *Malaprop* in Richard Sheridan's play *The Rivals* (1775) spoke of "an allegory on the banks of the Nile."

■ The misuse of a word for another one that sounds like it, as in

malapropism

"they won the world serious," is a _____.

(b)

■ Which of these two blunders involves a *malapropism?* (a) "Us boys went," (b) "a lecher course in history." (     )

■ "Every morning my mother exercises her abominable muscles."

malapropism

This sentence contains a *m_____*.

malapropism

■ Cross out each ridiculous misuse, known as a *m*_____, and write the correct word above it:

incandescent

Thomas Edison invented the indecent lamp.

frankincense

The wise men brought gifts of myrrh and frankfurters.

reservations

Our government put the Indians into reservoirs.

monarchy

The government of England is a limited mockery.

an imaginary
line

The equator is a menagerie lion that runs around the middle of the earth.

---

4. **euphemism** (yo͞o′fə-miz′əm): a mild expression substituted for a distasteful one. Example: "a morals charge" for "rape," "resting place" for "grave," "stylishly stout" for "fat."

5. **triteness:** dullness in expression or content; lack of freshness and creativity. *Triteness* occurs in story plots ("theft of diamonds"), in greeting cards ("just a note to say I am thinking of you"), and in speeches ("Dr. Fossil needs no introduction, so without further ado . . . .")

■ A mild, indirect expression to avoid a blunt, painful one is a

euphemism

*eu*_____ .

euphemism

■ To say that an ailing cat was "put to sleep" is a *eu*_____ .

triteness

Also the stale phrase is an example of *tr*_____ .

Examples:
   bathroom
   washroom
   powder room
   restroom

■ Hardly anybody goes to the toilet any more. Give two euphemisms we usually use for "toilet."

_____

_____

---

Write *trite* in front of any dull, unoriginal lines.

_____ a. I have decided to write my theme on the subject of dogs.

_____ b. Last week I was attacked by a four-legged flea plantation known as man's best friend.

_____ c. Sooner or later, after all is said and done, a senior citizen must face the prospect of retirement.

_____ d. When our birthday cake becomes a fire hazard, we consider retirement.

**Rhetoric    203**

Trite:
  a, c, e

euphemism

euphemisms
Examples: gee,
  my gosh, egad,
  holy, jeepers,
  jiminy crickets

1. (e)
2. (a)
3. (d)
4. (b)
5. (c)

acronym

initial

acronym

UFO

radar

UNESCO

_____ e. Everybody has had embarrassing moments, and I
am no exception.

■ A substitute expression that avoids the naming of deity (ex., "holy
gee," "for gosh sake," "by golly") is a *eu* _____.
Cite three other such softened oaths known as *eu* _____.

_____

_____


_____

## Quiz

Write the letter that indicates the best definition.

(    ) 1. rhetoric      a. tautology; wordiness
(    ) 2. redundancy    b. a mild substitute expression
(    ) 3. malapropism    c. staleness in expression
(    ) 4. euphemism     d. a ridiculous word blunder
(    ) 5. triteness       e. art of effective communication

6. **acronym** (ak′rə-nim): a word made up from the initial letters or
syllables of a title or phrase. Examples: MADD (Mothers Against
Drunk Drivers), WAC (Women's Army Corps).

■ If you don't want a jail or a new mall built in your neighborhood,
you are a NIMBY, which word is an *ac* _____ for "not
in my back yard."

■ The word "AWOL" is made up basically from the _____
[initial / final] letters of "absent without leave" and is therefore called
an *a* _____ .

■ Write the *acronym* for each of the following titles or phrases.

■ _____ unidentified flying object

■ _____ radio detecting and ranging

■ _____ United Nations Educational, Scientific, and
Cultural Organization

7. **antonym** (an'tə-nim): a word of opposite meaning. "Tall" and "short," "fast" and "slow," "smart" and "stupid" are pairs of *antonyms.*

8. **homonym** (hom'ə-nim): a word that sounds like another word but has a different meaning and usually a different spelling. Examples: "air" and "heir," "past" and "passed," "site" and "cite" are *homonyms.*

■ Pairs of words like "principle" and "principal," "block" and "bloc," are called *ho*_____.

*homonyms*

■ Pairs of words like "beautiful" and "ugly," "rich" and "poor," are called *an*_____ .

*antonyms*

■ "Dear" and "hateful" are _____ ; "dear" and "deer" are _____ .

*antonyms*
*homonyms*

■ "Bare" and "bear" are _____ ; "bare" and "clothed" are _____ .

*homonyms*
*antonyms*

---

9. **concreteness:** quality of being specific and of referring to particular things. *Concreteness* adds clarity and power to writing.

10. **connotation:** the suggestiveness and emotional associations of a word, apart from its denotation, or literal meaning. Propagandists often use words that seem honest but which, by their *connotations,* arouse prejudice.

■ Clarity of detail is called *con*_____ .

concreteness

■ Choose the *concrete* phrase: (a) "some young fellow," (b) "a shambling newsboy." ( )

(b)

■ Choose the *concrete* phrase: (a) "an interesting animal," (b) "a blue-bottomed ape." ( )

(b)

■ The feeling that surrounds a word is its *conn*_____ .

connotation

■ Underline three words with favorable *connotations* to describe an ancestor who absolutely refused to change his opinions about anything: obstinate, pig-headed, steadfast, hidebound, bigoted, staunch, unflinching.

steadfast
staunch
unflinching

■ Which news headline has unfavorable *connotations?* (a) "Mayor and Wife Invite Friends to Housewarming," (b) "Facts Bared About Mayor's New Love-Nest." ( )

(b)

## Quiz

Write the letter that indicates the best definition.

1. (d)
2. (e)
3. (b)
4. (a)
5. (c)

(   ) 1. acronym     a. exactness; specificness
(   ) 2. antonym     b. word with same sound
(   ) 3. homonym     c. suggestive qualities; overtones
(   ) 4. concreteness     d. word made from initials
(   ) 5. connotation     e. word with opposite meaning

---

**11. prose:** writing or speech which is not poetry. Most communication—whether of newspapers, magazines, or conversation—is *prose*.

(a)

■ *Prose* is the language of (a) ordinary conversation and writing, (b) Longfellow's "The Village Blacksmith." (   )

prose

■ All of your life you have been talking in _____ [poetry / prose].

prose

■ Essays by Michael Montaigne, Charles Lamb, and Robert Benchley are all written in _____ [poetry / prose].

(b)

■ A *prose* composition requires (a) rhyming, (b) no rhyming. (   )

---

**12. exposition:** writing which explains or informs. *Exposition* is one of four traditional types of discourse, the others being *description, narration,* and *argumentation.*

**13. précis** (prā′sē): a short condensed version of a piece of writing. The *précis* is shorter than the original but it maintains something of the same phrasing, tone, order, and proportion of ideas.

exposition

■ Writing that is explanatory is called _____ [narrative / exposition].

précis

■ Summarizing a composition but preserving the original phrasing and tone results in a *pr*_____ .

(a)

■ The *précis* of a magazine article or essay (a) shortens it, (b) expands it. (   )

exposition
(b)

■ To set forth information is the function of *ex*_____; so the natural language of *exposition* is (a) poetry, (b) prose. (   )

(a)

■ A good subject for *exposition* might be (a) symbolism in Melville's *Billy Budd,* (b) an imaginary dialogue between two lovesmitten Eskimos. (    )

(a)

■ Although the *précis* of a composition is much shorter than the original, it usually retains (a) some of the original phrasing and tone, (b) the minor details. (    )

---

14. **plagiarism** (plā′jə-riz′əm): copying the language or ideas of another author and presenting them as one's own; includes the lifting of phrases and sentences from research sources without using quotation marks. *Plagiarism* results in severe penalties at most colleges.

15. **paraphrase** (par′ə-frāz′): to restate a passage in different words. The researcher must *paraphrase* borrowed material or place it within quotation marks, and must credit the source in either case.

plagiarism

■ Copying somebody else's writing without giving proper credit is called *pl* _____ .

paraphrase

■ To restate a borrowed passage in one's own words is to *pa* _____ .

credit

■ Whether one *paraphrases* a passage or quotes it, he or she should _____ [credit / ignore] the original source.

(a)

■ *Plagiarism* is (a) literary theft, (b) permissible borrowing. (    )

plagiarism

(b)

■ To avoid the serious offense of _____ , one might (a) change a word now and then in borrowed material, (b) use quotes around each borrowed passage and credit the original writer. (    )

(b)

plagiarism

■ If a line is too individual or clever for easy *paraphrasing* the researcher should (a) steal it, (b) place it in quotation marks. (    )

Then, if he also credits the source, he will avoid *p* _____ .

---

## Quiz

Write the letter that indicates the best definition.

1. (d)
2. (e)

(    ) 1. prose      a. a restatement in one's own words

(    ) 2. exposition      b. a condensation; a shortened version

(     ) 3. précis        c. literary theft
(     ) 4. plagiarism      d. ordinary nonpoetic language
(     ) 5. paraphrase     e. informative writing; one type of essay

---

**16. ellipsis** (i-lip′sis): the omission of words, as from quoted material, usually indicated by three dots or asterisks. *Ellipsis* may be used to shorten a quoted passage but not so as to change the meaning or to remove surgically any damaging evidence.

■ "But, in a larger sense, we cannot dedicate . . . this ground." The three dots indicate (a) an ellipsis, (b) a pause while Lincoln took a drink. (    )

(a)

■ The omission of words from a quoted passage is called an

ellipsis

*el* _____ .

three

■ The *ellipsis* is indicated by _____ [three / seven] dots.

■ If your research source says, "Poe drank, although very infrequently, during this period" and you write it as "Poe drank . . . during

improper

this period," you are making _____ [proper / improper] use

ellipsis

of _____ .

---

**17. begging the question:** assuming what has yet to be proved. *Begging the question* is a fallacy of logic, as when we say, "Shouldn't all those crooks at City Hall be turned out of office?" or "It's a waste of money to give that murderer a trial—just string 'im up!"

**18. post hoc** (pōst hok′): assuming that one thing caused another merely because it happened earlier. This term for a fallacy of logic is from the Latin phrase *post hoc, ergo propter hoc,* which literally means "after this, therefore because of this."

begging

■ To take something for granted without proof is _____ *the question.*

■ "Why must a useless course like history be made compulsory?"

question

The word that *begs the* _____ and needs proving

"useless"

is _____ ["useless" / "course"].

■ When an Indian dance gets credit for causing the rain that falls the

*post hoc*

next day, the reasoning behind such credit is called *p* _____

*h* _____ .

*post hoc*

begs

(b)

(a)

*hominem*

(a)

*sequitur*

does not

*non sequitur*

*ad hominem*

■ The fallacy of assuming that two events that follow each other must have a cause-effect relationship is called _____ _____ .

■ "We must not permit a pornographic book like *The Catcher in the Rye* to be kept in our library." The word that _____ *the question* and needs proving is (a) "permit," (b) "pornographic." (   )

■ A young pugilist wearing a certain bathrobe scored a knockout in one round; thereafter he insisted on wearing that same robe, never cleaned, to every fight of his career. He believed in (a) *post hoc* reasoning, (b) hygiene. (     )

---

19. **ad hominem** (ad hom′ə-nəm): appealing to a person's prejudices or selfish interests rather than to his reason; attacking an opponent rather than sticking to the issue. The Latin phrase *argumentum ad hominem* means "argument at or to the man."

20. **non sequitur** (non sek′wi-tər): a conclusion that does not follow from the evidence presented. The Latin phrase *non sequitur* means "it does not follow."

■ In a debate about state lotteries, an attack on your moral character is an *ad*_____ .

■ *Ad hominem* implies that the real issue of the argument gets (a) overlooked, (b) close attention. (     )

■ "My husband loves Italian motion picture films, so I think he'll enjoy the chicken cacciatora I am going to cook for him." The reasoning here involves a *non*_____ .

■ In a *non sequitur* the conclusion _____ [does / does not] follow from the evidence presented.

■ "Schopenhauer was very pessimistic and nobody should read his essays." The conclusion is not justified by the evidence, and we have a n_____ s_____ .

■ "Better vote against this school bill, Smedley; your kids have graduated already and you'll just get soaked for more taxes." The argument here is a_____ h_____ .

---

Write the letter that indicates the best definition.

1. (c)
2. (d)
3. (e)
4. (a)
5. (b)

(　　) 1. ellipsis　　　　　　a. appeal to prejudice
(　　) 2. begging the question　b. an illogical conclusion
(　　) 3. *post hoc*　　　　　c. omission of words
(　　) 4. *ad hominem*　　　　d. assuming without proof
(　　) 5. *non sequitur*　　　e. after this, therefore because of this

---

**21. bandwagon device:** persuasion to join the popular or winning side. "To climb aboard the bandwagon" means to shift one's vote to the apparent winner.

bandwagon

■ "Three out of four smoke Hempos!" Such ads that suggest that we join the majority use the *b* _____ *device*.

win

■ The *bandwagon device* tells us to vote for Jim Snurd because he is going to _____ [lose / win] by a landslide.

bandwagon

(b)

■ "Three million sold already!" Whether this pitch refers to Klunker cars, to horseburgers, or to albums by the Five Lunatics, it uses the *b* _____ *device* and it urges you to do (a) the rational thing, (b) what the crowd is doing. (　　)

---

**22. faulty dilemma** (di-lem′ə): the offering of only two alternatives when more than two exist. "We must wipe out the Pootzians or we will perish." Such talk illustrates the *faulty dilemma,* since it ignores the possibility of peaceful coexistence.

**23. analogy** (ə-nal′ə-jē): an extended comparison to clarify an idea; a comparison of things which are alike in certain ways and therefore presumably alike in other ways. *Analogies* can illustrate an idea but they do not prove it.

dilemma

■ "Either the man is boss in a home or the woman will rule." Such logic presents a *faulty d* _____ .

analogy

■ Comparing man to an eagle that must rule its own nest is an *an* _____ .

illustrate

■ *Analogies* _____ [prove / illustrate] ideas.

■ "The early bird catches the worm, so I'll be up at dawn and find a job." This is reasoning by _____ .

analogy

■ "Don't touch alcohol or you'll end up in the looney bin." This choice is the *f*_____ *d*_____ .

faulty dilemma

■ The *faulty dilemma* forces one to choose from _____ [two / all of the] possibilities.

two

■ Bede's *Ecclesiastical History* (eighth century) likens our life to the quick flight of a sparrow through a lighted hall at night. This is an *a*_____ .

analogy

---

24. **Socratic irony** (sə-krat′ik): the device of pretending to be ignorant and asking questions in order to trap the opponent into obvious error. Socrates uses *Socratic irony,* for instance, to refute a husky Athenian who argues that might makes right.

■ The man who uses *Socratic irony* asks a series of innocent-sounding questions (a) because he is stupid, (b) because he is leading his opponent into self-contradiction. (    )

(b)

■ To employ *S*_____ *irony* one must (a) ask adroit questions to draw out the other fellow's ignorance, (b) talk constantly in an opinionated fashion. (    )

Socratic

(a)

■ If falsely accused of plagiarism you might use *Socratic* _____ to clear yourself by saying, (a) "I'm innocent, teacher; I swear I'm innocent!" (b) "Very interesting—now where is this passage which I have stolen?" (    )

irony

(b)

---

### Quiz

Write the letter that indicates the best definition.

1. (b)
2. (d)

3. (a)

4. (c)

(    ) 1. bandwagon device    a. an extended comparison

(    ) 2. faulty dilemma    b. argument for joining the popular side

(    ) 3. analogy    c. refuting by means of clever but innocent-sounding questions

(    ) 4. Socratic irony    d. offering two alternatives when more exist

**25. fragment:** an incomplete sentence. *Fragments* are often considered the unpardonable sin in freshman themes, though they are acceptable in exclamations, dialogue, and certain types of informal writing.

**26. comma splice:** the use of a comma between main clauses where a period or semicolon should be used. Example: "Jack London wrote about supermen and superdogs, he became a rich socialist."

Before each of the following write *fragment, comma splice,* or *correct.*

comma splice

■ _____ H. L. Mencken was pungent and opinionated, I never thought he was dull.

fragment

■ _____ Alexandre Dumas being about the most imaginative novelist I had ever read.

fragment

■ _____ Because the *Bhagavad* teaches complete unselfishness, humility, and goodness.

correct

■ _____ Elvis died.

Before each of the following write *fragment, comma splice,* or *correct.*

comma splice

■ _____ The British loved Kipling, however, he was never poet laureate.

fragment

■ _____ A scholarly analysis, which reads like a detective story, of the Shakespeare sonnets, particularly those dealing with the Dark Lady.

correct

■ _____ My brother can't write like Chaucer, but he spells like him.

---

**27. infinitive** (in-fin'i-tiv): a verbal form that consists usually of "to" plus a verb, as "to walk." The *infinitive* can do the work of a noun, adjective, or adverb.

**28. participle** (pär'ti-sip'əl): a verbal adjective. "Flying in a battered plane, I had some frightening moments." Here "flying," "battered," and "frightening" are *participles*.

infinitive

■ A phrase like "to paint" is an *in* _____ .

■ A verbal adjective—like "honking" in "honking geese" is a

participle

*p* _____ .

■ "Attacking his critics, James Fenimore Cooper began to waste valuable writing time." "Attacking" is a _____, "to waste" is an _____, and "writing" is a _____ .

■ "To strive, to seek, to find, and not to yield." This final line of Tennyson's poem "Ulysses" (1842) contains four _____ .

■ Inserting words between "to" and the verb in an *infinitive* results in a *split infinitive,* a phrasing which often sounds awkward. Which phrase has a split infinitive? (a) "to as soon as possible analyze Chekhov's play," (b) "to analyze Chekhov's play as soon as possible. (   )

■ "Shakespeare was able to find several gripping themes in the chronicles of Holinshed." Here "to find" is an *i*_____ and "gripping" is a *p*_____ .

A *participle* that does not clearly modify the right word is a *dangling participle.* After each of the following write *dangler* or *correct.*

■ Becoming six years old, my mother got a divorce. _____

■ Echoing Emerson, Walt Whitman spoke of man's divinity. _____

■ If stewed, you will enjoy these prunes. _____

---

29. **parallelism** (par′ə-lel′iz-əm): similarity of grammatical structure given to similar ideas. *Parallelism* in phrasing brings out *parallelism* in ideas.

■ Consider the sentence, "Fritz loves fishing, climbing, and to yodel." It has faulty *par*_____ but would become acceptable if the phrase "to yodel" were changed to the word *y*_____ .

■ "Gunder has vowed to work, to save money, and that he will succeed in business." This sentence has _____ [acceptable / faulty] *parallelism.*

■ Which has better *parallelism?* (a) "I came and after I saw the enemy they were conquered by me," (b) "I came, I saw, I conquered." (   )

for

parallelism

■ Lincoln referred to "government of the people, by the people, _____ [for / to help] the people" and achieved structural *pa* _____ .

---

**30. idiom:** an accepted phrase that is contrary to the usual language pattern. *Idioms* are natural, supple, and often very informal. Examples: "catch cold," "give in," "hint at," "knock off work," "pick a fight."

idioms

■ Phrases like "comes in handy" and "takes after his father" are *id* _____ .

(a)

■ Although *idioms* violate normal language construction, they are (a) proper and acceptable, (b) colorful but unusable. (     )

idiom
(b)

■ Another peculiar English phrasing, known as an *id* _____ is (a) "walk with me," (b) "angry with me." (     )

(b)

■ Which is an *idiom?* (a) "became a loafer," (b) "went to the dogs." (     )

idiomatic

■ Ernest Hemingway achieved vigor and naturalness in his stories by using _____ [formal / idiomatic] English.

---

## Quiz

Write the letter that indicates the best example.

1. (e)
2. (c)
3. (a)
4. (d)
5. (f)
6. (b)

|   |   |   |   |
|---|---|---|---|
| (     ) | 1. fragment | a. | *"To err* is human." |
| (     ) | 2. comma splice | b. | We grabbed a bite. |
| (     ) | 3. infinitive | c. | "Here comes Lulu, get the hymn book." |
| (     ) | 4. participle | d. | "'The Lottery' is a *terrifying* story." |
| (     ) | 5. parallelism | e. | "Whereas Irving knew the Catskills." |
| (     ) | 6. idiom | f. | He lived; he loved; he died. |

## REVIEW TEST

Supply the missing word in each sentence.

1. Copying material without giving proper credit is *pl*_____.
2. The ridiculous misuse of a word for another that sounds like it is a *mal*_____.
3. A word like "WAVE," made up from the initials of a title, is an *ac*_____.
4. A mild word substituted for a blunt one is a *eu*_____.
5. Prose composition that explains or sets forth is *ex*_____.
6. Ordinary writing that is not poetry is called *pr*_____.
7. A word of opposite meaning is an *an*_____.
8. A word with the same sound but different meaning is a *ho*_____.
9. A conclusion which "does not follow" from the evidence is a n_____
   *se*_____.
10. Needless repetition or wordiness is *re*_____.
11. An accepted phrase that defies normal language patterns is an *id*_____.
12. The verbal "grinning" in "grinning faces" is a *pa*_____.
13. An incomplete sentence is a *fr*_____.
14. Propaganda urging one to follow the crowd is the *b*_____ *device*.
15. An omission of words, indicated by three dots, is an *el*_____.

Write *True* or *False*.

_____ 16. *Concreteness* refers to the use of clear, specific detail.
_____ 17. *Post hoc* logic is considered valid in science.
_____ 18. *Begging the question* means assuming without proof.
_____ 19. An argument *ad hominem* sticks to the main issue.
_____ 20. *Triteness* adds color and vigor to one's style.
_____ 21. To use *Socratic irony* means to argue and fall into one's own trap.
_____ 22. In the *faulty dilemma* one must choose from an incomplete set of alternatives.
_____ 23. *Comma splice* refers to the omission of a comma.

**Rhetoric    215**

_____ 24. The following contains *parallelism:* "We will fight with guns, with bombs, and with fists."

_____ 25. *Rhetoric* is the art of persuasive writing and speaking.

---

Write the letter that indicates the best completion.

(     ) 26. An *analogy* is (a) a proof, (b) an exaggeration, (c) a comparison, (d) a stale expression.

(     ) 27. An example of an *infinitive* is (a) "the critic Mencken," (b) "criticizing," (c) "to criticize," (d) "to critics."

(     ) 28. A *précis* is (a) an explanation, (b) an expansion, (c) a quotation, (d) a condensation.

(     ) 29. A *paraphrase* is (a) a restatement, (b) a quotation, (c) a line of poetry, (d) a wordy passage.

---

Match each word with its definition.

(     ) 30. participle       a. dull, worn-out phrasing

(     ) 31. triteness        b. suggestiveness

(     ) 32. connotation      c. verbal adjective

(     ) 33. plagiarism       d. literary theft

---

## Key to Review Test

Check your test answers with the following key. Deduct 3% per error from a possible 100%.

| | | |
|---|---|---|
| 1. plagiarism | 12. participle | 23. False |
| 2. malapropism | 13. fragment | 24. True |
| 3. acronym | 14. bandwagon | 25. True |
| 4. euphemism | 15. ellipsis | 26. (c) |
| 5. exposition | 16. True | 27. (c) |
| 6. prose | 17. False | 28. (d) |
| 7. antonym | 18. True | 29. (a) |
| 8. homonym | 19. False | 30. (c) |
| 9. *non sequitur* | 20. False | 31. (a) |
| 10. redundancy | 21. False | 32. (b) |
| 11. idiom | 22. True | 33. (d) |

Score: _____ %

---

# 15

# Eliminating Wordiness

PARTIAL LIST

a ~~highly talented~~ genius, **12**
audible ~~to the ear~~, **12**
autobiography ~~of his life~~, **14**
~~basic~~ fundamentals, **12**
bisect an angle ~~in two~~, **11**
~~completely~~ demolished, **11**
~~completely~~ unanimous, **9**
consensus ~~of opinion~~, **25**
continue ~~on~~, **20**
cooperated ~~together~~, **12**
crazy ~~in the head~~, **6**
~~each and~~ everyone, **34**

enormous ~~in size~~, **12**
~~final~~ conclusion, **9**
food ~~to eat~~, **4**
green ~~in color~~, **12**
~~like, man~~, **31**
many ~~in number~~, **10**
meet ~~up with~~, **34**
mopped ~~up~~ the floors, **18**
~~needless to say~~, **15**
~~personally~~ I thought, **6**
~~really very~~, very lucky, **28**
reason . . . is ~~because~~, **16**

round ~~in shape~~, **34**
short ~~in stature~~, **12**
~~short~~ ten-minute break, **34**
soprano ~~singer~~, **24**
twenty minutes ~~in time~~, **34**
until dawn ~~in the morning~~, **7**
visible ~~to the eye~~, **1**
ways ~~and means~~, **34**
widow ~~woman~~, **12**
~~you know~~, **31**

An author came down from his mountain cabin every week for groceries. He saw a big neon sign above a fish store: FRESH FISH SOLD HERE. "Cut out the word 'here' and save electricity," he advised the shopkeeper. "Everybody knows you're selling it here, not in Oslo."

"Great idea!" said the shopkeeper.

The following week the sign read: FRESH FISH SOLD. "Cut out the word 'sold,'" advised the author. "Everybody knows you're not giving the fish away."

"Great idea!" said the shopkeeper.

The following week the sign read: FRESH FISH. "Cut out the word 'fresh,'" advised the author. "Everybody knows you're not advertising last year's fish."

The following week the sign read: FISH. "And that's the minimum to advertise my fish," said the shopkeeper.

The author sniffed the air. "Cut out the word 'fish' too," he said. "We can smell your fish from the top of the mountain."

The author had a point. We should cut unnecessary words from our writing.

An old newspaper editor pointed to a line written by a cub reporter. It read, "At 7 P.M. Wednesday evening Sven Johnson was killed by a fatal bullet through his head." Said the editor: "You don't need 'evening' because 'P.M.' takes care of that. You don't need 'fatal' because 'killed' takes care of that. Please cut unnecessary words from your writing."

That's the theme of this chapter: Cut unnecessary words from your writing.

## EXERCISES

COVER THIS STRIP

---

**1.**

Cut unnecessary words from your writing. Consider the following sentence.

The ketchup stain on my tuxedo was visible to the eye.

■ Is a stain often seen by, say, the ear, the nose, or the elbow?

no _____

■ Don't readers already know that seeing is the job of the eye?

yes _____

to the eye ■ Three unnecessary words in the sentence are _____.

---

**2.**

Look for unnecessary words.

We sat on the hilltop and admired the sunset in the west.

no ■ Do we often see sunsets in the east? _____

■ Don't readers already know that the sun has a habit of setting in
yes the west? _____

in the west ■ Three unnecessary words in the sentence are _____.

---

**3.**

Using too many words to express an idea is known as wordiness or
redundancy.

avoid ■ Good writers _____ [love / avoid] redundancy.

---

**4.**

Look for unnecessary words.

The homeless in our city need food to eat.

■ Would the homeless need food, say, to patch their pants or to nail a fence? _____

no

■ Don't readers already know that food is for eating? _____

yes

■ Two words that should be crossed out are _____.

to eat

## 5.

Consider these two sentences.

■ Our clubs cooperated together since the month of April.

*Hint:* What does the Latin prefix *co* mean? _____

~~together~~
~~the month of~~
together

■ We estimate a sale of about five hundred hot dogs, more or less.

*Hint:* Isn't every estimate an approximation? _____

Now cross out the unnecessary words.

~~about~~
~~more or less~~
yes

## 6.

Cross out unnecessary words.

■ Personally I thought Rico had gone crazy in the head.

~~Personally~~
~~in the head~~

## 7.

Cross out unnecessary words.

■ I sold my jalopy for the sum of thirty dollars.

■ Uncle Buck played poker until dawn in the morning.

~~the sum of~~

~~in the morning~~

## 8.

Cross out unnecessary words.

■ My new rug measures ten feet in length by six feet in width.

■ Never before in the past had nations joined together to fight pollution.

~~in length~~
~~in width~~
~~in the past~~
~~together~~

**9.**

Cross out unnecessary words.

~~first~~
~~final~~

■ I was fascinated by Shakespeare's *Hamlet* from ~~first~~ introduction to ~~final~~ conclusion.

~~completely~~
~~woman~~

■ The jury was ~~completely~~ unanimous in its support of the widow ~~woman~~.

---

**10.**

Cross out unnecessary words.

~~in number were~~
~~the personal~~
~~. . . who~~

■ Many ~~in number were~~ the personal friends who attended Joe Bingle's funeral.

~~in color~~
~~to the touch~~

■ Our baby's eyes are blue ~~in color~~ and its feet are soft ~~to the touch~~.

---

**11.**

Cross out unnecessary words.

~~together~~
~~completely~~

■ Two days after the twins passed a driver's test, their cars collided ~~together~~ and were ~~completely~~ demolished.

~~in two~~

■ Geometry students can bisect an angle ~~in two~~ with ruler and compass.

---

**12.**

Cross out unnecessary words.

~~in stature~~
~~in size~~

■ Although I am short ~~in stature~~, my ears are enormous ~~in size~~, and my face looks like a taxicab with the doors open.

---

**Quiz**

Cross out unnecessary words. If a phrase looks acceptable, write *OK* in front of it.

1. ~~in color~~
2. OK
3. ~~woman~~
4. ~~completely~~

1. green ~~in color~~
2. the male prisoner
3. a widow ~~woman~~
4. ~~completely~~ demolished

5. audible to the ear
6. cooperated together

7. an estimate of profits
8. a stain on my tuxedo

---

**13.**

Rewrite in eight words.

Coach Roach
taught me the
fundamentals of
soccer.

■ Coach Roach taught me the basic fundamentals of the game of soccer, you know what I mean?

_____

_____

---

**14.**

Rewrite in five words.

Lincoln
Steffens
wrote an
autobiography.

■ In the case of Lincoln Steffens, he wrote an autobiography of his own life.

_____

_____

---

**15.**

Rewrite in five words.

Albert Einstein
was a genius.

■ Needless to say, Albert Einstein was a highly talented genius.

_____

_____

---

**16.** A common redundancy is "The reason . . . is because." It's like saying, "The cause is because."

_Redundant:_ The reason Noah didn't play cards is because an elephant stood on the deck.

_Acceptable:_ The reason Noah didn't play cards is that an elephant stood on the deck.

_Better:_ Noah didn't play cards because an elephant stood on the deck.

Rewrite the following sentence.

■ The reason I'm tardy is because I helped an old lady cross a busy street.

I'm tardy because I helped an old lady cross a busy street.

_____

_____

_____

**17.**

Rewrite the following sentences.

■ The reason McGinty lost the election is because he wouldn't kiss the babies.

McGinty lost the election because he wouldn't kiss the babies.

_____

_____

■ The reason my kitten likes tennis is because its daddy is in the racket.

My kitten likes tennis because its daddy is in the racket.

_____

_____

**18.** The word *up* can be cut without loss from some phrases.

Cross out *up* where it is unnecessary.

■ This morning I mopped up the floors and swept up the sidewalk. Then I looked up and saw a robin.

mopped ~~up~~
swept ~~up~~

**19.**

Cross out *up* where it is unnecessary.

■ I watched the groggy fighter try to get up in the final seconds but time was up. That night I wrote up the sport story, polished up the paragraphs, then carefully folded up the manuscript.

wrote ~~up~~
polished ~~up~~
folded ~~up~~

**20.**

Continue means "keep on."

■ Is it logical to write "continue on," which means "keep on on"?

no _____

**21.**

Cross out unnecessary words.

continue ~~on~~
proceed ~~on~~

■ We will continue on with the five o'clock news, after which we will proceed on with interviews.

---

**22.** Sentences that begin with "There is" or "There are" often gain force if they are restated without those introductory phrases. Consider:

    a. There were three strangers entering the Boodle Bank.
    b. Three strangers entered the Boodle Bank.

b

Which is the punchier opening line for a short story? (    )

---

**23.**

Restate this sentence, eliminating *there*.

Thousands of
mental patients
own guns.

■ There are thousands of mental patients who own guns.

_____

_____

**24.**

Rewrite the sentence, eliminating *there*.

A fly was
swimming in
my soup.

■ There was a fly swimming in my soup.

_____

_____

**25.** *Consensus* means "a general opinion."

■ The phrase "consensus of opinion" is an example of the

wordiness

_____ [crispness / wordiness] that careful writers usually

avoid

_____ [avoid / love].

consensus

■ We are due for an earthquake soon, according to a _____
[consensus / consensus of opinion] of experts.

_____

**26.**

consensus

■ More women should enter politics, according to a *con*_____
of congressional leaders.

■ News item: "The consensus of opinion of fashion designers is that dresses will be shorter next summer." What must be cut in that sentence (not counting dresses)? _____

_____

**27.** The words *very* and *really* are overused and can often be deleted without loss.

Restate in seven words.

■ We're really proud of our very outstanding debate team.

_____

_____

**28.**

Restate in twelve words.

■ The guest speaker, in my very humble opinion, was really very, very lucky to get cold cash for hot air.

_____

_____

**29.**

Rewrite in eleven words.

■ Dad was really a baseball pitcher, and I was really his very first screwball.

_____

_____

**30.**

Cross out every useless *really* in the following passage.

really anxious
really enjoyed
really believe
really out-
standing

four

mature

■ I was really anxious for school to begin this fall. I have always really enjoyed studying and meeting people, and I really believe that the opportunities here at Knockwurst College are really outstanding.

■ In the foregoing passage, the word "really" can be cut _____ times without loss; in fact, these deletions have resulted in a more _____ [redundant / mature] style.

_____

Cross out unnecessary words in the following sentences.

1. ~~The reason~~
   ~~. . . is~~
2. ~~on~~
3. ~~up~~
4. ~~really~~ . . .
   ~~really~~
5. ~~very, very~~

1. The reason Art was arrested is because he hit a police car.
2. The audience was applauding or swatting mosquitoes, so Joe continued on.
3. Take this shovel and clean up your apartment.
4. The restaurant promised really huge steaks—like manhole covers. They really tasted like manhole covers too.
5. Bill's room was so very, very dirty that his dog buried a bone in the rug.

---

**31.** The words *like, you know, you understand,* and *man* can be used correctly, but when used loosely they become a blemish in conversation.

Cross out unnecessary words, then count how many words are left in the sentence.

■ I like Betty, you understand, but, man, I can't like marry her, you know.

8

[14 words, cut to _____ words]

■ We like drove past her house, man, and you know she was like kissing the man from like Texas you understand.

13

[21 words, cut to _____ words]

■ You know the route to army headquarters, and you understand you'll be expected—at age fourteen—to fight like a man.

22

[22 words, cut to _____ words]

---

**32.** A good writer makes every word count. He doesn't use a windy, worn-out phrase if a simple word or two can do the job.

Restate in one word.

now

■ _____ in this day and age

believe

■ _____ am of the opinion

---

**33.**

Restate in one word.

because
(or *since*)

■ _____ in view of the fact that

| | |
|---|---|
| if | ■ _____ in the event that |
| No. | ■ _____ I must admit that my reply to the query just put to me is in the negative. |

---

**34.**

Restate in one word.

| | |
|---|---|
| except | ■ _____ with the exception of |
| Please | ■ _____ I would appreciate it if |

---

**35.**

Restate in one word.

| | |
|---|---|
| now | ■ _____ at this point in time |
| meet | ■ _____ come in contact with |

---

## Quiz

Each of these sentences contain a redundancy. Cross out any unnecessary words.

1. ~~herewith~~
2. ~~singer~~
3. ~~and means~~
4. ~~to death~~
5. ~~below~~

6. ~~Each and~~
7. ~~in time~~

8. ~~short~~
9. ~~up with~~
10. ~~in shape~~
    . . . ~~in color~~
11. ~~like~~ . . .
    ~~man you~~
    ~~know~~

1. The registration card you requested is enclosed herewith.
2. The guest artist was Lily Pons, the colorature soprano singer.
3. The prisoners' committee planned ways and means to escape.
4. Smith's body was found stabbed and strangled to death.
5. The flames forced Knute to leap from the third floor to the ground below.
6. Each and everyone on our team won a trophy.
7. The customer ahead of me spent twenty minutes in time gossiping with the bank teller.
8. Our orchestra will now take a short ten-minute break.
9. I never dreamt I would meet up with the president.
10. Try to pick cantaloupes that are round in shape and yellow in color.
11. If like you smoke in bed, man, take out blanket insurance, you know.

Cross out redundancies in the following sentences. Write *OK* in front of any sentence that has no redundancy.

_____    1. The circus giant was well paid, but the little midget got a small salary.

_____    2. Personally I believe most holidays are the invention of greeting card companies.

_____    3. To the hungry, give food; to the thirsty, give water to drink.

_____    4. I wore a kelly green suit—the jacket belonged to Kelly and the pants to Green.

_____    5. Our beautiful yacht was dashed against the boulders and completely demolished.

_____    6. North Dakota has two seasons: winter and the month of July.

_____    7. After nine holes of golf, Mr. Rockefeller reluctantly gave the caddy the sum of ten cents.

_____    8. Randy had girl trouble. He had no girl friends of the female sex, and that was the trouble.

_____    9. The reason I call him Bulova is because he's a watch dog.

_____    10. Bart estimates that by 2020 the world population will be in the neighborhood of ten billion.

_____    11. Our grandchildren may never see a sky that's blue in color.

_____    12. I loved the sleepy atmosphere of Porkville, except when the wind blew the wrong way.

_____    13. Our problem in geometry class was to trisect an angle into three angles.

_____    14. Few readers are able to predict the final outcome of this detective story.

_____    15. Helen Keller, deaf and blind, wrote a notable autobiography of her life.

_____    16. All my little debts will be combined together into one massive debt.

_____    17. Our nation was conceived in liberty and dedicated to the proposition that all men are created equal.

_____    18. Joe sells old, out-of-date *Newsweek*s to dentists for their waiting rooms.

_____    19. After Homer ate the "mushrooms," he turned green in color.

**Eliminating Wordiness**    **227**

_____ 20. Mrs. Vandersnoot's rugs were so thick we needed snowshoes to continue on to the television set.

_____ 21. We looked ahead with hopeful optimism to our basketball game with Ameba High School.

_____ 22. One country music singer couldn't spell Tennessee two years ago, and now you know he like owns half of it.

_____ 23. Our sleepy village will develop into a vast slum unless we do some advance planning.

_____ 24. In my personal opinion, I think Jack the Ripper is still alive and he is doing my laundry.

_____ 25. In this modern day and age we can now pollute the environment far more efficiently than the ignorant Indians could.

## Key to Review Test

Check your test answers with the following key. Deduct 4% per error from a possible 100%.

| | | |
|---|---|---|
| 1. ~~little~~ | 10. ~~in the neighborhood of~~ | 19. ~~in color~~ |
| 2. ~~Personally~~ | 11. ~~in color~~ | 20. ~~on~~ |
| 3. ~~to drink~~ | 12. OK | 21. ~~hopeful~~ |
| 4. OK | 13. ~~into three angles~~ | 22. ~~you know~~ . . . ~~like~~ |
| 5. ~~completely~~ | 14. ~~final~~ | 23. ~~advance~~ |
| 6. ~~the month of~~ | 15. ~~of her life~~ | 24. ~~In my personal opinion~~ |
| 7. ~~the sum of~~ | 16. ~~together~~ | 25. ~~In this modern day and~~ |
| 8. ~~of the female sex~~ | 17. OK | ~~age~~ |
| 9. ~~The reason~~ . . . ~~is~~ | 18. ~~old~~ | |

Score: _____ %

# 16

# Figures of Speech

*Abraham Lincoln said that a man should preach "like a man fighting off a swarm of bees" (simile); that "we must save the good old ship of the Union on this voyage" (metaphor); that we must "bind up the nation's wounds" (personification). Figures of speech are a trademark of the imaginative writer. A random survey of William Shakespeare, Emily Dickinson, Herman Melville, or Jim Murray would reveal a galaxy of similes, metaphors, hyperboles, oxymorons. Your familiarity with such terms can help you in two ways: As an analyst of literary passages you can more ably identify and appreciate the stylistic devices used; as a creative writer you can gain sparkle and vigor by using a greater variety of figures of speech.*

## EXERCISES

COVER THIS STRIP

1. **simile** (sim′ə-lē): a figure of speech comparing two unlike things, usually with "like" or "as." Example: "She has a figure like an hourglass—and not a minute of it wasted."
2. **metaphor** (met′ə-fôr′): a figure of speech in which one thing is said to be another thing, without "like" or "as," or in which a likeness is implied. Example: "All the world's a stage"; "My boss barked out his orders."

Before each example write *simile* or *metaphor*.

metaphor

■ _____ Boston was a beehive.

simile

■ _____ Orville has a head like a granite block.

simile

■ _____ Teacher's heart is as big and soft as an overripe pumpkin.

metaphor

■ _____ My mother-in-law sailed into the room.

simile, metaphor

■ An expressed comparison between unlike things, with "like" or "as," is a _____ ; an implied comparison is a _____ .

Write *simile* or *metaphor*.

metaphor

■ _____ Mabel was a dynamo, but she got short-circuited.

simile

■ _____ He looks like a dishonest Abe Lincoln.

metaphor

■ _____ The Buick purred down the freeway.

3. **alliteration:** the repetition of an initial sound in words or accented syllables close together. *Alliteration* abounds in "the big brutal battles of *Beowulf.*"
4. **onomatopoeia** (on′ə-mat′ə-pē′ə): the use of words whose pronunciation suggests their meaning. *Onomatopoeic* words are common: *boom, hiss, murmur, zoom, moan, hum, chug, sizzle, cuckoo, glug.*

onomatopoeia

■ Using words that sound like what they mean is *on* _____ .

| | |
|---|---|
| alliteration | ■ Using the same initial letter in neighboring words is *al* _____ . |
| (b) | ■ Which line of poetry by Robert Herrick contains *alliteration?* (a) "The liquefaction of her clothes," (b) "I sing of brooks, of blossoms, birds and bowers." (   ) |

Before each example write *alliteration* or *onomatopoeia.*

| | |
|---|---|
| onomatopoeia | ■ _____ The locomotive snorted and hissed—then went chug-ah! |
| alliteration | ■ _____ What a tale of terror now their turbulency tells! |
| alliteration | ■ _____ That lazy, lovable lunatic. |
| onomatopoeia | ■ _____ He dived on his belly—plop, splash. |

---

5. **hyperbole** (hī-pûr′bə-lē): a gross exaggeration for rhetorical effect. Examples: "The new blonde typist made errors by the barrel, but nobody noticed."
6. **litotes** (lī′tə-tēz′): a figure of speech in which a point is made by a denying of its opposite; a kind of understatement; for example, "It's no small matter"; "Rockefeller was no pauper"; "The prisoner approached the gallows without enthusiasm."

| | |
|---|---|
| litotes | ■ Denying the opposite of what you mean is *li* _____ . |
| hyperbole | ■ Gross exaggeration is *hy* _____ . |
| (b) | ■ A *hyperbole* might say that the village boozer (a) drank several bottles of beer, (b) made the local brewery go on a twenty-four hour shift. (   ) |
| (b) | ■ An example of *litotes* is (a) "The mackerel had a bad odor," (b) "The mackerel did not smell like Chanel No. 5." (   ) |

Before each example write *hyperbole* or *litotes.*

| | |
|---|---|
| hyperbole | ■ _____ The mosquitoes were rangy and enterprising, and they'd siphon a quart of blood before you noticed them. |
| hyperbole | ■ _____ There's enough poetry on the boys' washroom walls to put Shakespeare out of business. |

litotes ▪ _____ Gangster Al Capone did not exactly win the Best Citizen award.

litotes ▪ _____ Those cigarettes didn't do your lungs any good.

## Quiz

Write the letter that indicates the best example.

1. (c)
2. (e)
3. (f)
4. (d)
5. (b)
6. (a)

(    ) 1. alliteration    a. a hairdo like an unmade bed
(    ) 2. hyperbole    b. the *bar-r-room* of the trombones
(    ) 3. litotes    c. lively lads and lasses
(    ) 4. metaphor    d. Alice was sugar and cream.
(    ) 5. onomatopoeia    e. Lulu has an army of suitors.
(    ) 6. simile    f. Caruso was not a bad singer either.

7. **apostrophe** (ə-pos′trə-fē): addressing a personified object, or an absent person as though present. Example from Francis Thompson: "O world invisible, we view thee."

8. **metonymy** (mi-ton′ə-mē): a figure of speech in which the name of a thing is used for something else associated with it; virtually synonymous with *synecdoche*. Example: "The sailor was warned to stay away from the skirts."

▪ In *apostrophe* the poet is emotionally involved with some absent

to it

person or some personified object and speaks directly _____ [to it/ of it].

metonymy
(a)

▪ "He was addicted to the bottle" is *met*_____ because "bottle" is associated with (a) liquor, (b) glassware. (    )

Before each example write *apostrophe* or *metonymy*.

metonymy ▪ _____ Dinner is $2.95 a plate.

metonymy ▪ _____ Melvin has read Tennessee Williams.

apostrophe ▪ _____ Robert Burns: "O Scotia! my dear, my native soil!"

metonymy ▪ _____ The White House announces . . . .

(a)

▪ Which line involves *apostrophe*?—(a) William Wordsworth: "Milton! thou shouldst be living at this hour," (b) John Masefield: "Oh London Town's a fine town." (    )

9. **oxymoron** (ok′si-mōr′on): a combination of two apparently contradictory words. Example: "dazzling darkness," "devout atheism," "lively corpse."

10. **antithesis** (an-tith′i-sis): The strong contrast of expressions, clauses, sentences, or ideas within a balanced grammatical structure. Example: "Life is short; art is long," "Give me liberty or give me death."

oxymoron

■ A seeming contradiction like "clever idiot" is an *ox*_____ .

■ "We must all hang together, or assuredly we shall all hang separately." This famous utterance by Franklin in 1776 illustrates

antithesis, does    *ant*_____, since it _____ [does / does not] present a contrast of ideas in a balanced pattern.

■ Which ending results in *antithesis?* "Johnny was in the church basement making taffy, and (a) wondering if Jimmy ever had so much

(b)    fun," (b) "Jimmy was in the theater balcony making love." (    )

oxymoron    ■ "Militant pacifism" is an *ox*_____, and Sir Philip Sidney's reference to "living deaths, dear wounds, fair storms, and

oxymorons    freezing fires" includes four *ox*_____ .

noisy    ■ An *oxymoron* might refer to a "_____ [strange / noisy]

attractive    silence" or to an "_____ [attractive / unusual] repulsiveness."

■ A contrast of ideas expressed as a balanced sentence is known as

antithesis    *ant*_____ .

■ An example of *antithesis* is (a) "You do not have to cut off your fingers to write shorthand," (b) "A cat has its claws at the end of the

(b)    paws; a comma has its pause at the end of the clause." (    )

---

11. **personification** (pər-son′ə-fə-kā′shən): the giving of human qualities to something that is not human; for example, "stern-faced Duty" and "the murmuring pines."

12. **pathetic fallacy** (fal′ə-sē): attributing human feelings to inanimate things: an aspect of personification. In *Modern Painters* (1856) John Ruskin objects to the *pathetic fallacy,* or falseness, in phrases like "the cruel crawling foam" or "weeping skies."

■ *Personification,* like "the brow of the hill," give human qualities to

(b)    (a) people, (b) nonhuman things. (    )

fallacy

(a)

(a)

(a)

pathetic
(b)

■ *Personification* is referred to as the *pathetic f*_____ when trees or skies are not merely likened to humans but are even endowed with (a) human feelings, (b) divine qualities. (    )

■ Which line involves *personification?* (a) Samuel Coleridge: "The one red leaf, the last of its clan, / That dances as often as dance it can," (b) Alfred Tennyson: "Comrades, leave me here a little, while as yet 'tis early morn." (    )

■ Which line involves *personification?* (a) William Shakespeare: "Blow, winds, and crack your cheeks," (b) Christina Rossetti: "This Advent moon shines cold and clear." (    )

■ The type of *personification* which attributes feelings to things, known as the *p*_____ *fallacy,* is suggested by (a) "in the teeth of the wind," (b) "the wailing wind." (    )

---

## Quiz

Write the letter that indicates the best example.

1. (d)
2. (b)
3. (c)
4. (a)
5. (f)
6. (e)

(    ) 1. apostrophe        a. her bold shyness
(    ) 2. antithesis        b. Man proposes; God disposes.
(    ) 3. metonymy          c. The farmer hired three hands.
(    ) 4. oxymoron          d. Here's to thee, oh Alma Mater!
(    ) 5. pathetic fallacy  e. the eye of the storm
(    ) 6. personification   f. the groaning branches of fruit
                              (special type of personification)

---

13. **allusion** (ə-lōō′zhən): a passing reference to something; an indirect mention. Milton's poetry is peppered with classical *allusions,* that is, references to passages in world literature.

allusion

■ Mentioning Achilles or Sancho Panza or Blake's "The Tyger" would be a literary *al*_____ .

(a)

■ A man makes a Biblical *allusion* if he refers to his wife as his (a) "rib," (b) "ball and chain." (    )

allusion

■ "Everything that Tanya touches turns to gold." The writer has made a passing reference, or _____ , to the story of King Midas.

allusion
(a)

■ "Well, I'll be a monkey's cousin!" This comment embodies an indirect reference, or _____, to (a) Darwinism, (b) Jeffersonian democracy. (   )

---

14. **irony** (i′rə-nē): saying the opposite of what is meant, by way of mockery: known as *verbal irony;* in general, the contrast between what is and what might reasonably be expected ("The Nudnick police station was burglarized"); see also *irony of fate* (Chapter 19, frame 16) and *Socratic irony* (Chapter 14, frame 24).

(b)

■ When peace-loving Stephen Crane says, "War is kind," he is probably (a) serious, (b) ironic. (   )

irony
(b)

■ "That's right," says your father, "have a good time, forget your homework, become a bum!" His advice is an example of *i*_____ because he really means (a) exactly what he says, (b) the opposite of what he says. (   )

irony

■ In "A Modest Proposal" (1729) Johathan Swift urges with tongue in cheek, or with *i*_____, that Englishmen should eat Irish infants.

(a)

■ Verbal *irony* is a form of (a) sarcasm, (b) eulogy. (   )

(b)

■ The baseball coach uses *irony* when he says, "You struck out five times—(a) such rotten luck!" (b) such a marvelous athlete!" (   )

---

15. **symbol** (sim′bəl): an object or a story element which has a basic meaning yet which also has another meaning; for example, a dove is a bird of the pigeon family yet it also stands for peace. In Hawthorne's *The Scarlet Letter,* the minister keeps putting his hand to his heart, a natural gesture but also a *symbol* of hidden guilt.

symbol

■ A flag, a cross, or a handclasp may stand for something beside itself and thus each may be a *sy*_____ .

(a)

■ Appropriate *symbols* to suggest old age might be (a) withered leaves and dry ashes, (b) budding flowers and gushing waters. (   )

(b)

■ *Symbolism* in fiction can exist (a) only in concrete objects such as an ivory leg, or livid scar, a white whale, (b) in objects, characters, gestures, situations, etc. (   )

symbol
(a)

■ As the Hemingway hero lies mortally wounded, he sees the buzzards circle closer and closer. The buzzards are a s_____ of (a) death, (b) hope. (       )

## Quiz

Write the letter that indicates the best definition.

1. (c)
2. (a)
3. (b)

(       ) 1. allusion       a. mockery by expressing opposites
(       ) 2. irony          b. that which stands for something else
(       ) 3. symbol         c. a casual reference to something

## REVIEW TEST

Supply the missing word in each sentence.

1. A gross exaggeration is a *hy*_____.
2. The repetition of initial letters in words is *al*_____.
3. Saying the opposite of what is really meant, in order to ridicule, is known as *ir*_____.
4. A comparison using "like" or "as" is a *si*_____.
5. Use of words that sound like what they mean is *on*_____.
6. Addressing the absent as though present is known as *ap*_____.
7. Naming of a thing to represent something closely associated with it is *me*_____.
8. "I was a stricken deer." Cowper's figure of speech is a *me*_____.
9. "The sun peered at me." This figure of speech is *pe*_____.
10. "Darkness visible." Milton's contradictory phrase is an *ox*_____.

---

Name the figure of speech in each example. The first letter of each answer is given.

| | |
|---|---|
| 11. lovely Lulu from Laredo | *a* _____ |
| 12. a head shaped like a Persian melon | *s* _____ |
| 13. Eat another plate. | *m*_____ |
| 14. a beach not without its beer cans and litter | *l* _____ |
| 15. Boom, crash, clang went the drum section. | *o* _____ |
| 16. Her brain is a storage vault. | *m*_____ |
| 17. The bitter sweetness of farewell. | *o* _____ |
| 18. Kay's wardrobe closet is about fifty yards long. | *h* _____ |
| 19. The pansies closed their little eyes. | *p* _____ |
| 20. O Eve, Eve, why did you eat the forbidden fruit? | *a* _____ |
| 21. He generously gave the church all of two cents. | *i* _____ |
| 22. Sam spends much; he earns little. | *a* _____ |
| 23. Respect the scepter, the sword, the flag. | *s* _____ |

24. We spoke of Plato, Chartres, Waterloo, Einstein's theory, and the art of Chaplin.

a _____

25. the grieving, melancholy clouds

p _____

f _____

## Key to Review Test

Check your test answers with the following key. Deduct 4% per error from a possible 100%.

1. hyperbole
2. alliteration
3. irony
4. simile
5. onomatopoeia
6. apostrophe
7. metonymy
8. metaphor
9. personification

10. oxymoron
11. alliteration
12. simile
13. metonymy
14. litotes
15. onomatopoeia
16. metaphor
17. oxymoron
18. hyperbole

19. personification
20. apostrophe
21. irony
22. antithesis
23. symbols
24. allusions
25. pathetic fallacy

Score: _____ %

# 17

# Name Derivatives

1. *aphrodisiac*
2. *boycott*
3. *chauvinism*
4. *cynic*
5. *Darwinism*
6. *Frankenstein monster*
7. *herculean*
8. *jabberwocky*
9. *laconic*

10. *Lilliputian*
11. *machiavellian*
12. *maudlin*
13. *maverick*
14. *mentor*
15. *nimrod*
16. *odyssey*
17. *Pyrrhic victory*
18. *quixotic*

19. *robot*
20. *solon*
21. *spoonerism*
22. *stentorian*
23. *tantalize*
24. *utopian*
25. *vandal*

*The names of people and places are imbedded in our language. The commonest forms are simple adjectives like "Shakespearean" or "Siamese." But when someone like Louis Pasteur or John L. McAdam discovers or develops something of wide use, we get words like "pasteurize" or "macadamize." From literature and mythology come a horde of words such as "cereal" (from "Ceres," goddess of the grain), "jovial" (from "Jove"), and "yahoo" (from Jonathan Swift's* Gulliver's Travels, *1726).*

*The name words in Chapter 17 are a cultural heritage and are sure to turn up in your reading. Learning their source will make it easier to remember their meaning. Four supplementary exercises (optional) on name words will be found at the end of this chapter.*

## EXERCISES

COVER THIS STRIP

1. **aphrodisiac** (af′rə-diz′i-ak): arousing sexual desire. An *aphrodisiac* is any drug, food, or agent which excites lust; it is named after *Aphrodite,* the goddess of love.

2. **boycott:** to refuse to deal or associate with, in order to coerce or punish. Captain Charles *Boycott* was shunned by the Irish Land League in 1880 for refusing to reduce land rents.

■ An *aphrodisiac* increases one's (a) beauty, (b) sexual desire. ( )

(b)

■ Any music, perfume, or food which increases sexual desire is an

aphrodisiac

*aph* _____ .

■ When Aldous Huxley refers to a certain juice as "tart and *aphrodisiac,*" he means the drink will arouse (a) hostility, (b) lustfulness. ( )

(b)

shun

■ To *boycott* is to _____ [trade with / shun].

■ Those who *boycott* a restaurant (a) avoid the place, (b) hold luncheon meetings there. ( )

(a)

■ Grandfather claims that most so-called adult movies merely act as

aphrodisiac

an *aph* _____ . He says we should stay away from such motion

boycott

pictures—that is, we should *bo* _____ them.

3. **chauvinism** (shō′vin-iz′əm): fanatical or blind patriotism. Nicolas *Chauvin* became ridiculous with bragging about his superloyalty to Napoleon and France.

4. **cynic** (sin′ik): one who has a sneering disbelief in human sincerity and goodness. The *Cynics* were ancient Greek philosophers who maintained that virtue was the goal of life and who, as a result, became very critical of other people and their motives.

■ The Nazi conviction that Hitler and Germany could do no wrong

chauvinism

was *ch* _____ .

(a)

■ The patriotism of a *chauvinist* is (a) extreme, (b) moderate. ( )

| | |
|---|---|
| chauvinism | ■ The intense national spirit known as *ch*_____ is manifested in most countries by (a) impartial criticism of national policy, (b) much flag-waving. (    ) |
| (b) | |
| (a) | ■ A *cynical* person is (a) suspicious and sarcastic, (b) agreeable and innocent. (    ) |
| (b) | ■ The *Cynic* Diogenes, who kept looking for an honest man, obviously thought that most people are (a) virtuous, (b) lacking in virtue. (    ) |
| cynic | ■ One who sneers at our motives is a *cy*_____, and such a person would have a low opinion of fanatical patriotism, known as |
| chauvinism | national *ch*_____, or, possibly, of the delusion that males are |
| chauvinism | the superior sex, known as male *c*_____. |

5. **Darwinism:** the theory of evolution that plants and animals transmit slight hereditary variations to future generations and that those forms survive and develop that are best suited to their environment. *Darwinism* involves, in brief, the concepts of natural selection and of the survival of the fittest.

| | |
|---|---|
| Darwinism | ■ According to the theory of evolution, known as *Dar*_____, species of plants and animals (a) have been changing and developing from earlier species, (b) have always been as they are now. (    ) |
| (a) | |
| (b) | ■ Nature permits a species to survive, according to *Darwinism,* if that species (a) has moral goodness, (b) adapts itself to its environment. (    ) |
| Darwinism | ■ Those species that have the most efficient claws, fins, or teeth, according to _____ *ism,* are the most likely (a) to be wiped |
| (b) | out, (b) to survive and perpetuate themselves. (    ) |

### Quiz

Write the letter that indicates the best definition.

| | |
|---|---|
| 1. (d) | (    ) 1. aphrodisiac |
| 2. (c) | (    ) 2. boycott |
| 3. (a) | (    ) 3. chauvinism |
| 4. (b) | (    ) 4. cynic |
| 5. (e) | (    ) 5. Darwinism |

a. fanatical patriotism
b. a suspicious, sarcastic pessimist
c. refuse to deal with
d. tending to excite lust
e. evolution of species through the survival of the fittest

**6. Frankenstein monster** (frank'ən-stīn'): anything that becomes a danger to its creator. In Mary Shelley's novel *Frankenstein* (1818) a natural philosopher named *Frankenstein* creates a repulsive monster which gets out of control and murders him.

(a)

■ The *Frankenstein monster* becomes (a) a threat to its inventor, (b) a faithful, useful servant. (   )

Frankenstein

(b)

■ The monster gets out of control and kills *Fr*_____. One must remember that *Frankenstein* is the name of (a) the treacherous monster, (b) the scientist who created the monster. (   )

Frankenstein
(a)

■ A *Fr*_____ monster among us today, threatening its creators, is (a) the thermonuclear bomb, (b) the bicycle. (   )

---

**7. herculean** (hur'kyoo lē'ən): very powerful and courageous. *Hercules,* son of Zeus, performed twelve tremendous labors which Hera imposed on him.

(a)

■ A *herculean* task demands (a) power and courage, (b) wit and grace. (   )

herculean

herculean
(a)

■ The job of digging the Panama Canal was *her*_____;

another tremendous, *h*_____ job was construction of (a) Hoover Dam, (b) Fido's new doghouse. (   )

(b)

■ Like all *herculean* heroes, steel-drivin' John Henry was courageous and (a) highly educated, (b) powerful. (   )

---

**8. jabberwocky:** nonsensical talk. "Jabberwocky" is an amusing nonsense poem in Lewis Carroll's *Through the Looking Glass* (1872).

jabberwocky
(b)

■ Nonsense talk is called *jab*_____. To understand *jabberwocky* is (a) easy, (b) almost impossible. (   )

■ Which of the following lines is *jabberwocky?* (a) "He did not wear his scarlet coat," (b) "'Twas brillig, and the slithy toves. . . ."

(b)

(   )

jabberwocky
(a)

■ To accuse a congressman of *jab*_____ is to imply that his talk is (a) meaningless, (b) unpatriotic. (   )

---

**9. laconic** (lə-kon'ik): brief; pithy. The *Laconians* were thrifty with words; they replied to an enemy ultimatum with one word: "If."

**10. Lilliputian** (lil'ə-pū'shən): very small; a tiny person. On the island of *Lilliput,* described in Swift's *Gulliver's Travels,* the men and women are six inches tall.

laconic

■ Most classified ads are _____ [laconic / wordy].

brief

■ A *laconic* answer is _____ [redundant / brief].

Lilliputian
(a)

■ To say that a presidential candidate is "*Lil*_____ in talents" is (a) insulting to him, (b) flattering to him. (   )

tiny

■ A *Lilliputian* house is _____ [huge / tiny].

laconic

■ Political candidates tend to be wordy rather than *la*_____ .

Lilliputians

■ Gulliver meets the Brobdingnagians, a race of highly intelligent giants who are quite the opposite of the tiny *Li*_____*s.*

## Quiz

Write the letter that indicates the best definition.

1. (d)
2. (e)
3. (b)
4. (a)
5. (c)

(   ) 1. Frankenstein monster    a. brief; concise
(   ) 2. herculean    b. gibberish; doubletalk
(   ) 3. jabberwocky    c. tiny
(   ) 4. laconic    d. a threat to its own inventor
(   ) 5. Lilliputian    e. powerful; requiring great strength and bravery

**11. machiavellian** (mak'i-ə-vel'i-ən): crafty and deceitful in political strategy. In *The Prince* (1513), Niccolo *Machiavelli,* a Florentine diplomat, describes ways to grasp and maintain political power.

**12. maudlin** (môd'lin): tearfully emotional or sentimental; foolishly drunk. Mary *Magdalen* was depicted by medieval painters with her eyes red and swollen from weeping.

maudlin

■ Sentimental people often revel in their tearful memories and become *mau*_____ .

| | |
|---|---|
| unstable | ■ One who is *maudlin* is emotionally _____ [stable / unstable] |
| weep over | and perhaps inclined to _____ [dissect / weep over] a dead bird. |
| | ■ Bribes, double dealing, and false promises are common to |
| machiavellian | *mac* _____ diplomacy. |
| unscrupulous | ■ The *machiavellian* politician is hard-boiled and _____ [honorable / unscrupulous] with no time for tearful loyalties and |
| maudlin | *m* _____ sentiment. |
| maudlin | ■ The woman who weeps softly into her beer is *ma* _____. |
| machiavellian | ■ The diplomat who thinks "Anything goes" is *ma* _____. |

13. **maverick** (mav'ər-ik): a person of unorthodox ideas who tends to act independently of parties and factions. Samuel *Maverick* (circa 1850), a Texas rancher, would not brand his calves, and they were called *mavericks.*

| | |
|---|---|
| | ■ An independent-minded congressman who can't be counted on to |
| maverick | vote with his party is sometimes called a *mav* _____. |
| (b) | ■ A *maverick* is (a) a conformist, (b) a nonconformist. (    ) |
| | ■ Henry David Thoreau, who defied his government by refusing to |
| maverick | pay his poll tax, was a *m* _____. |
| | ■ Ralph Waldo Emerson believed in self-reliance and genuine indi- |
| defend | viduralism, and so his essays tend to _____ [defend / attack] |
| maverick | a man's right to be a *m* _____. |

14. **mentor** (men'tər): a wise and loyal adviser; a trusted teacher. In Greek legend, *Mentor* gives wise counsel to Odysseus and his son Telemachus.

| | |
|---|---|
| mentor | ■ A head football coach is sometimes referred to as a _____ [monitor / mentor]. |
| counselor | ■ A *mentor* is a trusted _____ [wife / counselor]. |

mentor

(a)

■ You might refer to your English professor as your *m*_____ .
After all, *Mentor* was Telemachus' (a) wise teacher, (b) mortal enemy. (     )

---

**15. nimrod:** a hunter. *Nimrod,* the grandson of Ham, is described as a mighty hunter in Genesis 10:8.

(a)

■ A store for *nimrods* sells (a) shotguns, (b) women's purses. (     )

Nimrod

hunter

nimrods

■ The Bible mentions *Nim*_____ , who was a mighty

_____ [wrestler / hunter].

■ Our western elk have been decimated by _____
[nimrods / hotrods].

---

### Quiz

Write the letter that indicates the best definition.

1. (b)
2. (a)
3. (e)
4. (c)
5. (d)

(     ) 1. machiavellian    a. weakly or tearfully emotional
(     ) 2. maudlin    b. politically crafty; unscrupulous
(     ) 3. maverick    c. a counselor
(     ) 4. mentor    d. a hunter
(     ) 5. nimrod    e. a nonconformist

---

**16. odyssey** (od′ə-si): a long eventful journey. Homer's *Odyssey* describes ten adventurous years of wandering by *Odysseus* on his homeward voyage after the fall of Troy.

odyssey

■ In Steinbeck's *The Grapes of Wrath* (1939) the Joads make an adventurous *od*_____ from Oklahoma to California.

odyssey
(b)

■ A long journey, such as was made by Lewis and Clark, is called an

*o*_____ if it is (a) quick and direct, (b) wandering and with unexpected delays. (     )

odyssey

(a)

■ Colorful wanderings such as those of Odysseus are known as

an _____—and one would probably use the word *odyssey* to describe one's (a) two-year trip across Asia by donkey, (b) overnight flight to Chicago. (     )

---

**17. Pyrrhic victory** (pir´ik): a too costly victory. *Pyrrhos* defeated the Romans at Asculum, 279 B.C., but lost so many men that he exclaimed, "One more such victory and we are undone!"

■ A *Pyr*_____ *victory* is (a) an overwhelming success, (b) extremely expensive. (     )

■ A baseball team which wins a practice game but loses its short stop and its star pitcher in a bone-breaking collision has won a *P*_____ *victory.*

■ A nation which drains its resources to win a small military objective has won a *Pyrrhic v*_____, that is, a rather _____ [wonderful / hollow] triumph.

---

**18. quixotic** (kwik-sot´ik): idealistic but ridiculously impractical. Don *Quixote,* the hero of a novel by Cervantes (1615), is a romantic visionary, a tilter at windmills, but one of God's fools.

■ Idealists like Don Quixote are *qu*_____; they tend to be (a) level-headed and conventional, (b) impulsive and romantic. (     )

■ Critics condemned Woodrow Wilson's plan for a League of Nations as *qu*_____, that is, (a) visionary, (b) cynical. (     )

■ The American Transcendentalists were full of visionary and *q*_____ schemes, such as the Brook Farm experiment, a truly _____ [practical / impractical] undertaking.

---

**19. robot** (rō´bət): a human-like machine or a machine-like human. *R.U.R., Rossum's Universal Robots* (1923), a satiric play by Karel Kapek, introduced the word *robot* into our language.

**20. solon** (sō´lən): a wise lawmaker. *Solon* is referred to in Plato's "The Symposium" as "the revered father of Athenian Laws."

■ Legislators are often called *so*_____.

■ Automatons are *ro*_____.

■ Normally one might expect to see *solons* in _____ [factories / Congress] and *robots* in _____ [factories / Congress].

---

**Left margin answers:**

Pyrrhic
(b)

Pyrrhic

victory

hollow

quixotic
(b)

quixotic, (a)

quixotic

impractical

solons

robots

Congress

factories

■ A person who must perform the same simple mechanical operation day after day becomes a kind of *r*_____ .

■ *Robots* have (a) passions and free will, (b) only automatic reactions. (     )

■ Our laws are formulated by *s*_____ .

■ The word *solon* has traditionally suggested a _____ [wise / featherheaded] lawmaker.

## Quiz

Write the letter that indicates the best definition.

| (     ) 1. odyssey | a. a wise lawmaker |
| (     ) 2. Pyrrhic victory | b. a costly triumph |
| (     ) 3. quixotic | c. visionary; impractical |
| (     ) 4. robot | d. a wandering journey |
| (     ) 5. solon | e. an automaton |

**21. spoonerism:** an accidental transposition of sounds in adjacent words. The Rev. W. A. *Spooner* of New College, Oxford, used to make comic blunders like "our queer old dean" for "our dear old queen."

■ *Spoonerisms* like "nosey little cook" for "cozy little nook" involve (a) transposed sounds, (b) gross exaggerations. (     )

■ "It is kistumary to cuss the bride" is a *sp*_____ .

■ Another _____ *ism* is "half-warmed fish" for (a) "half-formed wish," (b) "half-hearted kiss." (     )

■ The phrase "tons of soil" is a *spoonerism* for "sons of toil," and "well boiled icicle" is a *sp*_____ for "well _____ _____."

**22. stentorian:** extremely loud. *Stentor* is described by Homer in *The Iliad* as a Greek herald with the voice of fifty men.

■ Challenging the Trojans in the distance required a *st*_____ voice.

(b)

stentorian
(a)

was not

■ A *stentorian* voice is like (a) a whisper, (b) a bellow. (    )

■ Of course, *st*_____ tones are quite acceptable in (a) a football stadium, (b) a college library. (    )

■ The Greek herald named Stentor _____ [was / was not] silent as the Sphinx.

___

**23. tantalize:** to tease and torment by withholding what is offered. *Tantalus* was tormented in Hades by water and fruit that he could never quite reach.

smell

■ A hungry cat is *tantalized* when it is allowed to _____ [eat / smell] a roast chicken.

tantalize
(b)

■ We usually tease, or *tan*_____, by (a) giving gifts, (b) withholding satisfactions. (    )

tantalized
(b)

■ A famished beggar is _____*zed* as he walks (a) through a forest, (b) past a bakery. (    )

___

**24. utopian** (ū-tō′pi-ən): impossibly ideal, especially in social organization. Sir Thomas More's *Utopia* (1516) describes a flawless government and society—imaginary, of course.

(b)

■ Dreamers envision a *utopian* social order in which everything will be (a) lousy, (b) practically perfect. (    )

utopian

■ A nation without wars, without crime, without poverty? That would be *ut*_____.

utopian
(a)

■ Edward Bellamy's *Looking Backward* (1887) describes a *u*_____ society of the year 2000, wherein conditions would presumably be vastly (a) improved, (b) worse. (    )

(b)

■ Ivor Brown speaks of H. G. Wells' "charting of Utopias," meaning that Wells explored (a) African jungles, (b) plans for ideal societies. (    )

___

**25. vandal:** a person who willfully or ignorantly mars or destroys property, especially what is beautiful or valuable. The *Vandals* were a Germanic people who ravaged Gaul and Spain and sacked Rome in A.D. 455.

vandals
(b)

vandal

vandal
(b)

vandal

■ Window smashers and tire slashers are *van*_____;
in short, they are public (a) benefactors, (b) menaces. (    )

■ Whoever painted those vulgar words all over our elementary
school is a *va*_____, and a poor speller, too.

■ A beauty-defacing rascal, or *v*_____, might be found
(a) drawing a famous ruin, (b) ruining a famous drawing. (    )

■ Were Venus de Milo's arms broken off by a *v*_____, or
did she chew her fingernails too much?

_____

## Quiz

Write the letter that indicates the best definition.

<table>
<tr><td>1. (e)</td><td>(    ) 1. spoonerism</td><td>a. to tease and torment</td></tr>
<tr><td>2. (d)</td><td>(    ) 2. stentorian</td><td>b. a destroyer of property</td></tr>
<tr><td>3. (a)</td><td>(    ) 3. tantalize</td><td>c. ideal; existing only in theory</td></tr>
<tr><td>4. (c)</td><td>(    ) 4. utopian</td><td>d. loud as a trumpet</td></tr>
<tr><td>5. (b)</td><td>(    ) 5. vandal</td><td>e. turned-around syllables</td></tr>
</table>

# REVIEW TEST

Write the word studied in this chapter that will complete the sentence.

1. A voice of Homeric loudness is *st* _____ .
2. A hunter is sometimes called a *ni* _____ .
3. A slip of the tongue involving transposed syllables is a *sp* _____ .
4. A general refusal to deal with somebody is a *bo* _____ .
5. Winning a contest at tremendous cost is a *Py* _____ *v* _____ .
6. To be tearfully, drunkenly sentimental is to be *ma* _____ .
7. A drug or other agent which excites lust is an *ap* _____ .
8. An automaton or mechanical person is a *ro* _____ .
9. One who maliciously defaces public property is a *va* _____ .
10. A wise lawmaker is a *so* _____ .
11. A device that becomes a threat to its own creator is a *Fr* _____ *m* _____ .
12. Patriotism carried to a fanatical extreme is *ch* _____ .
13. A long wandering journey is an *od* _____ .
14. A nonconformist acting independently of party is a *ma* _____ .
15. The concepts of natural selection and of the survival of the fittest are basic to *Da* _____ .

---

Write *True* or *False*.

_____ 16. A *Lilliputian* would probably be an effective basketball center.

_____ 17. A *herculean* task requires great strength and endurance.

_____ 18. *Jabberwocky* is clear, standard English.

_____ 19. A *mentor* is a wise counselor or teacher.

_____ 20. A *cynic* tends to distrust people's motives.

---

Write the letter that indicates the best completion.

( ) 21. A *utopian* plan is (a) economical, (b) practical, (c) democratic, (d) visionary.

( ) 22. A *machiavellian* leader is (a) unscrupulous, (b) honorable, (c) self-sacrificing, (d) naive.

( ) 23. A *laconic* comment is (a) flattering, (b) windy, (c) short, (d) amusing.

(    ) 24. A *quixotic* undertaking is (a) expensive, (b) impractical, (c) popular, (d) dull.

(    ) 25. To *tantalize* is (a) to inoculate, (b) to tickle, (c) to tease, (d) to eat.

## Key to Review Test

Check your test answers with the following key. Deduct 4% per error from a possible 100%.

| | | |
|---|---|---|
| 1. stentorian | 10. solon | 19. True |
| 2. nimrod | 11. Frankenstein monster | 20. True |
| 3. spoonerism | 12. chauvinism | 21. (d) |
| 4. boycott | 13. odyssey | 22. (a) |
| 5. Pyrrhic victory | 14. maverick | 23. (c) |
| 6. maudlin | 15. Darwinism | 24. (b) |
| 7. aphrodisiac | 16. False | 25. (c) |
| 8. robot | 17. True | |
| 9. vandal | 18. False | |

Score: _____ %

## SUPPLEMENTARY EXERCISES

### Exercise 1

1. **argosy** (är′gə-sē): a merchant ship or fleet of ships (from *Ragusa,* a Dalmatian port).

2. **behemoth** (bi-hē′məth): a huge animal (alluded to in *Job* 40:15–24).

3. **Boswell:** a friend and biographer (from James *Boswell,* who wrote *The Life of Samuel Johnson,* 1791).

4. **derrick:** crane; hoist (from Derrick, a seventeenth-century London hangman).

5. **draconian** (drā-kō′nē-ən): harsh, cruel (from Draco, a Greek lawmaker).

6. **galvanize:** to startle; to excite; to electrify (from L. Galvani, an Italian physicist).

7. **hector:** to browbeat; to bully; to pester (from Hector, the Trojan hero of Homer's *Iliad*).

8. **jezebel** (jez′ə-bel′): a shameless, wicked woman (from the wife of King Ahab, in *II Kings* 9:7, 30).

---

### Quiz

Write the letter that indicates the best definition.

| | | |
|---|---|---|
| 1. (e) | ( ) 1. argosy | a. to bully; to annoy |
| 2. (c) | ( ) 2. Boswell | b. to electrify; to startle |
| 3. (h) | ( ) 3. behemoth | c. a biographer |
| 4. (d) | ( ) 4. derrick | d. a crane |
| 5. (g) | ( ) 5. draconian | e. a fleet of merchant ships |
| 6. (b) | ( ) 6. galvanize | f. a shameless woman |
| 7. (a) | ( ) 7. hector | g. cruel; inhumanly severe |
| 8. (f) | ( ) 8. jezebel | h. a hippopotamus-like animal |

---

### Exercise 2

1. **martinet** (mär′tə-net′): a very strict disciplinarian (from General Jean Martinet, a seventeenth-century French drillmaster).

2. **masochism** (mas′ə-kiz′əm): the obtaining of pleasure, particularly sexual pleasure, from being hurt (from Leopold von Sacher-Masoch, an Austrian author).

3. **mecca:** a place attracting many people; a goal (from Mecca, a holy city of the Moslems).

4. **mesmerize:** to hypnotize (from Franz Mesmer, a German physician).

5. **panjandrum** (pan-jan′drəm): an exalted official (from a character invented by Samuel Foote, English dramatist).

6. **pharisaical** (far′i-sā′i-kəl): self-righteous; hypocritical (from the Pharisees in the New Testament).

7. **pickwickian:** benevolent, naive, and blundering (from Mr. Samuel Pickwick in Dickens' *Pickwick Papers,* 1836).

8. **Portia** (pôr′shə): a female lawyer (from the heroine of Shakespeare's *The Merchant of Venice,* 1596).

---

## Quiz

Write the letter that indicates the best definition.

| | | | |
|---|---|---|---|
| 1. (f) | ( ) 1. martinet | a. the goal of many travelers |
| 2. (d) | ( ) 2. masochism | b. an official of lofty importance |
| 3. (a) | ( ) 3. mecca | c. lady lawyer |
| 4. (e) | ( ) 4. mesmerize | d. the enjoyment of being hurt |
| 5. (b) | ( ) 5. panjandrum | e. to hypnotize |
| 6. (h) | ( ) 6. pharisaical | f. a rigid disciplinarian |
| 7. (g) | ( ) 7. pickwickian | g. good-hearted, naive, muddled |
| 8. (c) | ( ) 8. Portia | h. self-righteous, censorious |

---

## Exercise 3

1. **protean** (prō′ti-ən): changeable; readily taking on different shapes (from Proteus in Greek mythology).

2. **rodomontade** (rod′ə-mon-tād′): bragging; blustering (from Rodomonte, a boastful king in Ariosto's *Orlando Furioso,* 1516).

3. **sadism** (sad′iz-əm): the obtaining of pleasure, particularly sexual pleasure, from hurting others (from the author Count de Sade, who describes brutal sexual aberrations).

4. **sardonic** (sär-don′ik): scornful; sneering; cynical (from a poisonous Sardinian plant causing laughter-like convulsions).

5. **serendipity** (ser′ən-dip′i-tē): a knack for making lucky discoveries by accident (from the story, "The Three Princes of Serendip," whose heroes made lucky finds).

6. **Shylock:** a relentless creditor (from the usurer in Shakespeare's *The Merchant of Venice,* 1597, who wants his pound of flesh).

7. **titian** (tish′ən): auburn; reddish yellow (from the artist Titian, who often painted women's hair this shade).

8. **yahoo** (yä′hoō): a crude or vicious person (from the brutish Yahoos in *Gulliver's Travels*).

## Quiz

Write the letter that indicates the best definition.

| | | |
|---|---|---|
| 1. (f) | (  ) 1. protean | a. the enjoyment of inflicting pain |
| 2. (h) | (  ) 2. rodomontade | b. a hard-fisted creditor |
| 3. (a) | (  ) 3. sadism | c. reddish yellow |
| 4. (g) | (  ) 4. sardonic | d. a bestial person |
| 5. (e) | (  ) 5. serendipity | e. a knack for lucky finds |
| 6. (b) | (  ) 6. Shylock | f. changeable in form |
| 7. (c) | (  ) 7. titian | g. cynical; scornful |
| 8. (d) | (  ) 8. yahoo | h. boasting; blustering |

## Exercise 4

1. **Adonis** (ə-don′is): an extremely handsome young man (from Adonis, who was loved by Aphrodite but was killed by a wild boar).

2. **Amazon:** any tall, strong, or athletic woman (from the Amazon women who helped the Trojans fight the Greeks).

3. **Babbitt:** a smug, conventional, uncultured businessman (from George Babbitt, a character in a Sinclair Lewis novel).

4. **bacchanalia** (bak′ə-nā′li-ə): drunken parties; orgies (from Bacchus, god of wine).

5. **bedlam** (bed′ləm): a scene of noisy confusion (from Bethlehem, a lunatic asylum in London).

6. **gargantuan** (gär-gan′choō-ən): huge; gigantic (from Gargantua, the enormous prince in Rabelais' *Gargantua and Pantagruel*).

7. **micawberish:** ever optimistic and cheerful (from the Dickens character Micawber, who keeps saying, "Something will turn up").

8. **Spartan:** brave, hardy, stoical (from the Spartan soldiers who practiced austerity and self-discipline).

**Quiz**

Write the letter that indicates the best definition.

| | | | |
|---|---|---|---|
| 1. (c) | ( ) 1. Adonis | a. mad, noisy disorder |
| 2. (f) | ( ) 2. Amazon | b. hardy; lacking luxury |
| 3. (g) | ( ) 3. Babbitt | c. a handsome male |
| 4. (d) | ( ) 4. bacchanalia | d. drunken orgies |
| 5. (a) | ( ) 5. bedlam | e. enormous; very large |
| 6. (e) | ( ) 6. gargantuan | f. a female warrior |
| 7. (h) | ( ) 7. micawberish | g. a middle-class conformist |
| 8. (b) | ( ) 8. Spartan | h. optimistic |

# 18

# Psychology

*A cynic has said that psychology "tells us what everybody knows, in language that nobody understands." His comment is more witty than accurate. Actually, psychology, which is the study of human behavior, tells us many things we don't know about ourselves and in language we can learn to understand quite well. In fact, the terms of psychology must be understood if we are to qualify in such diverse areas as social work, law, and medicine; or if we are to analyze the fiction of Faulkner, the poetry of Jeffers, the dramas of O'Neill.*

*Chapter 18 stresses twenty-five basic terms of psychology, and presents fifty more definitions in a supplementary list. As you fill in the frames, try to relate the terms to people you have known or read about. Can you think of anyone with a* neurosis, *a* psychosomatic *illness, or a trace of* narcissism? *Have you yourself had a* traumatic *experience? Are you a* sibling *(or would you knock a person down for calling you that)? Words become more meaningful when you see how they apply to the life around you.*

## EXERCISES

COVER THIS STRIP

**1. ambivalence** (am-biv′ə-ləns): conflicting feelings, such as love and hate, toward the same person or thing. You may have a deep affection for your parents and yet be angry because they interfere with your decisions; your attitude toward them, then, is one of *ambivalence.*

■ A child wants to pet a strange "doggie" but is fearful. The conflict

ambivalence

of feelings is called *amb_____* .

■ Felix wants to order the giant hot fudge sundae but he doesn't want

ambivalence

to get fat. His attitude toward the sundae is one of *am_____* .

■ A star basketball player has *ambivalent* feelings toward his coach. This means that the athlete (a) can shoot with either hand, (b) has

(b)

contradictory emotions. (    )

■ Wilmer wants to ask Alice for a date but worries that she will turn him down; Alice loves Jerry but has fits of jealousy when he talks to other girls; Jerry craves alcohol but realizes that it can ruin him.

ambivalence

These conflicting attitudes illustrate *am_____* .

possible

■ It is _____ [possible / impossible] for a person to be both attracted and repelled by something. The condition is

ambivalence

called *a_____* .

**2. aptitude** (ap′tə-tōōd′): the natural ability to acquire a skill or type of knowledge. A test of musical *aptitude,* for example, does not measure achievement but predicts future performance.

■ A high score in a mechanical-*aptitude* test means (a) that you have unusual ability as a mechanic, (b) that you could be trained to be a

(b)

good mechanic. (    )

■ An achievement test measures what you can do now; an

aptitude

*apt_____* test predicts what you will be able to do with training.

■ Glenna is extremely athletic, and although she has never played

aptitude

tennis she probably has an *ap_____* for it.

**258    Psychology**

■ Harvey is an excellent speller and scores high in a finger-dexterity test; apparently he _____ [does / doesn't] have an *a*_____ for typewriting.

does
aptitude

---

**3. claustrophobia** (klô′strə-fō′bē-ə): morbid fear of being in enclosed or narrow places.

■ Linus feels stifled and fearful in an elevator or a closet. He has *cl*_____ .

claustrophobia

■ *Claustrophobia* manifests itself in an abnormal fear of (a) small rooms, (b) heights. (     )

(a)

■ A phobia involves excessive fear in the absence of real danger. The excessive fear and anxiety of a clerk who must work in a small, windowless office may be due to *cl*_____ .

claustrophobia

■ A person with *claustrophobia* would probably feel comfortable (a) in a meadow, (b) in a trunk. (     )

(a)

---

**4. compensation:** an attempt to make up for an undesirable trait by exaggerating a socially approved one.

■ A student who is weak in academic courses may try to excel in athletics—an example of *com*_____ .

compensation

■ *Compensation* is an effort to excel in one activity in order to make up for a feeling of _____ [inferiority / accomplishment] in another.

inferiority

■ Napoleon, Hitler, and Stalin were of short stature, and their drive for political power was probably a form of *co*_____ .

compensation

■ Igor was embarrassingly poor in athletics, so he tried doubly hard to become a _____ [success / failure] as a debater, an effort known as *c*_____ .

success
compensation

---

**5. dipsomania:** an abnormal craving for alcoholic liquors.
**6. kleptomania:** an abnormal tendency to steal.

| | |
|---|---|
| kleptomania | ■ An irresistible impulse to steal is *klep*_____; an insatible desire for alcohol is *di*_____. |
| dipsomania | |
| | ■ Emotional disturbances have been cited as a cause of *dipsomania,* |
| drink | or the tendency to _____ [steal / drink], and *kleptomania,* |
| steal | or the tendency to _____ [steal / drink]. |
| | ■ Alcoholics Anonymous is an excellent organization for those |
| dipsomania | whose problem is *di*_____. |
| | ■ "Stealing lingerie?" said the judge. "Looks like a case of |
| kleptomania | *kl*_____. Ten days should be enough. After all, this is your first slip." |
| | ■ *Kleptomania* is associated with (a) overeating, (b) shoplifting. |
| (b) | ( ) |
| | ■ *Dipsomania* is associated with (a) boozing, (b) pocket picking. |
| (a) | ( ) |

---

### Quiz

Write the letter that indicates the best definition.

|   |   |
|---|---|
| 1. (e) | ( ) 1. ambivalence    a. fear of small enclosures |
| 2. (c) | ( ) 2. aptitude    b. alcoholism |
| 3. (a) | ( ) 3. claustrophobia    c. capacity to learn |
| 4. (f) | ( ) 4. compensation    d. irresistible stealing |
| 5. (b) | ( ) 5. dipsomania    e. conflicting feelings |
| 6. (d) | ( ) 6. kleptomania    f. making up for a shortcoming |

---

7. **ego** (ē′gō): the conscious part of the personality, which has to deal with the id, the superego, and external reality, according to Freud. The *ego* does our logical thinking.

8. **id:** the primitive, instinctive, aggressive part of our personality. The pleasure-loving *id,* with which we are born, seeks immediate gratification regardless of consequences, but it is later held in check by the superego and ego, says Freud.

9. **superego:** the moralistic part of the personality which acts as a conscience to control the ego and the id. The *superego* is a product of parental and social training, and it sets up standards of right and wrong.

■ A baby is like a little animal; it is swayed by the raw, instinctive part of its personality, the *i*_____.

id

■ From its environment the child absorbs a sense of what is right and wrong. This developing conscience has been called the *su*_____.

superego

■ The self-aware, thinking part of the mind is called the *e*_____.

ego

■ The unconscious parts of the mind include the primitive drives, or *i*_____, and the conscience, or *su*_____. The conscious part of the mind, which does our thinking, is the *e*_____.

id, superego

ego

■ The uncontrolled impulses of the *id* are likely to be _____ [encouraged / condemned] by society. Such uncontrolled impulses would probably produce (a) rapists, burglars, gluttons, (b) priests, teachers, saints. (    )

condemned

(a)

■ Traditional values and ideals of society are represented by the *su*_____. The *superego* strives for (a) pleasure, (b) perfection. (    )

superego
(b)

■ The conscious, thinking part of you is called the *e*_____. The *ego* operates according to the _____ [reality / pleasure] principle.

ego

reality

■ Personalities can be distorted, says Freud, if either the animalistic *i*_____ or the moralistic *s*_____ is too strong. One's behavior should be controlled by the conscious aspect of the mind, the *e*_____.

id, superego

ego

■ The concept of an *id, ego,* and *superego* was first developed by (a) Sigmund Freud, (b) Charles Darwin. (    )

(a)

10. **extrasensory perception** (ESP): ability to gain knowledge without use of the known senses. *ESP* refers to telepathy, clairvoyance, or any other means of perceiving external events of communicating by mental rather than physical means.

(a)

■ *Extrasensory perception* would be operative if you could send a message by (a) brain waves, (b) Western Union. (    )

extrasensory perception

■ *ESP* is an acronym for *ex* _____ *per* _____ .

■ You dream that your best friend is calling for help, and the next day he falls down a well. Precognition, as illustrated here, is a type of

extrasensory perception

*ex* _____ *p* _____ .

■ Most psychologists do not as yet believe in *extrasensory perception*

ESP

(usually abbreviated _____ ).

■ The term *ESP* does *not* refer to (a) clairvoyance, (b) precognition, (c) telepathy, (d) short-wave radio. (    )

(d)

---

11. **free association:** the free, unhampered, rambling talk by a patient by which his repressions are discovered.

12. **psychoanalysis** (sī′kō-ə-nal′ə-sis): a system of mental therapy, devised by Freud, whereby through free association and dream analysis certain conflictual material is released from the unconscious.

■ Freud's technique of treating mental illness is known as

psychoanalysis

*psy* _____ .

free association

■ Rambling from one topic to another is called *fr* _____

*as* _____ . This activity is common during sessions of

psychoanalysis

*psy* _____ .

■ The purpose of *psychoanalysis* is to help the patient overcome problems that are basically (a) mental, (b) physical. (    )

(a)

■ A mental shock that occurred in infancy might be disclosed during

psychoanalysis
free association

a session of *ps* _____ by means of *fr* _____

*as* _____ .

■ Through *free association* one's unconscious wishes find (a) concealment, (b) verbal expression. (    )

(b)

■ Psychologists do not accept all of Freud's theories, but he is respected as the father of *p* _____ *sis*.

psychoanalysis

Write the letter that indicates the best definition.

1. (f)
2. (d)
3. (b)
4. (e)
5. (c)
6. (a)

(   ) 1. ego          a. Freud's system of treatment
(   ) 2. id           b. conscience, or moral control
(   ) 3. superego     c. rambling monologue
(   ) 4. ESP          d. seat of animalistic impulses
(   ) 5. free association   e. thought transference
(   ) 6. psychoanalysis    f. thinking part of the mind

---

**13. hallucination** (hə-lōo'sə-nā'shən): the apparent witnessing of sights and sounds that do not exist.

hallucination

■ "Yesterday upon a stair / I saw a man who wasn't there. . . ." The poet seems to have had a *hal* _____ .

(a)

■ The sights and sounds of a *hallucination* are (a) imaginary, (b) actual. (   )

hallucination

■ Macbeth imagines that he sees the murdered Banquo sitting in front of him; Macbeth is experiencing a *ha* _____ .

(b)

■ *Hallucinative* drugs make one's sense impressions more (a) dependable, (b) undependable. (   )

---

**14. hypochondria** (hī'pə-kon'drē-ə): excessive worry about one's health; anxiety about minor or imaginary ailments.

**15. psychosomatic** (sī'kō-sō-mat'ik): referring to a physical disorder caused by emotional stress.

hypochondria

■ Every morning Wilhelm gets up worried, looks at his tongue, and swallows thirty pills; his problem is *hyp* _____ .

(a)

■ A *hypochondriac* usually believes that his health is (a) failing, (b) perfect. (   )

psychosomatic

■ Gus's ulcers act up when he works under pressure; his illness is probably *psy* _____ .

psychosomatic
(a)

■ Disorders such as asthma, dermatitis, and high blood pressure are sometimes *ps* _____ , that is, caused by (a) emotional stress, (b) bacterial infection. (   )

| | |
|---|---|
| hypochondria | ■ Julius with his imaginary illnesses suffers from *hy*_____; he caught his last disease from the *Reader's Digest.* His wife Lydia, overfearful of germs, boils dishes three times before using them; she |
| hypochondria | also suffers from *h*_____. |
| psychosomatic | ■ Soldiers have sometimes developed a paralysis from fear of combat; such paralysis is _____ *ic.* |

---

16. **narcissism** (när′si-siz′əm): abnormal self-love; erotic pleasure obtained from admiration of one's own body or mind.
17. **Oedipus complex** (ed′ə-pəs): sexual attraction to the parent of the opposite sex and hostility for the parent of the same sex.

| | |
|---|---|
| narcissism | ■ *Narcissus* admired his own physical features; thus, Freud refers to such self-love as *nar*_____. |
| (b) | ■ *Narcissism* involves a lack of concern for other people and extreme concern for (a) narcotics, (b) one's self. (    ) |
| Oedipus complex | ■ *Oedipus* loved his mother and hated his father; thus, Freud refers to a similar stage in child development as the *Oed*_____ *com*_____. |
| Oedipus complex | ■ Little Jasper is competing with his father for the love of his mother; Jasper's feelings are referred to as the *O*_____ *c*_____. |
| narcissism | ■ The pretty people in TV commercials often say, "I love my hair— so soft and fragrant," "My skin is baby-smooth," "My breath is twenty-four hours sweet and fresh, thanks to Putro"; such conceited lines suggest *nar*_____. |
| (b) | ■ The *Oedipus complex* involves rivalry for the love of the parent of (a) the same sex, (b) the opposite sex. (    ) |
| narcissism | ■ A person who is obsessed with his or her own handsome appearance is exhibiting *na*_____. |

---

## Quiz

Write the letter that indicates the best definition.

1. (e)
2. (d)
3. (a)
4. (c)
5. (b)

(    ) 1. hallucination     a. of illness caused by emotions
(    ) 2. hypochondria     b. love-mother, hate-father phase
(    ) 3. psychosomatic     c. self-love
(    ) 4. narcissism     d. anxiety about one's health
(    ) 5. Oedipus complex     e. seeing what is nonexistent

---

**18. psychosis** (sī-kō′sis): a mental disorder such as paranoia or schizophrenia that involves very serious disorganization of the personality; insanity.

**19. paranoia** (par′ə-noi′ə): a mental disorder marked by delusions of persecution or of grandeur.

**20. schizophrenia** (skit′sə-frē′nē-ə): a mental disorder marked by splitting of the personality, a retreat from reality, and emotional deterioration.

(a)
(b)

■ *Psychotic* people are (a) irrational, (b) rational. (    ) They tend to (a) cope with reality, (b) withdraw from reality. (    )

paranoia

■ The delusion that people are plotting behind your back and are "out to get you" is a symptom of *par*_____.

(a)

■ Another common symptom of *paranoia* is the delusion of (a) grandeur, (b) inferiority. (    )

schizophrenia

■ Stanley sits silently for hours, possibly in a fixed position. Such withdrawal from reality is usually known as *sch*_____.

(a)

■ A *schizophrenic* tends to be (a) withdrawn and mute, (b) the life of the party. (    )

paranoia

■ Delusions of grandeur ("I am Napoleon," "I am Jesus Christ") are symptoms of *pa*_____.

(b)

■ A major mental disorder is (a) neurosis, (b) a psychosis. (    )

psychosis

■ Hardening of blood vessels in the brain of an elderly person may result in a serious mental disorder, or *ps*_____.

schizophrenia

■ The *psychotic* who is rigid and unresponsive probably suffers from *sc*_____; the *psychotic* who shouts "They conspire against me—I'll kill them—I'll rule the world!" probably suffers from

paranoia

*pa* _____ .

---

**21. rationalization** (rash'ən-ə-liz-ā'shən): justifying of unreasonable behavior by presenting false but plausible reasons to oneself or to others.

conceal

■ To *rationalize* one of our misdeeds is to _____ [reveal / conceal] the real motives behind it.

■ Whenever Buster, who is overweight, orders another double banana split, he says: "I have to keep up my strength." Buster's excuse

rationalization

is an example of *rat* _____ .

(b)

■ Big Country invades rich Little Country, saying, "We will restore better government." Big Country is probably indulging in (a) pure altruism, (b) rationalization. ( )

rationalization

■ Self-justification, known as *ra* _____ , is probably being used when a football coach explains a 79-6 loss this way: "We lost because (a) we were outplayed"; (b) them umpires was prejudiced."

(b)

( )

---

**22. regression:** going back to earlier, less mature behavior as an escape from a present conflict.

■ Six-year-old Wilmer sees his new baby sister get all the attention, so he begins to wet his pants again. He is trying to solve his conflict

regression

by *reg* _____ .

less

■ *Regression* involves a change to _____ [more / less] mature behavior.

■ A young housewife keeps running back to the security of her

regression

parental home. This, too, is probably *reg* _____ .

■ A man loses his wife or his job and gets drunk. His escape to the

child

irresponsible condition of a _____ [child / adult] is

regression

*r* _____ .

**23. sibling:** a brother or sister.

siblings

■ The Grunches have three sons and two daughters, a total of five *sib* _____ .

siblings

■ Suppose you have an older sister and a younger brother. This means that you have two *si* _____ .

are not

■ Your cousins _____ [are / are not] your *siblings*.

is not

■ Wally, an only child, _____ [is / is not] a *sibling*.

sibling

■ Competition and jealousy between two brothers, between two sisters, or between a brother and a sister are aspects of *s* _____ rivalry.

---

**24. trauma** (trou′mə): an emotional shock which has a lasting effect.

major

■ A trauma is a _____ [minor / major] emotional shock.

(a)

■ Nellie has nightmares ever since her car accident. Its effect has been (a) traumatic, (b) salutary. (    )

trauma

■ Incest or other forms of sexual molestation can cause serious *tr* _____ in children.

trauma
(b)

■ The effects of an emotional shock, or *t* _____ , are (a) temporary, (b) lasting. (    )

---

**25. voyeur** (vwä-yûr′): a Peeping Tom; one who obtains sexual gratification by looking at sexual objects or acts, especially secretively.

(a)

■ A *voyeur* peeks into windows hoping to see (a) sexual acts, (b) television programs. (    )

voyeur

(b)

■ A Peeping Tom, also known as a *vo* _____ , derives particular pleasure from (a) exhibiting his body, (b) peeking in secret at the nakedness of others. (    )

(b)

■ Two men are using telescopes. The *voyeur* is the fellow peering (a) at Jupiter, (b) into bedrooms. (    )

an immature

■ Children go through a stage of intense curiosity about sex. Consequently, *voyeurism* is considered to be _____ [a mature / an immature] way of achieving sexual fulfillment.

## Quiz

Write the letter that indicates the best definition.

1. (e)
2. (c)
3. (h)
4. (b)
5. (g)
6. (d)
7. (a)
8. (f)

( ) 1. psychosis — a. a lasting emotional shock
( ) 2. paranoia — b. justifying with false reasons
( ) 3. schizophrenia — c. delusions of grandeur and persecution
( ) 4. rationalization — d. a brother or sister
( ) 5. regression — e. serious mental disorder (general term)
( ) 6. sibling — f. a Peeping Tom
( ) 7. trauma — g. escape via less mature behavior
( ) 8. voyeur — h. splitting of personality

## REVIEW TEST

Write the word studied in this chapter that will complete the sentence.

1. Abnormal self-love is *na* _____ .
2. Morbid fear of small, enclosed places is *cl* _____ .
3. That part of the unconscious mind that acts as a conscience is the *su* _____ .
4. A brother or sister is a *si* _____ .
5. A splitting of the personality and withdrawal from reality is *sc* _____ .
6. Conflicting feelings, like love and hate, for the same person are known as *amb* _____ .
7. A son's desire for his mother and rivalry with his father is the *Oed* _____ *c* _____ .
8. Physical illness caused by emotional stress is *ps* _____ .
9. Reverting to less mature behavior as an escape is *reg* _____ .
10. Excessive desire for alcohol is *di* _____ .
11. Abnormal anxiety about one's imagined illnesses is *hy* _____ .
12. A compulsion to do shoplifting is *kl* _____ .
13. A lasting emotional shock is a *tr* _____ .
14. One who peeks into windows to see sex acts is a *vo* _____ .
15. Uncle Fritz claims he is General Grant and that the neighbors are plotting to poison him. Fritz has symptoms of *pa* _____ .

---

Write *True* or *False*.

_____ 16. The purpose of an *aptitude* test is to measure achievement.

_____ 17. The *ego* is the conscious part of the personality.

_____ 18. *Hallucinations* can be caused by drugs.

_____ 19. *Free association* is a technique used in psychoanalysis.

_____ 20. A *psychosis* is a fairly common, minor nervous ailment.

_____ 21. Unusually keen vision and hearing are referred to as *extra-sensory perception (ESP)*.

_____ 22. The *id,* which is powerful during one's infancy, passes out of existence when one reaches maturity.

_____ 23. A certain blind girl tried doubly hard to master the piano; her efforts are a form of *compensation.*

_____ 24. *Rationalization* means logical reasoning, the avoidance of fallacy.

_____ 25. *Psychoanalysis* is a method of treating mental illness.

## Key to Review Test

Check your test answers with the following key. Deduct 4% per error from a possible 100%.

| | | |
|---|---|---|
| 1. narcissism | 10. dipsomania | 19. True |
| 2. claustrophobia | 11. hypochondria | 20. False |
| 3. superego | 12. kleptomania | 21. False |
| 4. sibling | 13. trauma | 22. False |
| 5. schizophrenia | 14. voyeur | 23. True |
| 6. ambivalence | 15. paranoia | 24. False |
| 7. Oedipus complex | 16. False | 25. True |
| 8. psychosomatic | 17. True | |
| 9. regression | 18. True | |

Score: _____ %

1. **abnormal psychology:** the study of abnormal behavior, including neurosis, psychosis, and other mental disorders.
2. **acrophobia** (ak′rə-fō′bē-ə): a fear of high places.
3. **aggression:** behavior that aims to hurt someone or what he stands for.
4. **amnesia** (am-nē′zhə): partial or total loss of memory; specifically, forgetting one's own identity.
5. **atavism** (at′ə-viz′əm): reversion to an earlier ancestral characteristic.
6. **behaviorism:** the doctrine that man reacts automatically, like a machine, to stimuli.
7. **clairvoyance** (klâr-voi′əns): the alleged ability to see objects or to know things beyond the range of the senses.
8. **compulsion:** an irresistible impulse to perform an irrational act.
9. **conditioned reflex:** a response set off by a second stimulus associated with the primary stimulus; for example, secretion of saliva set off in Pavlov's dog by a dinner bell.
10. **defense mechanism** (mek′ə-niz′əm): an unconscious adjustment to block out unpleasant memories, feelings, or knowledge.
11. **dementia praecox** (di-men′shə prē′koks): former term for schizophrenia.
12. **dissociation** (di-sō′sē-ā′shən): a splitting apart of mental elements, involving loss of control over memory and motor processes.
13. **dualism:** the state of being twofold; the theory that a man consists of two entities—body and mind.
14. **Electra complex:** a daughter's unconscious sexual attachment to her father and hostility to her mother.
15. **empathy:** one's participating in the feelings and spirit of another person or thing.
16. **exhibitionism:** a tendency to behave so as to attract attention; self-exposure.
17. **extrovert** (eks′trō-vûrt): a person actively interested in his environment and other people rather than in himself.
18. **fixation:** an abnormal attachment to some person, object, or idea.
19. **Freudian** (froi′dē-ən): pertaining to Sigmund Freud's methods of psychoanalysis, which emphasize the techniques of free association and transference and try to give the patient an insight into his unconscious conflicts and motives.
20. **gustatory** (gus′tə-tôr′ē): relating to the sense of taste.
21. **hysteria** (hi-ster′ē-ə): emotional frenzy marked by sensory and motor disturbances.
22. **identification:** the putting of oneself in the place of someone else and unconsciously sharing his admirable qualities.
23. **infantilism** (in-fan′tə-liz′əm): extreme immaturity of mind and body in an adult.
24. **inhibition** (in′i-bish′ən): the blocking of one impulse by another.
25. **intelligence quotient** (I.Q.): the mental age multiplied by 100 and then divided by the actual age.
26. **introspection:** analysis of one's own mental and emotional states.
27. **intuition** (in′too-ish′ən): awareness of something without conscious reasoning.
28. **kinesthetic** (kin′is-thet′ik): pertaining to muscle sense or the sensation of position, movement, and tension in the body.
29. **libido** (li-bē′dō): the drive for sex gratification.
30. **masochism** (mas′ə-kiz′əm): the deriving of sexual pleasure from being hurt or humiliated.

31. **maturation** (mach′oo-rā′shən): completion of growth process in the body and the accompanying behavioral changes.
32. **megalomania** (meg′ə-lō-mā′nē-ə): delusions of wealth, power, and self-importance.
33. **melancholia** (mel′ən-kō′lē-ə): a mental disorder characterized by extreme gloominess and depression of spirits.
34. **neurasthenic** (nūr′əs-then′ik): afflicted with fatigue, worry, pains, etc., because of emotional conflicts.
35. **neurosis** (nū-rō′sis): an emotional disorder, less severe than a psychosis, characterized by anxieties, obsessions, compulsions, and physical complaints.
36. **obsession:** an idea or desire that haunts the mind.
37. **parapsychology** (par′ə): the study of clairvoyance, telepathy, and other apparently supernatural phenomena.
38. **phobia** (fō′bē-ə): any irrational or morbid fear.
39. **pleasure principle:** automatic adjustment of one's thoughts to secure pleasure and to avoid pain.
40. **projection:** ascribing one's own motives to someone else, thus relieving one's ego of guilt feelings.
41. **psychedelic** (sī′ki-del′ik): of a mental state, usually drug-induced, marked by entrancement and blissful aesthetic perceptiveness.
42. **psychodrama:** the acting out of situations related to one's problem, as a form of cathartic therapy.
43. **Rorschach test** (rôr′shäk): the analysis of personality by means of responses to ink-blot designs.
44. **sadism** (sad′iz-əm): the deriving of sexual pleasure from hurting one's partner.
45. **stimulus** (stim′yoo-ləs): anything that excites an organism, organ, or part into activity.
46. **subjective:** reflecting a person's feelings and thinking rather than objective reality.
47. **sublimation:** the channeling of psychic energy into socially acceptable activities.
48. **subliminal** (sub-lim′ə-nəl): below the level of consciousness but perceptible by the subconscious.
49. **synapse** (si-naps′): the point where a nerve impulse passes from one neuron to the next.
50. **xenophobia** (zen′ə-fō′bē-ə): fear or hatred of strangers and foreigners.

---

# 19
# Fiction

*People read fiction mainly for pleasure. As with music or painting or pizza-making, however, one derives increased pleasure the more he knows about his subject. A college student should be aware of the different types of novels: Gothic, Victorian, epistolary, picaresque, existentialist, and so on. He should recognize such attributes as suspense, local color, stream of consciousness, and motivation. A student can enjoy fiction without knowing a myth from a moth, but he can appreciate fiction better and discuss it more intelligently if he understands some technical terms associated with it.*

*Study the definitions carefully. Fill in the blanks without looking back to the top of the frame.*

## EXERCISES

COVER THIS STRIP

1. **novel:** a long fictitious prose story of some complexity, involving characters, scenes, and action. The first English *novel* is usually said to be Samuel Richardson's *Pamela,* published in 1740; the first American novel is William Hill Brown's *The Power of Sympathy* (1789).

2. **novelette:** a short novel, about fifty to a hundred pages long, also called a *novella.* Example: Ernest Hemingway's *The Old Man and the Sea* (1952).

fictitious

■ A *novel* is a long _____ [factual / fictitious]

does

story which _____ [does / does not] involve characters and action.

novelette

■ If sixty pages long, a story is usually called a *n*_____ .

novel

■ Samuel Richardson's *Pamela,* a lengthy fictitious story, was the first English *n*_____ .

novelette

■ Herman Melville's fictitious story *Benito Cereno* (1856) is about seventy pages long and can be referred to as a _____ .

longer

■ A *novelette* is _____ [shorter / longer] than a short story

shorter

and _____ [shorter / longer] than a novel.

3. **plot:** the central plan of action in a story or play; the author's arrangement of episodes. The story consists of certain events in chronological order, whereas the *plot* is the form into which the author organizes those events.

4. **coincidence** (kō-in'sə-dəns): the remarkable occurrence of certain events at the same time, apparently by chance. Example: Longfellow's Evangeline is separated from her lover Gabriel and, years later, as an old nurse, she finds him by chance just as he is dying in an alms-house.

(b)

■ By the *plot* of a novel we mean (a) its general subject, (b) its arrangement of action. (     )

coincidence

■ When Huck Finn, by sheerest chance, arrives at a distant farmhouse on the very day when Tom Sawyer is expected there, it is *co*_____ .

| | |
|---|---|
| less | ■ The overuse of *coincidences* in a story tends to make the *plot* _____ [more / less] believable. |
| (a) | ■ Aristotle says in his *Poetics* that the most important element of tragedy is *plot,* by which he means (a) the plan of action, (b) the moral tone. (    ) |
| plot | ■ O. Henry stresses the plan of action, or *p*_____, but unfortunately his *plot* usually hinges on some incredible chance meet- |
| coincidence | ing, or *c*_____ . |

5. **suspense:** uncertainty as to the outcome; anxiety caused by a tense situation. *Suspense* is an indispensable ingredient of the mystery thriller and the melodrama.
6. **flashback:** an interruption in a story or play to present action which occurred earlier. *Flashback* breaks up the orderly time sequence but often gains psychological value.

| | |
|---|---|
| (a) | ■ *Suspense* refers to (a) uncertainty, (b) pleasure. (    ) |
| flashback | ■ In the play *Death of a Salesman,* Willy Loman is shown remembering and reliving a hotel episode of an earlier period. This is a *fl*_____ . |
| past | ■ The *flashback,* often very effective in drama, jumps to the _____ [past / future]. |
| suspense | ■ During the fourth act of his five-act plays Shakespeare has the unhappy problem of keeping alive the uncertainty and tension known as *su*_____ . |
| (a) | ■ The maintaining of *suspense* is especially important in the (a) mystery story, (b) essay. (    ) |
| suspense | ■ The condemned killer is strapped to the electric chair in a scene fraught with _____ ; then suddenly we see him, years earlier, as a boy scout winning a prize at Sunday school. This time |
| flashback | shift is called _____ . |

7. **anachronism** (ə-nak′rə-niz′əm): representing something as happening in the wrong historical period. An *anachronism*

occurs in *Julius Caesar* when Cassius says, "The clock has stricken three."

anachronism

■ Raphael's depiction of the Holy Family in medieval clothing is an *an* _____ .

(b)

■ An *anachronism* is an error involving (a) bad grammar, (b) the wrong period of time. (    )

anachronism

■ In a western film, critics noticed a time-flaw, or *an* _____: above the Indians could be seen (a) an eagle, (b) a commercial airplane. (    )

(b)

anachronism

■ It would also be a historical error, or *an* _____ , to show Abraham Lincoln using (a) an electric shaver, (b) a feather pen. (    )

(a)

---

## Quiz

Write the letter that indicates the best definition.

1. (g)
2. (e)
3. (b)
4. (a)

5. (d)

6. (f)
7. (c)

(    ) 1. anachronism    a. a full-length fictitious story
(    ) 2. coincidence    b. a shift to earlier events
(    ) 3. flashback    c. anxiety as to how things will turn out
(    ) 4. novel    d. a fictitious story shorter than a novel but longer than fifty pages
(    ) 5. novelette    e. the simultaneous occurrence of unrelated incidents
(    ) 6. plot    f. the pattern of story action
(    ) 7. suspense    g. an event misplaced in history

---

8. **setting:** the physical and spiritual surroundings or environment in which the story takes place. The *setting* of Sinclair Lewis's *Main Street* (1920) is a midwestern village.

9. **local color:** picturesque details—of customs, dialect, and scenery—that bring out a specific story setting. *Local color* is prominent in Bret Harte's portrayal of mining camps, saloons, riffraff, and mining lingo.

background

■ *Setting* refers to the story's _____ [action / background].

setting

■ Nathaniel Hawthorne's *The Scarlet Letter* (1850) has a Puritan village as its background, or *s* _____ .

(a)

local

setting

(a)

(b)

■ *The Scarlet Letter* reflects *local color* in (a) the pillory, Puritan garments, and pious talk, (b) the vengeance theme. (    )

■ Jesse Stuart's depiction of the dialect, garb, cabins, and oddities of the Kentucky backwoods people supplies the _____ *color* to this _____ [setting / anachronism].

■ The *setting* of Truman Capote's *In Cold Blood* (1965) is (a) a Kansas town, (b) the slaying of a family. (    )

■ Sarah Orne Jewett was a *local colorist,* since her stories depict customs, dialect, and setting that exist (a) anywhere, (b) only in Maine. (    )

---

10. **point of view:** the writer's way of telling the story, whether as participant or as observer, whether as seen by one character or by many characters, whether with objectivity or with editorial comment. *Tom Sawyer* is told in the third person from an omniscient *point of view,* but *Huckleberry Finn* is told in the first person from Huck's *point of view.*

(a)

view

first

should not

point, third

■ A writer of fiction decides at the outset through whose eyes the story action will be seen; in other words, he chooses and sticks to a definite (a) point of view, (b) local color. (    )

■ In Poe's "The Tell-Tale Heart" (1843) the narrator says, "I loved the old man," and we know that the *point of* _____ is _____ [first / third] person.

■ Suppose you write a novelette from the first person point of view. Then the secret thoughts and conversations of various nonpresent characters probably _____ [should / should not] be described.

■ Horatio Alger pointed out that his "hero" was "poor but honest"— the _____ *of view* is _____ [first / third] person.

---

11. **characterization** (kar′ik-tər-i-zā′shən): the portrayal of people, their physical and spiritual traits and peculiarities. Good *characterization* is consistent and three-dimensional, developed largely by action and dialogue rather than merely by flat abstract description.

**12. motivation:** that which causes a character to do what he does. What *motivations* cause Macbeth to murder Duncan?

characterization

■ The way people are portrayed is *ch*_____.

motivation

■ The passion, grievance, or need which impels a character to act as he does is his *mot*_____.

motivation

■ Men will not kill, seek divorces, or chase whales without sufficient *mot*_____.

characterization

■ Thomas Wolfe portrayed people so that you came to know their yearnings, their impulses, and their warts—this was effective *ch*_____.

motivation
characterization

■ The sudden reform of sinners and drunkards at the end of sentimental stories is usually without sufficient *m*_____—it suggests faulty *ch*_____.

_____

**13. protagonist** (prō-tag′ə-nist): the main character of a drama or fictional work. Hamlet, Ivanhoe, Huck Finn, and Brer Rabbit are *protagonists* of literary pieces.

**14. anti-hero:** a protagonist who lacks the noble spirit or admirable life purposes usually found in a heroic figure. Modern fiction depicts many an aimless, sinful *anti-hero*.

protagonist

anti-hero

■ The chief character of a novel or drama is known as its *pro*_____. If this *protagonist* is an ordinary, fault-ridden fellow with low aspirations he is an *an*_____.

protagonist

anti-hero

■ Clyde Griffith, as the central character of Theodore Dreiser's *An American Tragedy* (1925), is the novel's *pro*_____; and since Clyde is depicted as a stupid, blundering killer he is also an _____.

is not

■ A minor character, like Polonius in *Hamlet,* _____ [is / is not] the *protagonist.*

against

■ Since *anti* means _____ [around / against], the Greek play character who opposes the main character is called

antagonist

the _____ [antagonist / protagonist].

■ The *anti-hero* of a modern novel usually has a flock of

_____ [inspirational / shabby] traits.

---

**15. stream of consciousness** (kon'shəs-nis): thoughts and feelings of a character presented as an unceasing, disjointed sequence. *Stream of consciousness* presents a flow of random, fragmented, semi-articulate thoughts from all levels of consciousness and unconsciousness, often as a kind of unpunctuated *interior monologue*.

■ The interior monologue—the puns and the jumble of impressions in James Joyce's *Ulysses* (1922) reflects the protagonist's *stream*

*of* _____ .

■ The thoughts in *stream of consciousness* are (a) uniform and coherent, (b) disjointed and fragmentary. (    )

■ Authors like William Faulkner and Virginia Woolf, using

_____ *of consciousness* techniques, have depicted the flow of human thought as a kind of (a) interior monologue, (b) an unbroken

chain of logic. (    )

---

## Quiz

Write the letter that indicates the best definition.

(    ) 1. setting      a. the main character or hero
(    ) 2. local color      b. the cause of a character's action
(    ) 3. point of view      c. an unadmirable protagonist
(    ) 4. characterization      d. how people are portrayed
(    ) 5. motivation      e. picturesque, distinctive details
(    ) 6. protagonist      f. background of the action
(    ) 7. anti-hero      g. the outlook from which the action is described
(    ) 8. stream of consciousness      h. jumbled thoughts and feelings

---

**16. irony of fate** (ī'rə-nē): the way that destiny twists or foils the plans of men. Thomas Hardy's characters get a glimpse of happiness but by some *irony of fate* they fail to achieve it.

fate
(b)

■ The *irony of* _____ has a way of providing (a) the expected reward, (b) the unexpected disaster. (    )

(a)

■ In Stephen Crane's "The Open Boat" (1898) the unselfish oiler, who is possibly the most deserving of life, is the only man who drowns. This illustrates (a) the irony of fate, (b) that this is the best of all possible worlds. (    )

irony
(b)

■ The _____ *of fate* would be illustrated if the fire department building (a) needed painting, (b) burned down. (    )

---

17. **epistolary novel** (i-pis′tə-ler′ē): a novel written in the form of a series of letters. The eighteenth-century *epistolary novel* told a story through an exchange of letters, or epistles, usually between the adventurous heroine and a female friend.

18. **picaresque novel** (pik′ə-resk′): a novel that has a vagabond hero who goes from one adventure to another. *Picaresque novels* such as Tobias Smollett's *Roderick Random* (1748) were popular during the eighteenth century.

epistolary

■ Samuel Richardson's *Pamela* (1740) and *Clarissa Harlowe* (1748) consist entirely of fictional letters and are called *e* _____ *novels.*

(b)

■ An epistle is (a) the wife of an apostle, (b) a letter. (    )

picaresque

■ Mark Twain's *Huckleberry Finn* (1884), with its young rogue, episodic adventures, and satire, resembles the *pic* _____ *novel.*

picaresque
(b)

■ The vagabond hero of a *pic* _____ *novel* is usually involved in (a) a single episode, (b) a series of adventures. (    )

epistolary

■ J. P. Marquand's *The Late George Apley* (1936), which is told by means of letters, is a modern *ep* _____ novel.

picaresque

rogue
(b)

■ The protagonist of a *pic* _____ *novel* is a _____ [gentleman / rogue] who usually (a) stays in one place, (b) travels from one adventure to another. (    )

---

19. **Gothic novel:** a horror tale often involving a haunted castle, secret passages, mysterious noises and crimes. Mary Godwin Shelley's *Frankenstein* (1818) is a *Gothic novel*.

20. **Victorian novel:** an English novel written during the reign of Queen Victoria, 1837–1901, and reflecting—unthinkingly or satirically—the leisurely literary style, "decent" tastes, and empty respectability of that period. Distinguished *Victorian novels* were written by Charles Dickens, Thomas Hardy, William Thackeray, Samuel Butler, George Eliot, and others.

■ Novels involving haunted castles and clanking chains—such as *The Mysteries of Udolpho* (1794), by Anne Radcliffe—

Gothic                  are _____ [Gothic / picaresque].

■ Complacency, prudishness, and moral earnestness are common to

Victorian               the bulky *V*_____ *novel* of the nineteenth century.

Frankenstein            ■ The *Gothic novel,* such as _____ [*David Copperfield /*
(b)                     *Frankenstein*], stressed (a) cheerful events, (b) terror. (     )

■ Horace Walpole's bloodcurdling *The Castle of Otranto* (1764) was

Gothic                  typically _____ [agnostic / Gothic] in dealing with
                        (a) ghosts and madmen, (b) childhood sweethearts and business suc-
(a)                     cess. (     )

■ English authors like Dickens and Hardy wrote slow-paced

Victorian               *V*_____ *novels* during the _____ [eighteenth /
nineteenth              nineteenth] century.

---

21. **science fiction:** fantasies about time machines, space travel, and future marvels, made credible by technical detail. Modern *science fiction* began with Jules Verne and H. G. Wells.

22. **whodunit** (ho͞o-dun′it): a murder story dealing with the detection of the criminal; a detective story. The *whodunit*—from "Who did it?"—began with Edgar Allan Poe and Sir Arthur Conan Doyle and is now an extremely popular type of fiction.

■ A novel about spaceships and interplanetary wars is called

science                 *sc*_____ *fiction*. It deals with (a) actual events, (b) fantastic
(b)                     incidents not yet realized. (     )

■ A novel by Dashiell Hammett which ends in the capture of a slayer

whodunit                is a *wh*_____ .

■ Edgar Rice Burroughs' story of a battle between earthlings and Martians is classified by the librarian under (a) science, (b) science fiction. (    )

(b)

science

■ Ray Bradbury's *Fahrenheit 451* (1953) and Aldous Huxley's *Brave New World* (1932) contain sharp social comment but are fantasies of future technology and are classed as _____ *fiction.*

whodunit

detective

■ An Erle Stanley Gardner murder yarn is a _____ ; in other words, it is a _____ [detective /science] story.

---

### Quiz

Write the letter that indicates the best definition.

1. (f)
2. (d)
3. (g)

4. (e)
5. (c)
6. (a)
7. (b)

(    ) 1. irony of fate    a. fantasies about space travel
(    ) 2. epistolary novel    b. a detective story
(    ) 3. picaresque novel    c. a morally righteous novel of the Dickens-Hardy era
(    ) 4. Gothic novel    d. a novel in letter form
(    ) 5. Victorian novel    e. a grotesque horror story
(    ) 6. science fiction    f. unexpected twist of destiny
(    ) 7. whodunit    g. a story of a vagabond's adventures

---

**23. allegory:** a symbolic story in which the actions and characters have a secondary set of meanings; the simultaneous telling of parallel stories. John Bunyan's *Pilgrim's Progress* (1678) is a very obvious *allegory.*

(a)

■ A story like Swift's *Gulliver's Travels* (1726) with two sets of meanings is (a) an allegory, (b) a coincidence. (    )

■ If Herman Melville's *Moby Dick* (1851) is symbolic and tells several distinct parallel stories, as critics claim, then it is an

allegory

*al* _____ .

(b)

■ *Piers Plowman* (fourteenth century) is called an *allegory* because (a) it deals with country life, (b) its simple action has a secondary, spiritual interpretation. (    )

allegory
(b)

■ A long symbolic story such as Samuel Butler's *Erewhon* (1872) is known as an *al*_____ because it has (a) one level of meaning, (b) two or more levels of meaning. (     )

24. **satire:** wit, irony, or sarcasm used to ridicule abuses and follies. Outstanding *satire* has been written by Horace, Juvenal, Swift, Byron, Rabelais, Voltaire, Lewis Carroll, and others.

25. **social criticism:** the exposure of faults in various aspects of society. The *social criticism* of Sinclair Lewis hits at small town gossip, middle-class conformity, racial discrimination, and medical quackery.

social

■ Harriet Beecher Stowe's *Uncle Tom's Cabin* (1852) attacks slavery and therefore represents important *so*_____ *criticism.*

satire

■ Had Mrs. Stowe used sarcasm and wit, her criticism might have taken the form of *sa*_____ .

satirists

■ James Thurber and Aldous Huxley wittily ridiculed modern follies and may therefore be called _____ [sadists / satirists].

satire

social

(b)

criticism


(a)

■ Jonathan Swift's *Tale of a Tub* (1704) directs laughter at the faults of Englishmen and is thus *sa*_____ as well as _____ *criticism.*

■ The intention of *satire* is (a) to honor, (b) to ridicule. (     )

■ Another story involving *social* _____ is (a) John Steinbeck's *The Grapes of Wrath* (1939), exposing the miserable plight of the Okies, (b) Henry W. Longfellow's *Hiawatha* (1855), depicting an Indian romance. (     )

26. **sentimentalism:** excessive emotionalism, with emphasis on tender feelings and tears; called ***sensibility*** during the eighteenth century. Whereas *sentiment* is an expression of delicate, sensitive feelings, *sentimentalism* suggests a soft-heartedness that is gushy and insincere.

27. **realism:** the presentation of everyday life as it is, in accurate, photographic detail rather than in a romanticized way. *Realism* began as a nineteenth-century literary movement that tried to

reflect actual life, using commonplace characters and depicting their ordinary impulses, problems, and surroundings.

■ In early American novels such phrases as "the sympathetic tears gushed down her cheeks" suggest literary *sent*_____.

sentimentalism

■ Sinclair Lewis's description of the dullness and dirtiness of Main Street is one of *re*_____.

realism

■ *Sentimentalism* refers to soft emotions that are _____ [quiet and restrained / excessive].

excessive

■ *Realism* shows people and their surroundings as they _____ [are / ought to be].

are

■ *Sentimentalism,* whether in love poetry or in commercial greeting cards, is emotionally (a) honest and reasonable, (b) overdone. (     )

(b)

■ William Dean Howells' *The Rise of Silas Lapham* (1885) reflects ordinary people and their problems and achieves *r*_____.

realism

■ The scene describing the death of Little Nell, a classic tear-jerker by Dickens, illustrates _____.

sentimentalism

---

**28. naturalism:** an extension of realism tending to stress sordidness and sexuality and to portray man as a soulless animal shaped by his environment and heredity. *Naturalism* is a leading modern literary movement; it denies supernaturalism and looks at man as a puppet lacking free will.

■ Literary *naturalism* portrays man as (a) a noble creation of God, (b) an animal molded by his environment. (     )

(b)

■ The extension of realism known as *nat*_____ gives close attention to (a) sordidness and sexuality, (b) beauty and high ideals. (     )

naturalism

(a)

■ The *naturalistic* novels of Theodore Dreiser depict man as _____ [god-like / brutish] and as _____ [molded by / rising superior to] his environment.

brutish, molded by

---

**29. existentialism** (eg′zis-ten′shə-liz′əm): a view of life which maintains that man is alone in a purposeless universe and that he must exercise his own free will to oppose a hostile environment. This *existentialist* theme of man's total responsibility to himself in the midst of conformist pressures is reflected in the fiction of Jean-Paul Sartre, Albert Camus, Franz Kafka, and others.

**30. alienation** (al′yə-nā′shən): a separation from others and from participation; loss of affection. Man's sense of *alienation* from established society is a recurring theme in today's fiction.

■ Literary *existentialism* stresses (a) the aloneness of man and the hostility of his environment, (b) the togetherness of mankind and the values of living. (     )

(a)

■ The young anti-hero of Camus' *The Stranger* (1946) lacks religion, love, or human involvements; thus, the novel reflects *ex*_____

existentialism

alienation

and illustrates man's essential _____ [brotherhood / alienation].

■ When man loses his faith and sees himself as a short-lived animal

alienation
(a)

in an uncaring world, his sense of *al*_____ is usually (a) increased, (b) decreased. (     )

■ *Existentialism* maintains that man must make his choices in a

purposeless

_____ [meaningful / purposeless] existence.

existentialism

(b)

■ *Alienated* man, as depicted in the fiction of *ex*_____, tends to see life as (a) noble and spiritual, (b) absurd and pointless. (     )

## Quiz

Write the letter that indicates the best definition.

1. (d)
2. (e)
3. (g)
4. (a)

5. (c)

6. (h)

7. (f)

8. (b)

(   ) 1. allegory
(   ) 2. satire
(   ) 3. social criticism
(   ) 4. sentimentalism

(   ) 5. realism

(   ) 6. naturalism

(   ) 7. existentialism

(   ) 8. alienation

a. emotionalism in excess
b. separation from others
c. portrayal of life as it is
d. a story with a secondary
   interpretation
e. a witty, often sophisticated attack
   on follies
f. Sartre's doctrine of man's
   responsibility to himself.
g. an exposure of social faults, often
   serious in tone
h. an extension of realism, emphasizing
   sordidness

# REVIEW TEST

Supply the missing word in each sentence. The first letter of each answer is given.

1. A long symbolic story in which characters and events have a secondary set of meanings is an *al* _____ .

2. The background or environment in which the story action takes place is the *se* _____ .

3. Telling a story through an exchange of letters is the method of an *ep* _____ novel.

4. Bringing out the personalities and individual traits of people in a story is *ch* _____ .

5. An extended horror story dealing, for example, with haunted castles and madmen is a *G* _____ novel.

6. Picturesque detail which brings out a particular story setting is *local c* _____ .

7. The portrayal of an event or object in the wrong historical period is an *an* _____ .

8. Each man is alone and must make his own decisions in a meaningless universe, according to *ex* _____ .

9. A protagonist without noble qualities is an *an* _____ .

10. A remarkable chance occurrence of events at the same time is a *co* _____ .

---

Write *True* or *False*.

_____ 11. *Motivation* is the moving about or traveling which takes place in a story.

_____ 12. In *stream of consciousness* the thoughts emerge in clear and logical fashion.

_____ 13. *Sentimentalism* is excessive emotionalism.

_____ 14. *Naturalism* focuses on the pleasanter and nobler aspects of life.

_____ 15. The *Victorian novel* was written by such authors as Charles Dickens, Thomas Hardy, and George Eliot.

_____ 16. *Science fiction* sometimes deals with interplanetary travel.

_____ 17. A *whodunit* is a detective story.

_____ 18. The *irony of fate* implies that man usually gets what he expects and deserves.

_____ 19. A *novelette* is an essay, somewhat longer than a novel.

_____ 20. *Social criticism* refers to the evaluation of the style, merits, and shortcomings of a book.

Write the letter that indicates the best completion.

(    ) 21. The *plot* of a novel is its (a) plan of action, (b) moral, (b) background, (d) social criticism.

(    ) 22. The *protagonist* of a *picaresque* novel is usually (a) a maiden, (b) a nobleman, (c) a lover, (d) a scamp.

(    ) 23. Man's *alienation* refers to his (a) relatives, (b) foreign extraction, (c) aloneness in society, (d) sinfulness.

(    ) 24. A *novel* is a long (a) life story, (b) fictitious story, (c) essay, (d) poem or play.

(    ) 25. Most *satire* involves (a) suspense, (b) flashback, (c) sentimentalism, (d) irony and sarcasm.

## Key to Review Test

Check your test answers with the following key. Deduct 4% per error from 100%.

| | | |
|---|---|---|
| 1. allegory | 10. coincidence | 19. False |
| 2. setting | 11. False | 20. False |
| 3. epistolary | 12. False | 21. (a) |
| 4. characterization | 13. True | 22. (d) |
| 5. Gothic | 14. False | 23. (c) |
| 6. color | 15. True | 24. (b) |
| 7. anachronism | 16. True | 25. (d) |
| 8. existentialism | 17. True | |
| 9. anti-hero | 18. False | |

Score: _____ %

1. **anthology:** a collection of essays, stories, poems, or plays. An *anthology* is often used in college English classes.
2. **commonplace book:** a collection of miscellaneous thoughts, verses, and quotations jotted down for possible later use. Ben Jonson kept a *commonplace book* entitled *Timber*, which includes references to his friend William Shakespeare.
3. **expatriate** (eks-pā′trē-it): one who has left his native land. After World War I, many American *expatriates*, such as Gertrude Stein and Ernest Hemingway, lived and wrote in Paris.
4. **folklore:** the traditional legends, sayings, beliefs, and customs of the people. American *folklore* includes proverbs, riddles, superstitions, ballads, hunting and fishing yarns, and tales of the mountaineer and the cowboy.
5. **incunabula** (in′kyoo-nab′yoo-lə): books printed before 1500. *Incunabula* such as Sir Thomas Malory's *Le Morte d'Arthur*, printed by William Caxton in 1485, are rare treasures today.
6. **lampoon:** a coarsely humorous attack in prose or verse ridiculing someone. The *lampoon* is a particularly strong or malicious brand of satire.
7. **Lost Generation:** a term used by Gertrude Stein to describe the generation of young men and women who were disillusioned by World War I, and the nature of society, and who had therefore forsaken the traditional cultural values. The *Lost Generation* included writers such as Ernest Hemingway, F. Scott Fitzgerald, and John Dos Passos.
8. **motif** (mō-tēf′): a distinctive unifying feature or theme which recurs throughout a work. Ahab's passion for vengeance is a dominant *motif* in *Moby Dick*.
9. **myth:** an old story about gods or racial heroes which explains such things as the origin of the sun and the seasons or of social upheaval; also refers today to a prevailing concept of human nature such as the *myth* of Yankee ingenuity, the *myth* of progress, and the *myth* of the alienated man; also refers sometimes to the fictitious milieu of a particular literary work, as J. R. R. Tolkien's *myth* of the hobbits. Certain poets, such as Blake, Yeats, and T. S. Eliot, have created *myths* as framework for their poetry.
10. **narrative:** a story or an account of happenings. *Narratives* relate action, either factual or fictional, as in diaries, travel literature, ballads, and stories.
11. **Nobel prize** (nō-bel′): an annual prize awarded in Stockholm, Sweden, to the outstanding writer or idealistic literature. Past winners include Sinclair Lewis, 1930; Eugene O'Neill, 1936; T. S. Eliot, 1948; William Faulkner, 1949; Ernest Hemingway, 1954; John Steinbeck, 1962; Saul Bellow, 1976; Isaac Singer, 1978.
12. **novel of manners:** a novel, often satiric, that reflects the customs and habits of a particular social class of a certain period. Novels of manners have been written by Jane Austen, Edith Wharton, and John P. Marquand.
13. **parable** (par′ə-bəl): a short simple story that illustrates a moral or spiritual truth. The Bible presents the *parable* of the prodigal son.
14. **parody** (par′ə-dē): comical imitation tending to ridicule an author or literary work. For example, Bret Harte's "Mrs. Judge Jenkins" (1871) is a *parody* of John Whittier's too-sentimental "Maud Muller" (1854).
15. **pornography** (pôr-nog′rə-fē): obscene writing designed to arouse sexual desire. By definition of the Supreme Court, *pornography* has no redeeming social value.
16. **primitivism:** the belief that primitive cultures are superior in many ways to our corrupt and complicated civilization and that people close to nature have better qualities

than those in cities. Rousseau, Cooper, and Hemingway exhibit *primitivism* in their admiration for uncorrupted nature and for simple, red-blooded, earthy people.

17. **pseudonym** (soo'də-nim): a fictitious name or pen name: for example, George Eliot, *pseudonym* of Mary Ann Evans, who wrote *Silas Marner* (1861); Artemus Ward, *pseudonym* of the American humorist Charles F. Browne.

18. **redaction** (ri-dak'shən): the editing and reduction or revision of literary materials for publication. Magazine editors sometimes *redact* a popular novel and print a streamlined version.

19. **saga** (sä'gə): a story of heroic deeds, especially of medieval Icelandic heroes. The Viking *sagas* influenced Longfellow's poetry.

20. **synopsis** (si-nop'sis): a brief summary of the plot of a novel, drama, or other composition. A *synopsis* provides a quick general view of a subject without critical comment.

21. **tall-tale:** a yarn about incredible happenings, usually involving superhuman feats by a character. The remarkable deeds of Paul Bunyan and Davy Crockett occur in typical, humorous *tall-tales* of the frontier.

22. **tetralogy** (te-tral'ə-jē): a series, by a single author, of four related works. A *tetralogy* of dramas, consisting of three tragedies and a satyr play, were presented in sequence at the festival of Dionysus in Athens.

23. **thesaurus** (thi-sô'rəs): a treasury of words, with synonyms and antonyms classified and arranged to help writers. A dictionary and a *thesaurus* are indispensable to an author—talent helps, too.

24. **tone:** an author's attitude toward his material and his readers, whether reverent, jesting, cynical, impersonal, and so on. A nostalgic *tone* often pervades the lyric prose of Thomas Wolfe.

25. **trilogy** (tril'ə-jē): a series, by a single author, of three related works, as in fiction or drama. Eugene O'Neill's *Mourning Becomes Electra* (1931) is a *trilogy,* a series of three plays, in which the ancient Greek playwright Aeschylus's theme of fate haunts an American household.

# 20
# Poetry

*It is not enough to say of a verse, "How pretty that is" or "That's a remarkable phrase." To analyze a poem we must be familiar with certain basic technical terms. It is important to know the various figures of speech (see Chapter 16). We must also recognize such aspects of versification as hexameter, anapest, and assonance, and such types of poems as sonnet, epic, and dramatic monologue. Nor should we turn blank at the mention of blank verse, confusing it, perhaps, with free verse.*

*Analysis cannot hope to explain completely the mysterious nature of poetry, "untwisting all the claims that tie / The hidden soul of harmony"; yet a knowledge of poetic terms can be a real step toward a richer appreciation of poetry.*

## EXERCISES

COVER THIS STRIP

1. **scansion** (skan′shən): the analysis of verse to show its meter and rhyme scheme. *Scansion* marks include ˘ for an unaccented syllable, ′ for an accented syllable, and | for a foot division.

2. **foot:** the basic unit of verse meter, consisting usually of two or three syllables of which ordinarily one is stressed. The number of feet to the line determines the meter.

scansion

feet

■ Metrical analysis, or *sc*_____, tells you the number and type of _____ [feet / figures of speech] in each line of verse.

scansion
(b)

■ The process of poetic *sc*_____ is (a) emotional, (b) analytical. (     )

feet

scansion

■ The number of metric units, or _____ [bars / feet], in a line of verse is calculated by *sc*_____ .

three

■ The number of *feet* in Robert Burns' verse "Your locks were like the raven" is _____ [three / seven].

3. **iamb** (ī′amb): an unstressed syllable followed by a stressed syllable; for example, "tŏníght," "dĕný," "ănd nów," "mў lóve."

4. **trochee** (trō′kē): a stressed syllable followed by an unstressed syllable; for example, "fástĕr," "dámsĕl," "dýĭng," "flíng ĭt."

iamb

second

■ The *iambic* foot, or *ia*_____, consists of two syllables with the stress on the _____ [first / second] syllable.

trochee

first

■ The *trochaic* foot, or *tr*_____, consists of two syllables with the stress on the _____ [first / second] syllable.

Before each example of a metrical foot write *iamb* or *trochee*.

trochee

■ _____ hanging

iamb

■ _____ the sky

iamb

■ _____ to dream

| | |
|---|---|
| trochee | ■ _____ drink it |
| trochee | ■ _____ Edith |

Before each example of verse write *iambic* or *trochaic*.

| | |
|---|---|
| iambic | ■ _____ To be or not to be . . . |
| trochaic | ■ _____ Come and trip it as ye go. |
| iambic | ■ _____ I struck the board and cried . . . |

5. **anapest** (an′ə-pest′): two unstressed syllables followed by a stressed syllable; for example, "ŏf thĕ mén"; "tŏ rĕjóice"; "ĭntĕrfére."

6. **dactyl** (dak′til): a stressed syllable followed by two unstressed syllables; for example, "sińg tŏ thĕ"; "fléeĭng frŏm"; "rápĭdlў."

| | |
|---|---|
| anapest | ■ The *anapestic foot,* or *an*_____, consists of three sylla- |
| third | bles with the stress on the _____ [first / third] syllable. |
| dactyl | ■ The *dactylic* foot, or *da*_____, consists of three syllables |
| first | with the stress on the _____ [first / third] syllable. |

Before each sample metrical foot write *anapest* or *dactyl.*

| | |
|---|---|
| anapest | ■ _____ of the king |
| dactyl | ■ _____ laughing with |
| dactyl | ■ _____ fade in the |
| anapest | ■ _____ with Elaine |
| anapest | ■ _____ in despair |

Before each verse sample write *anapestic* or *dactylic.*

| | |
|---|---|
| dactylic | ■ _____ Maiden most beautiful, mother most bountiful . . . |
| anapestic | ■ _____ And the sheen of their spears was like stars on the sea |

7. **caesura** (si-zhoor′ə): a pause within the line of verse, indicated in scansion by two vertical lines, thus ‖. The *caesura* usually

coincides with a pause in the thought, as at a major mark of punctuation.

caesura
(b)

■ In scansion the pause known as the *ca*_____ is indicated by (a) a snaky line, (b) two vertical lines. (    )

■ Alexander Pope wrote, "One truth is clear, Whatever is, is right."

caesura
(b)

A pause known as a *c*_____ belongs after (a) "truth," (b) "clear." (    )

caesura
(a)

■ "Beowulf spake, bairn of Ecgtheow." The pause, or _____, belongs after (a) "spake," (b) "bairn." (    )

---

## Quiz

Write the letter that indicates the best definition or example.

1. (e)
2. (f)
3. (b)
4. (a)
5. (c)
6. (g)
7. (d)

(    ) 1. anapest      a. the basic unit of verse meter
(    ) 2. caesura      b. a foot like "tenderly"
(    ) 3. dactyl      c. a foot like "the stars"
(    ) 4. foot      d. a foot like "kissing"
(    ) 5. iamb      e. a foot like "in her home"
(    ) 6. scansion      f. a pause within the verse
(    ) 7. trochee      g. metrical analysis

---

8. **tetrameter** (te-tram′i-tər): a line of poetry containing four feet; example from Lord Tennyson of iambic *tetrameter:* "I come from haunts of coot and hern." Shorter lines are the *trimeter,* three feet; the *dimeter,* two feet; and the *monometer,* one foot.

9. **pentameter** (pen-tam′i-tər): a line of poetry containing five feet; example from John Keats of iambic *pentameter:* "When I have fears that I may cease to be."

10. **hexameter** (hek-sam′i-tər): a line of poetry containing six feet. Longer and less common than the *hexameter* line are the *heptameter,* seven feet, and the *octameter,* eight feet.

tetrameter

■ A verse containing four metrical feet is a *tet*_____.

pentameter

■ A verse containing five metrical feet is a *pen*_____.

hexameter

■ A verse containing six metrical feet is a *hex*_____.

three

■ The *trimeter* line has _____ [three / four] feet, and the

two

*dimeter* has _____ [two / five] feet.

hexameter

■ The Alexandrine, a line popular in French poetry, is composed of six iambic feet; in other words, it is in *iambic* _____ *meter.*

(b)

■ A *tetrameter* is to a pentameter as (a) six is to five, (b) four is to five, (c) five is to six. (    )

tetrameter

hexameter

■ A *pentameter* has one more foot than a _____ , and it has one less foot than a _____ .

four

■ The final foot of a line is sometimes shortened, or "truncated"; how many feet are there in William Blake's line, "Tyger! Tyger! burning bright"—not counting the feet on the tiger? _____
[three / four]

(a)

■ In other words, Blake's line is (a) trochaic tetrameter, (b) iambic trimeter. (    )

Scan the following versus.

iambic
pentameter
trochaic

■ Thomas Gray's "The curfew tolls the knell of parting day."
*i*_____ *p*_____ .

■ Thomas Carew's "He that loves a rosy cheek." _____

tetrameter

_____ .

iambic
hexameter

■ Edmund Spenser's "God helpe the man so wrapt in Errours endless traine!" _____ _____ .

anapestic
pentameter

■ Robert Browning's "And I paused, held my breath in such silence, and listened apart." _____ _____ .

dactylic
hexameter

■ The Bible's "How art thou fallen from heaven, O Lucifer, son of the morning!" _____ _____ .

---

11. **poetic license:** a writer's assumption that he may deviate from accepted standards of correctness for artistic effect. *Poetic license* has been cited to excuse violations of grammar, diction, rhythm, rhyme, and historical facts.

(b)

■ *Poetic license* is sometimes mentioned to excuse (a) lack of productivity, (b) departures from correctness. (    )

■ "The owl, for all his feathers, was a-cold." Here Keats has exercised *p* _____ *license* (a) to alter a fact, (b) to patch his iambic rhythm. (    )

■ Shakespeare's tampering with facts and dates in his historical dramas is usually attributed to (a) poetic license, (b) dishonesty. (    )

## Quiz

Write the letter that indicates the best definition.

(    ) 1. tetrameter      a. a verse with five feet
(    ) 2. pentameter      b. a verse with four feet
(    ) 3. hexameter       c. an author's right to break rules
(    ) 4. poetic license  d. a verse with six feet

12. **masculine rhyme:** a rhyme limited to the stressed last syllable; single rhyme. Example: "kiss" and "miss," "late" and "fate," "repent" and "consent."

13. **feminine rhyme:** a rhyme of two or three syllables, with the stress on the first syllable; also called double-rhyme or triple-rhyme. Example: "stranger" and "danger," "sleeping" and "creeping," "saddening" and "maddening."

■ In *masculine rhyme* the similarity of sounds appears in (a) the one stressed last syllable, (b) two or more syllables. (    )

■ Two-syllable rhyme, or double rhyme, is called *fem* _____ *rhyme.*

Before each part of rhyming words write *masculine* or *feminine.*

■ _____ "hate" and "fate"

■ _____ "sheep" and "sleep"

■ _____ "flicker" and "sicker"

■ _____ "complain" and "refrain"

■ _____ "glory" and "story"

14. **internal rhyme:** rhyming within the line; for example, "And nations rush faster toward disaster."

15. **inversion:** a reversal in the natural word order to help out the rhyme or rhythm. *Inversions* are now usually considered undesirable: "And them behold no more shall I."

internal

■ A rhyme between two words in the same line is called *in* _____ *rhyme.*

inversion

■ A turning about of the normal word order is called *in* _____ .

does

rhyme, does

■ "And oh what bliss if her I could kiss"—this verse _____ [does / does not] have *internal* _____ and _____ [does / does not] contain *inversion.*

Before each line of verse write either *inversion* or *internal* (for *internal rhyme*).

internal

■ _____ We were the first who ever burst

inversion

■ _____ In her attic window the staff she set

inversion

■ _____ The invited neighbors to the husking come

internal

■ _____ For the moon never beams without bringing me dreams

---

16. **consonance** (kon′sə-nəns): imperfect rhyme in which the words have identical consonant sounds but different vowel sounds. Example: "men" and "mean," "walk" and "weak," "fool" and "fail."

17. **assonance** (as′ə-nəns): imperfect rhyme in which the words have identical vowel sounds but different consonant sounds before and after. Example: "flame" and "rain," "night" and "pine," "blow" and "groan."

(b)

■ *Consonance* means imperfect rhyme with an identicality of (a) vowels, (b) consonants. (    )

(a)

■ *Assonance* means imperfect rhyme with an identicality of (a) vowels, (b) consonants. (    )

Before each imperfect rhyme write *consonance* or *assonance*.

consonance

■ _____ "cling" and "clang"

assonance

■ _____ "shame" and "raid"

consonance

■ _____ "note" and "night"

assonance

■ _____ "creep" and "flee"

(b)

■ *Consonance* appears in (a) "they hate their fate," (b) "my love doth live." (     )

(b)

■ *Assonance* appears in (a) "her fears and tears," (b) "to wink at him." (     )

---

## Quiz

Write the letter that indicates the best example.

1. (f)
2. (e)
3. (b)
4. (c)
5. (d)
6. (a)

(     ) 1. assonance  a. "think" and "drink"
(     ) 2. consonance b. "wonder" and "thunder"
(     ) 3. feminine rhyme c. "Who says the flag is but a rag?"
(     ) 4. internal rhyme d. "To me the angry words he spoke."
(     ) 5. inversion  e. "cord" and "card"
(     ) 6. masculine rhyme f. "plan" and "map"

---

18. **epic:** a long narrative poem that describes heroic adventures in an exalted style. The *folk* or primitive *epic,* such as *Beowulf* or the *Iliad,* was originally recited by a bard to nobility; the *literary epic,* such as Virgil's *Aeneid* or Milton's *Paradise Lost,* is a more unified and polished work intended for reading.

poem

■ An *epic* is a lengthy, dignified _____ [essay / poem] which deals with (a) the beauty of flowers, (b) the adventures of he-

(b)

roes. (     )

epic
(a)

■ A long narrative poem in exalted style is known as an

e_____; an example of an *epic* is (a) Homer's *Odyssey,* (b) Whittier's "The Barefoot Boy." (     )

(b)

■ An *epic* such as Milton's *Paradise Lost* has a length of several hundred (a) words, (b) pages. (     )

(a)

epic
(b)

■ The tone of an *epic* poem by Homer or Milton is (a) lofty and dignified, (b) vulgar and uninspiring. (     )

■ A long, dignified narrative poem, called an _____, deals with (a) humorous family situations, (b) heroic adventures. (     )

---

19. **heroic couplet:** two rhyming lines in iambic pentameter, usually expressing a complete, epigrammatic thought, a verse form favored by Alexander Pope. Example: "A little learning is a dangerous thing; / Drink deep, or taste not the Pierian spring."
20. **quatrain** (kwo′trān): a four-line stanza, variously rhymed. Example: "I never saw a moor, / I never saw the sea; / Yet know I how the heather looks, / And what a wave must be."

two

rhyme
(a)

quatrain


(b)


quatrain



third




couplet

Pope

complete

■ The *heroic couplet* consists of _____ [two / four] lines that _____ [rhyme / do not rhyme] and which usually express (a) a complete thought, (b) part of a run-on thought. (     )

■ A four-line stanza of poetry is called a *q*_____.

■ The rhyming pattern of *quatrains* is (a) always *abab,* (b) variable. (     )

■ Folk ballads make common use of the four-line stanza, or _____.

■ The rhyming pattern of the *quatrain* in Edward FitzGerald's *The Rubaiyat* (1859) is *aaba,* which means that its _____ [first / third] line is unrhymed.

■ The two-line rhyme known as the *heroic c*_____ was a favorite of _____ [Pope / T. S. Eliot], and it usually expresses a _____ [complete / incomplete] thought.

---

21. **sonnet:** a fourteen-line poem in iambic pentameter with a prescribed rhyming and structural pattern. The *English,* or *Shakespearean, sonnet* consists of three quatrains and a couplet, rhyming *abab cdcd efef gg;* the *Italian,* or *Petrarchan, sonnet* consists of an octave (having eight lines) followed by a sestet (having six lines) and rhymes *abba abba cde cde* (the rhyme scheme of the sestet may vary).

| | |
|---|---|
| fourteen (a) | ■ The *sonnet* is _____ [twelve / fourteen] lines long and is in iambic (a) pentameter, (b) hexameter. (    ) |
| sonnet, (a) | ■ If its fourteen lines consist of three quatrains and a couplet, the *s*_____ is (a) English, (b) Italian. (    ) |
| sonnet, (b) | ■ If its fourteen lines consist of an octave and a sestet, the _____ is (a) English, (b) Italian. (    ) |

---

**22. blank verse:** unrhymed iambic pentameter. *Blank verse* is used in the dramas of Shakespeare and Marlowe and in other serious English poetry such as Milton's *Paradise Lost.*

**23. free verse:** rhythmical lines of irregular length without fixed metrical pattern and usually without rhyme; also called *vers libre. Free verse* has the rhythms and cadences of natural speech.

| | |
|---|---|
| (b) | ■ The magnificent *blank verse* of *Macbeth* and *Julius Caesar* is a) rhymed, (b) unrhymed. (    ) |
| (a) | ■ *Blank verse* consists of lines that are unrhymed and (a) in iambic pentameter, (b) of various lengths and stresses. (    ) |
| free | ■ On the other hand, unrhymed lines of irregular length are *f*_____ *verse.* |
| free (b) | ■ A line of *vers libre,* or *f*_____ *verse,* has (a) five stresses, (b) no fixed metrical pattern. (    ) |
| free | ■ Walt Whitman, Amy Lowell, and Carl Sandburg often use lines of irregular length and rhythm, known as _____ *verse.* |
| is blank | ■ "For who would bear the whips and scorns of time"—this representative line from *Hamlet* _____ [is / is not] in iambic pentameter; and so this unrhymed drama is in _____ *verse.* |

---

**24. imagery** (im′ij-rē): the various appeals to the senses made by a literary passage; any descriptive phrasing and figures of speech which make us feel, see, hear, smell, taste. Examples: "fragrant hair," "gentle rain," "a swarm of golden bees," "The hare limped trembling through the frozen grass."

| | |
|---|---|
| (b) | ■ A poem has *imagery* if its phrases (a) show imagination, (b) describe how things look, smell, taste, sound, or feel. (    ) |

■ Phrases like "grassy tomb" or "jolly shepherds" are known as *im*_____ because they appeal to the reader's (a) curiosity, (b) senses. (    )

■ *Imagery* is in the phrase (a) "drunk the milk of Paradise," (b) "ultimate theological conclusions." (    )

■ *Imagery* is in the line (a) "The sanitary condition of the restaurant was unsatisfactory," (b) "A black fly landed on the cracked rim of the soup bowl and began to rub its hind legs together." (    )

■ The appeal to the senses known as *i*_____ is especially common in (a) poetry, (b) algebra. (    )

---

**25. objective correlative** (kə-rel′ə-tiv): the evoking of an emotion in the reader by the artist's use of such objects, events, or situations as will objectify that emotion or serve as a formula for that emotion. For a discussion of the *objective correlative,* see T. S. Eliot's "Hamlet and His Problems" (1919).

■ A poet uses the *objective correlative* to arouse an emotion. For example, to make us feel melancholy (gloomy) he may make references to (a) autumn . . . a wailing wind . . . dead leaves, (b) April . . . sweet showers . . . twittering swallows. (    )

■ A poet who wishes to convey a sense of frustration might also use the *ob*_____ *co*_____. Circle the letters of three phrases below that suggest frustration:

a.  green fields          d.  rosy-fingered dawn
b.  a caged eagle         e.  "Strike three!"
c.  the hearty embrace    f.  the sucking quicksand

■ The poet's emotion may be transferred to the reader by means of symbolic description, in a technique called the *objective* _____.

■ The *objective correlative* uses symbols and formulae for a specific emotion so that the reader will (a) be bewildered, (b) feel the same emotion. (    )

■ The phrase *ob*_____ *correlative,* referring to a method of arousing a particular _____ [idea / emotion] in a reader, was coined in 1919 by (a) T. S. Eliot, (b) Woodrow Wilson. (    )

---

## Quiz

Write the letter that indicates the best definition.

1. (g)
2. (f)
3. (e)
4. (c)
5. (b)
6. (d)
7. (a)
8. (h)

(     ) 1. epic     a. appeals to the senses

(     ) 2. heroic couplet     b. unrhymed iambic pentameter

(     ) 3. quatrain     c. a patterned fourteen-line poem

(     ) 4. sonnet     d. unrhymed verses of irregular length

(     ) 5. blank verse     e. a four-line stanza

(     ) 6. free verse     f. two rhymed lines in iambic pentameter

(     ) 7. imagery     g. a long poem about heroic achievements

(     ) 8. objective correlative     h. the use of various images and references to arouse a specific emotion

# REVIEW TEST

Supply the missing word in each sentence.

1. The basic unit of verse measure is the *f*_____.

2. The analysis of rhythm and meter is known as *sc*_____.

3. A long narrative poem describing heroic deeds is an *ep*_____.

4. A four-line stanza is a *q*_____.

5. Rhyming within a line of poetry is *i*_____ *rhyme*.

6. A pause within a line of verse is a *ca*_____.

7. A metrical line of four feet is a *t*_____.

8. A metrical line of six feet is a *h*_____.

9. A metrical foot consisting of a stressed syllable followed by an unstressed syllable is a *tr*_____.

10. Twisting poetic words into unnatural order is called *in*_____.

---

Write *True* or *False*.

_____ 11. The *anapest* consists of two unstressed syllables followed by a stressed syllable.

_____ 12. *Blank verse* uses an irregular number of metrical feet to the line.

_____ 13. An example of *consonance* is "green" and "grain."

_____ 14. The Shakespearean *sonnet* rhyme pattern is *abab cdcd efef gg*.

_____ 15. The *heroic couplet* is unrhymed.

_____ 16. A *poetic license* costs a small fee and entitles a qualified person to write verse.

_____ 17. The *objective correlative* is used to evoke an emotion.

_____ 18. A *pentameter* line consists of seven feet.

_____ 19. Examples of *feminine rhyme* are "writing" and "biting," "fashion" and "passion."

_____ 20. *Imagery* refers to ingenious twists of plot.

---

Write the letter that indicates the best completion.

( ) 21. An example of a *dactylic* foot is (a) "dancing," (b) "in the town," (c) "the farmer," (d) "tenderly."

**Poetry** 303

( ) 22. An example of an *iambic* foot is (a) "favor," (b) "depend," (c) "of a cloud," (d) "faltering."

( ) 23. An example of *masculine rhyme* is (a) "cringe" and "lunge," (b) "measure" and "treasure," (c) "ships" and "lips," (d) "dine" and "time."

( ) 24. *Free verse* has (a) regular meter, (b) speech rhythms, (c) rhyming restrictions, (d) stanzaic pattern.

( ) 25. An example of *assonance* is (a) "hate" and "lame," (b) "dinner" and "thinner," (c) "sink" and "drink," (d) "steal" and "stall."

## Key to Review Test

Check your test answers with the following key. Deduct 4% per error from 100%.

| | | |
|---|---|---|
| 1. foot | 10. inversion | 19. True |
| 2. scansion | 11. True | 20. False |
| 3. epic | 12. False | 21. (d) |
| 4. quatrain | 13. True | 22. (b) |
| 5. internal | 14. True | 23. (c) |
| 6. caesura | 15. False | 24. (b) |
| 7. tetrameter | 16. False | 25. (a) |
| 8. hexameter | 17. True | |
| 9. trochee | 18. False | |

Score: _____ %

1. **Alexandrine** (al-ig-zan′drin): a line composed of six iambic feet; an *iambic hexameter*. The Alexandrine is popular in French poetry.
2. **ambiguity** (ambə-gyoo′i-tē): an expression having two or more possibly contradictory meanings; also refers to multiple suggestiveness which enriches poetry. William Empson's *Seven Types of Ambiguity* (1931) explores the nature of such hinted suggestions.
3. **ars poetica** (ärz pō-et′i-kə): the art of poetry.
4. **carpe diem** (kär′pi dī′em): "seize the day," a Latin phrase implying that one must enjoy the present moment, for tomorrow may be too late. The *carpe diem* theme appeared in *Ecclesiastes'* "Eat, drink, and be merry" and has run through literature like a scarlet thread.
5. **Cavalier poetry:** graceful, sophisticated, witty verses written during the reign of Charles I (1625–1649) by lyric poets Thomas Carew, Sir John Suckling, Richard Lovelace, and others. *Cavalier poetry* deals typically with beloved maidens and constancy and the importance of enjoying the present moment.
6. **dramatic monologue:** a narrative poem in which a single speaker gives his version of a dramatic situation, meanwhile exposing his own personality quirks; for example, Robert Browning's "My Last Duchess" (1842), which tells a story and incidentally reveals the viciousness of the narrator himself.
7. **elegy** (el′i-jē): a formal, melancholy poem, often a lament for the dead. Notable *elegies* include Gray's "Elegy Written in a Country Churchyard" (1750) and Whitman's "When Lilacs Last in the Dooryard Bloom'd" (1866).
8. **enjambment** (en-jam′mənt): the running on of a sentence from one line of verse into the next without a pause at the end of the line. Such a run-on line is in contrast to the more customary end-stopped line.
9. **haiku** (hī′koo): a delicate Japanese poem of three unrhymed lines consisting of five, seven, and five syllables, respectively. The *haiku* usually alludes in some way to a season.
10. **in medias res** (in mē′di-əs rēz): in the midst of things, that is, in the middle of the narrative. Homer begins an epic *in medias res,* then describes in flashbacks those incidents which led to this crisis.
11. **invocation:** an appeal for inspiration and guidance from a deity or Muse, at the beginning of an epic. Homer's *Iliad* begins with an *invocation* to Calliope, the Muse of epic poetry.
12. **kenning:** a metaphorical compound name for something in Anglo-Saxon poetry. *Kennings* in *Beowulf* include "whale-road" for "sea" and "foamy floater" for "ship."
13. **laureate** (lôr′ē-it): a poet recognized as the most eminent in a country. Poets *laureate* of England have included Wordsworth, Tennyson, and Masefield.
14. **light verse:** short, light-hearted poems. Witty, sophisticated *light verse* has been written by Dorothy Parker, Ogden Nash, Phyllis McGinley, and others.
15. **metaphysical conceit:** an ingenious, sustained comparison between things apparently highly dissimilar. In "A Valediction: Forbidding Mourning" (1633) John Donne compares the souls of two lovers to the two legs of a compass.
16. **metaphysical poetry:** highly intellectual, philosophical poetry marked by clashing emotions, jarring versification, and startling conceits, as written by John Donne, George Herbert, and other seventeenth-century writers. *Metaphysical poets* were often intensely analytical of human emotions.

17. **New Criticism:** an approach which concentrates on textual explication of a poem rather than on social implications or historical aspects. Critics such as T. S. Eliot and Robert Penn Warren favor the "close reading" of a poem and judge it by the coherence of its own aesthetic structure.

18. **ottava rima** (ə-tä′və rē′mə): an eight-line stanza in iambic pentameter, rhyming *abababcc.* The *ottava rima* is used in Byron's "Don Juan" (1824) and in Yeats' "Sailing to Byzantium" (1928).

19. **Spenserian stanza:** a nine-line stanza or poem rhyming *ababbcbcC,* consisting of eight iambic pentameter lines followed by an Alexandrine. This stanzaic form is used in Spenser's "The Faerie Queene" (1596) and in Keats' "The Eve of St. Agnes" (1820).

20. **sprung rhythm:** a rhythm in which each foot begins with a stressed syllable followed by a varying number of unstressed syllables. *Sprung rhythm,* a term coined by Gerard Manley Hopkins, is illustrated in his line: "Look at the stars! look, look up at the skies!"

# 21
# Natural Science

*An atomic scientist once said, "Some day we'll be able to heat huge apartment buildings with one little piece of coal." His friend responded, "My landlord does that already."*

*Progress in natural science is accelerating on many fronts: atomics, communications, genetics, medicine, television, meteorology, and outer space. Unbelievable changes will yet be made during our lifetime. To keep pace, we must understand the vocabulary of science. Yet students have made astonishing errors: "Taxidermy is driving a cab"; "Humus is what makes you laugh"; "Genes are blue pants"; "A woofer is a big dog"; "Torques live in eastern Europe."*

*This chapter emphasizes thirty basic terms of natural science. Absorb those definitions. Also assimilate the supplementary list of seventy terms at the end of this chapter—they'll add muscle to your grip on science*

1. **acoustics** (ə-kōōs′tiks): the laws of sound; the sound-transmitting qualities of a room or hall.
2. **decibel** (des′ə-bel): a measure of the volume of a sound; one tenth of a bel.
3. **resonance** (rez′ə-nəns): reinforced vibration due to the vibration, at the same frequency, of another body.

decibel

■ Gene loved to turn up his boombox to a *d*_____ rating of ninety—that was before he went deaf.

resonance

■ Alice's Stradivarius violin has lovely *re*_____. Unfortunately, those who built this hall knew nothing about

acoustics

*ac*_____.

■ A *decibel* is a measure of (a) resonance, (b) sweetness, (c) loudness.
(c)                                    (     )

resonance

■ Pavaratti hit a high note and the *r*_____ shattered his favorite wine goblet.

acoustics

■ The *a*_____ of Hollywood Bowl are so splendid that a croaking frog sounds like an opera star.

4. **alchemy** (al′kə-mē): medieval chemistry which sought mainly to change lead into gold and to find the elixir of perpetual youth.
5. **fission** (fish′ən): the splitting of an atom, with release of energy.
6. **mutation** (myōō-tā′shən): variation from the parent type.

■ Splitting the nucleus of a heavy atom into nuclei of lighter atoms is

fission
(c)

called nuclear *f*_____, a process that releases (a) small fish, (b) honey, (c) atomic energy. (     )

alchemy

■ Chemistry was once known as *al*_____,

(b)

and the goal of most alchemists was to turn lead into (a) energy, (b) gold, (c) plastics. (     )

■ Suppose that among your thousand rose bushes you found one without thorns, and you were able with cuttings to produce a new,

mutation

thornless variety of rose—a true *mu*_____.

alchemy

You'd really get gold, unlike those early fumbling chemists who practiced a _____.

(c)

■ The tremendous power of a hydrogen bomb is the result of (a) dynamite, (b) fishin', (c) fission. (     )

mutation

■ Smith's dog Sheila has two tails, both of which she likes to wag, but all her puppies have one tail. Her freakish condition is, apparently, not a genuine m _____.

## Quiz

Write the letter that indicates the best definition.

1. (f)
2. (e)
3. (b)
4. (c)
5. (d)
6. (a)

(     ) 1. acoustics     a. reinforced vibration
(     ) 2. alchemy     b. a measure of loudness
(     ) 3. decibel     c. atom splitting
(     ) 4. fission     d. variation from ancestry
(     ) 5. mutation     e. medieval chemistry
(     ) 6. resonance     f. quality of sound in a hall

7. **ampere** (am′pēr): the standard unit of electric current, equal to the current sent by one volt through a resistance of one ohm.
8. **megaton** (meg′ə-tun): the explosive power of one million tons of TNT.
9. **seismic** (sīz′mik): pertaining to earthquakes.

(b)

■ Electric current is measured in (a) volts, (b) amperes, (c) megatons. (     )

(a)

■ A *megaton* is as destructive as how much TNT? (a) one million tons, (b) one thousands tons, (c) one million pounds. (     )

seismic

■ When the house began to shake, Gwen knew it was a *sei* _____ disturbance; so she ran dripping out of the bathtub and into the street.

ampere

■ Megan studies under a 100-watt lamp. The bulb takes an electric current of approximately one *a* _____.

seismic

■ Joe kidded that the *se* _____ earth movement was so great that his house now has a new zip code.

seismic

megaton

ampere

■ What a shaker! It registered _s_____ power of 6.3 on the Richter scale, far greater than a _meg_____. Benny followed his usual ritual—he stood in the doorway and screamed. Our house was left without any electric current, not a single _a_____.

___

10. **carcinogen** (kär-sin′ə-jən):  any substance that causes cancer.
11. **cardiac** (kär′dē-ak′):  referring to the heart area or to heart disease.
12. **therapy** (ther′ə-pē):  the treatment of disease.

cardiac

■ Jason had a fast heartbeat. An electrocardiogram (EKG) indicated he had no _ca_____ abnormalities. He'd merely fallen in love.

carcinogen

■ Don't smoke! Tobacco is a _c_____.

carcinogen

therapy

■ Melvin's job exposed him to lead dust, a _c_____. He developed a lung ailment for which he is receiving _th_____.

cardiac

therapy

■ Ole had a _c_____ bypass, and now takes mild exercise as _t_____.

therapy

cardiac

carcinogen

■ Medical experts are driving Sam crazy. One day they'll recommend buffalo milk as _t_____ for his _c_____ problem, and a week later they'll find that buffalo milk contains a dangerous _c_____.

___

### Quiz

Write the letter that indicates the best definition.

1. (c)
2. (a)
3. (f)
4. (e)
5. (b)
6. (d)

(    ) 1. ampere      a. cancer-causing substance
(    ) 2. carcinogen      b. relating to an earthquake
(    ) 3. cardiac      c. unit of electric current
(    ) 4. megaton      d. treatment for disease
(    ) 5. seismic      e. measure of explosiveness
(    ) 6. therapy      f. pertaining to the heart

13. **catalyst** (kat′ə-list): a substance that speeds up a chemical reaction but itself undergoes practically no change.
14. **osmosis** (oz-mō′sis): the passing of a fluid through a membrane to equalize pressures.
15. **viscera** (vis′ər-ə): the internal organs such as the intestines and liver.

■ Water molecules will pass through a membrane toward a sugar or mineral solution. This process, called *os*＿＿＿＿＿＿＿＿＿＿, is vital to plants and animals.

osmosis

■ The *viscera* include (a) the throat, (b) the kneecaps, (c) the intestines. (    )

(c)

■ Platinum particles serve as a *cat*＿＿＿＿＿＿＿＿＿ to speed the production of sulphuric acid. Like other *catalytic* agents the platinum (a) disappears, (b) is unchanged, (c) turns to sodium ash. (    )

catalyst

(b)

■ Roots of plants absorb water by the process of *os*＿＿＿＿＿.

osmosis

■ Jack the Ripper slashed viciously across the abdomen, exposing his victim's *vi*＿＿＿＿＿＿＿＿＿＿.

viscera

■ The alumni reunions was dull and listless until peppy Pattie arrived. What a social *ca*＿＿＿＿＿＿＿＿＿!

catalyst

■ Dissolved food materials pass by *o*＿＿＿＿＿ through the walls of the *v*＿＿＿＿＿ and are absorbed into the bloodstream.

osmosis
viscera

---

16. **centrifugal force** (sen-trif′yə-gəl): the force tending to push a thing *outward* from the center of rotation. (Opposed to *centripetal force* which tends to draw a thing *inward* toward the center of rotation.)
17. **inertia** (in-ûr′shə): the tendency of matter to remain at rest or to move at uniform velocity in a straight line unless acted upon by an external force.
18. **torque** (tôrk): a force tending to produce rotation.

■ The boulder resting in the park tends to stay at rest because of its *in*＿＿＿＿＿＿＿＿＿.

inertia

■ Whirl a rock on a string above your head and the rock tends to break away from you because of (a) centrifugal force, (b) centripetal force, (c) torque. (     )

■ When you use a screwdriver to rotate the head of a screw, you are applying *t*_____.

■ Unless acted on by other forces, a satellite in outer space tends to move at constant speed in a straight line. This property of matter is called *i*_____.

■ At the county fair you ride a speedy Loop-the-Loop in which you briefly ride upside down. Luckily, you are held up safely at the ceiling against gravity by an outward thrust known as (a) inertia, (b) centripetal force, (c) centrifugal force. (     )

■ The merry-go-round is kept rotating by a force known as (a) a troika, (b) a truck, (c) a torque. (     )

---

## Quiz

Write the letter that indicates the best definition.

(     ) 1. catalyst      a. outward push
(     ) 2. centrifugal force      b. seeping through membranes
(     ) 3. inertia      c. rotation producer
(     ) 4. osmosis      d. intestines
(     ) 5. torque      e. resistance to change
(     ) 6. viscera      f. chemical reaction spur

---

19. **congenital** (kən-jen′ə-təl): existing from birth.
20. **gene** (jēn): an element in the chromosomes that transmit hereditary characteristics.
21. **viable** (vī′ə-bəl): physically fitted to live, said of a fetus or a seed.

■ Dr. Shlepp says Mia's five-month fetus is *v*_____. The poet Byron was born lame—his was a *con*_____ deformity.

■ My big ears, like the ears of an alert jackass, are due to a

*g*_____ from my big-eared daddy, his only gift to me.

■ Our school principal must think I was born stupid, because he called me a c _____ idiot.

■ Bob's height, his hazel eyes, his ski-slope nose—each trait was determined by some g _____ from his parents.

■ We planted the seeds of corn that we found in the ancient Egyptian tomb, but they were no longer vi _____ .

■ Color blindness is a c _____ condition which is hereditary in families with a defective g _____ .

---

22. **humus** (hū′məs): organic matter in soils, produced by decay of vegetable and animal stuff.
23. **hybrid** (hī′brid): the offspring of two plants or animals of different varieties.
24. **maturation** (mach′ə-rā′shən): attainment of maturity; completion of growth.

■ The mule is a hy _____ animal, the offspring of a mare and a jackass.

■ Lucy uses a compost pile of decayed grass and food wastes, called hu _____ , to enrich her garden soil.

■ These oranges are green, and Junior shouldn't have picked them until they reached ma _____ . Junior's brains haven't reached m _____ either.

■ If you cross-pollinate tall and short garden peas, the first generation of the h _____ peas will be tall, according to Gregor Mendel's laws of heredity.

■ Your cabbages will achieve m _____ more quickly if you apply organic _____ to the soil.

■ Greater vigor usually results from the crossing of varieties, as is true of h _____ corn and h _____ barley.

---

## Quiz

Write the letter that indicates the best definition.

1. (c)
2. (e)
3. (b)
4. (f)
5. (a)
6. (d)

(    ) 1. congenital     a. full growth
(    ) 2. gene     b. organic soil
(    ) 3. humus     c. existing at birth
(    ) 4. hybrid     d. able to survive
(    ) 5. maturation     e. transmitter of traits
(    ) 6. viable     f. product of cross-breeding

---

**25. solar** (sō'lər): pertaining to the sun.

**26. solstice** (sol'stis): the time when the sun is furthest from the equator, at about June 21 and December 22.

**27. zenith** (zē'nith): the point in the sky directly over an observer: opposed to *nadir* (nādər), the lowest possible point.

solar

■ The earth is part of the *s*_____ system.

(c)

■ *Zenith* is located (a) on the horizon, (b) below you, (c) above you. (    )

(a)

■ Our summer *solstice* occurs at about (a) June 21, (b) March 21, (c) September 22. (    ), at which time the sun with respect to the equator will be (a) overhead, (b) furthest north, (c) furthest south. (    )

(b)

solar

■ A _____ eclipse is an eclipse of the sun.

(a)

■ Freddie was born at the time of our winter *solstice*. His birthday occurs in (a) December, (b) June, (c) September. (    )

zenith

■ In the tropics, only mad dogs and Englishmen are outside at noon while the sun is at its *z*_____.

---

**28. supersonic:** greater than the speed of sound; faster than 738 miles per hour.

**29. trajectory** (trə-jek'tə-rē): the path described by something hurtling through space, especially the path of a projectile.

**30. troposphere** (trop'ə-sfēr'): the atmospheric zone next to the earth that contains clouds and winds, below the stratosphere.

troposphere
supersonic

■ The blazing comet, descending from the stratosphere and dipping into our *tr*_____, was traveling with *su*_____ velocity.

■ Longfellow shot an arrow into the air and it fell to earth he knew not where, because he didn't keep an eye on its *tr*_____.

trajectory

trajectory
supersonic

■ Our military enemy misjudged the *tr*_____ of their rocket, so that it hurtled with almost *s*_____ speed into our donkey.

(a)

■ Clouds and rain occur in the (a) troposphere, (b) bathysphere, (c) stratosphere. (     )

(b)

■ When your pilot says, "We've just reached supersonic speed," you are moving at about (a) 350 mph, (b) 750 mph, (c) 7500 mph. (     )

## Quiz

Write the letter that indicates the best definition.

1. (d)
2. (f)
3. (a)
4. (c)
5. (e)
6. (b)

(     ) 1. solar
(     ) 2. solstice
(     ) 3. supersonic
(     ) 4. trajectory
(     ) 5. troposphere
(     ) 6. zenith

a. faster than sound
b. the highest point
c. path of a missile
d. pertaining to the sun
e. zone of air and clouds
f. beginning of summer or winter

**REVIEW TEST**

Write the word studied in this chapter that will complete the sentence.

1. The unit of electrical current—don't be shocked!—is the *a* _____.

2. The unit of volume of sound—you hear me!—is the *de* _____.

3. The explosive power of a million tons of TNT equals—barroom!—a *me* _____.

4. This zone of clouds and wind in which we breathe the smog—sniff, sniff!—is the *tr* _____.

5. A jet plane that flies faster than sound has—whee!—*su* _____ speed.

6. Heart stoppage—farewell!—is *ca* _____ arrest.

7. A seventh-month fetus is—wah!—*vi* _____.

8. At noon the summer sun is—phew!—at its *ze* _____.

9. A convulsive earth movement is—rumble, rumble!—a *s* _____ disturbance.

10. Early chemistry sought mainly to transmute metals—aha, gold!—and was known as *al* _____.

11. June 22 was the date of our summer *so* _____.

12. The mating of a male lion and a female tiger produces a *hy* _____ animal called a liger.

13. Bananas are picked green but they turn yellow when they reach *ma* _____.

14. A grindstone, to keep rotating, requires a force called *t* _____.

15. My piano teacher was born with six fingers on her left hand—a *con* _____ condition. But what great bass chords!

Write *True* or *False*.

_____ 16. A *carcinogen* is a *therapy* to prevent cancer.

_____ 17. A *catalyst* is a feline disease.

_____ 18. The *trajectory* is the path of a missile.

_____ 19. *Osmosis* often occurs in the *viscera*.

_____ 20. *Centrifugal force* pushes outward from the center of rotation.

Write the letter that indicates the best definition.

(    ) 21. acoustics      a. unit of heredity
(    ) 22. fission        b. comic talk
(    ) 23. gene          c. qualities of sound
(    ) 24. humus        d. relating to the sun
(    ) 25. solar         e. catching trout
                                  f. organic matter in soil
                                  g. splitting atoms

## Key to Review Test

Check your test answers with the following key. Deduct 4% per error from a possible 100%.

| | | |
|---|---|---|
| 1. ampere | 10. alchemy | 19. True |
| 2. decibel | 11. solstice | 20. True |
| 3. megaton | 12. hybrid | 21. c |
| 4. troposphere | 13. maturation | 22. g |
| 5. supersonic | 14. torque | 23. a |
| 6. cardiac | 15. congenital | 24. f |
| 7. viable | 16. False | 25. d |
| 8. zenith | 17. False | |
| 9. seismic | 18. True | |

Score: _____ %

# SUPPLEMENTARY LIST

1. **absolute zero:** the lowest possible temperature, theoretically—273.18 degrees C., at which molecular motion ceases.
2. **acceleration:** the increased rate of change in velocity.
3. **adaptation** (ad'əp-tā'shən): a change in structure or function by which an organism adjusts better to its environment.
4. **aerodynamics** (âr'ō-dī-nam'iks): the branch of physics that studies gases in motion, including their mechanical effects and other properties.
5. **aneroid barometer** (an'ə-roid'): an instrument which measures atmospheric pressure by its effect on the flexible top of a metal box containing a partial vacuum.
6. **anticyclone:** a high pressure area in which the spiral currents flow clockwise in the northern hemisphere.
7. **asexual** (ā-sek'shoo-əl): without sex; reproducing itself without sexual union.
8. **ballistics** (bə-lis'tiks): the science dealing with the flight behavior and impact of projectiles.
9. **Bessemer process** (bes'ə-mər): making steel by forcing a blast of air through molten pig iron to remove impurities.
10. **Bohr theory** (bōr): the theory of Niels Bohr that electrons absorb or radiate energy when changing orbits.
11. **Brownian movement:** the zigzag movement of microscopic particles suspended in fluids, caused by collisions with molecules.
12. **centripetal force** (sen-trip'ə-təl): the force tending to draw a thing inward toward the center of rotation.
13. **cretinism** (krē'tən-iz'əm): idiocy and deformity resulting from a congenital thyroid deficiency.
14. **cybernetics** (sī-bər-net'iks): a comparative study of computers and the human nervous system to help explain brain processes.
15. **cyclotron** (sī'klə-tron'): an apparatus that gives high velocity and energy to protons and deuterons so they can smash nuclear targets.
16. **dominant:** *genetics.* designating a hereditary character which prevails over and masks a *recessive* character.
17. **electrolysis** (i-lek'trol'ə-sis): the decomposition of a chemical solution by means of an electric current.
18. **electrostatics:** a branch of physics that deals with electricity at rest known as static electricity.
19. **foot-pound:** a unit of work, enough to raise a one-pound mass a distance of one foot.
20. **fulcrum** (ful'krəm): the support on which a lever turns.
21. **galvanic** (gal-van'ik): of electricity from a battery; convulsive; startling.
22. **generic** (jə-ner'ik): pertaining to a genus or class; having a broad general application.
23. **geocentric** (jē'ō-sen'trik): regarding the earth as center of the universe.
24. **geophysics** (jē'ō-fiz'iks): the physics of the earth, dealing with tides, winds, earthquakes, magnetic fields, etc.
25. **gynecology** (gī'nə-kol'ə-jē): the branch of medicine dealing with women's diseases.
26. **gyroscope** (jī'rə-skōp'): a rotating device, used to stabilize ships and planes.
27. **hermetic** (hûr-met'ik): airtight; completely sealed to keep air and liquids from getting in or out.

28. **histology** (hi-stol′ə-jē): the microscopic study of tissue structure.
29. **horticulture:** the cultivation or garden plants.
30. **hydraulic:** using water or other liquid: as, a *hydraulic* brake.
31. **hygrometer** (hī-grom′ə-tər): an instrument for measuring humidity.
32. **immunology:** the branch of medicine which deals with immunity to disease.
33. **isobar** (ī′sə-bär′): a line on a weather map connecting points having the same barometric pressure.
34. **isotope** (ī′sə-tōp′): any of two or more forms of a chemical element, each with its individual mass number and radioactive behavior.
35. **kinetic energy** (ki-net′ik): energy resulting from the motion of a body: opposed to *potential* energy.
36. **Lamarckism** (lə-mär′kiz-əm): Lamarck's evolutionary theory that acquired characteristics can be inherited.
37. **malleable** (mal′ē-ə-bəl): pliable; capable of being hammered and shaped without breaking: said of metals.
38. **materia medica** (mə-tēr′ē-ə med′ə-kə): drugs and other remedial substances.
39. **Mendelism** (men′də-liz′əm): Gregor Mendel's principles of heredity, which predict characteristics of the offspring in cross-breading.
40. **metabolism** (mə-tab′ə-liz′əm): the sum of physical and chemical processes which supply energy to the body.
41. **metallurgy** (met′ə-lûr′jē): the science of separating metals from ores and refining them for use.
42. **natural selection:** the adaptation of a species to its environment through survival of the fittest.
43. **oscillation** (os′ə-lā′shən): the fluctuation between maximum and minimum values, as of an alternating current.
44. **periodic table:** an arrangement of chemical elements by atomic number to exhibit groups and families.
45. **pituitary** (pi-tōō′ə-ter′ē): a gland at the base of the brain that secretes hormones affecting growth and metabolism.
46. **qualitative analysis:** the determining of the ingredients in a substance.
47. **quantum theory** (kwon′təm): the theory that radiant energy is not smooth flowing but discontinuous, and emitted in definite units called *quanta*.
48. **rectifier:** any device, such as a vacuum tube, which converts alternating current into direct current.
49. **serology** (si-rol′ə-jē): the science of serums.
50. **sextant** (seks′tənt): a navigational instrument used in determining latitude at sea.
51. **simian** (sim′ē-ən): pertaining to monkeys or anthropoid apes.
52. **spectrum:** a band of colors observed when a beam of white light passes through a prism.
53. **speleology** (spē′lē-ol′ə-jē): the science of exploring caves; spelunking.
54. **spirochete** (spī′rə-kēt′): any of a genus of spiral-shaped bacteria some of which cause syphilis, trench mouth, and yaws.
55. **spontaneous generation:** the discredited theory that living organisms can originate in nonliving matter.
56. **stalactite** (stə-lak′tīt): an icicle-shaped rocky deposit hanging from the roof of a cave: distinguished from a *stalagmite,* which projects upward from the floor of a cave.

57. **taxidermy** (tak′sə-dûr′mē): the art of stuffing animals.
58. **tetanus** (tet′ə-nəs): an infectious, often fatal disease, marked by muscle spasms and lockjaw.
59. **thrombosis** (throm-bō′sis): a clotting of blood, forming an obstruction to circulation.
60. **topography** (tə-pog′rə-fē): mapping the surface features of a region.
61. **toxemia** (tok-sē′mē-ə): blood poisoning.
62. **toxicology** (tok′sə-kol′ə-jē): the science of poisons.
63. **Ursa Major** (ur′sə mā′jər): the constellation of the seven stars that form the Big Dipper; literally, the *Great Bear.*
64. **valence** (vā′ləns): the combining capacity of an atom or radical compared with that of a hydrogen atom.
65. **vector** (vek′tər): a quantity, such as force or velocity, that has both magnitude and direction.
66. **ventral** (ven′trəl): pertaining to the belly; abdominal: opposed to *dorsal,* pertaining to the back.
67. **ventricle** (ven′tri-kəl): one of the two lower chambers of the heart.
68. **vernier** (vûr′nē-ər): an auxiliary device which makes possible a more precise setting of a measuring instrument or a tool.
69. **vivisection** (viv′i-sek′shən): cutting into a living animal body in the interests of experimental research.
70. **watershed:** a ridge of high land separating two river drainage basins.

# 22

# Fine Arts and Philosophy

*An alcoholic decided to give up drink. When he came home sober, his dog didn't recognize him and bit him. Master this chapter with its challenging supplementary lists and you'll be so smart and changed—well, look out for Rover.*

*Writing the answers is vital, of course, but it is only part of the job: You must also engrave those concepts into your memory. One student always inked answers on his arms and legs before attending class, and his skin graduated six months before he did.*

*Space being limited, the definitions in this chapter are also limited. If a concept puzzles or fascinates you, be sure to research the word in an encyclopedia or a computer database. Such inquisitiveness is self-rewarding and also will make your instructor very happy.*

---

### FINE ARTS

*andante,* **1**

*aria,* **2**

*calligraphy,* **4**

*ceramics,* **7**

*choreography,* **5**

*collage,* **10**

*monolith,* **8**

*mural,* **11**

*statuary,* **9**

*surrealism,* **12**

*tapestry,* **6**

*tempo,* **3**

---

*President Ulysses S. Grant said, "I only know two tunes. One of them is 'Yankee Doodle' and the other one isn't." Grant had rare talent as a war general but his mastery of music was not extensive. The well-rounded college student ought to feel at home in the concert hall and the art gallery.*

COVER THIS STRIP

1. **andante** (än-dän′tā): a moderately slow movement in music.
2. **aria** (ä′rē-ə): a melody for solo voices, as in an opera or oratorio, usually with instrumental accompaniment.
3. **tempo:** the rate of speed of a musical passage.

(b)

■ An operatic solo is know as an (a) area, (b) aria, (b) urea. (     )

(a)

■ When the director says, "Let's pick up the *tempo*," he wants you to (a) play faster, (b) play slower, (c) remove wastepaper. (     )

tempo

■ After the presto movement, and in slower t_____,

andante

came the melodious *an*_____ .

aria

■ Pavarotti ended his *a*_____ with a blast that almost cracked a window in the opera house.

tempo
(c)

■ Mozart's "Eine Kleine Nachtmusik" includes a tender melody played at a leisurely *t*_____ and labeled (a) anchovy, (b) antidote, (c) andante. (     )

aria

■ I tried to sing the operatic *a*_____ by Handel, but I couldn't handle Handel.

4. **calligraphy** (kə-lig′rə-fē′): the art of beautiful handwriting; fancy penmanship.
5. **choreography** (kōr′ē-og′rə-fē): the arranging of ballets and other stage dances.
6. **tapestry** (tap′əs-trē): a wall-hanging textile with a decorative design.

■ I penned my love note twenty times with exquisite care before I

calligraphy

was satisfied with the *ca*_____ .

■ *Choreography* deals with the art of (a) handwriting, (b) dancing, (c) chorus. (     )

(b)

■ "What's that rug doing on the wall?" I asked, and the museum

tapestry

guide sneered, "That's a *ta*_____ ."

(c)

■ To learn elegant penmanship, take a course in (a) tapestry, (b) choreography, (c) calligraphy. (    )

(c)

■ A *tapestry* is usually distinguished by its (a) poetry, (b) tap dances, (c) pictorial design. (    )

(b)

■ *Calligraphy* is to *choreography* as handwriting is to (a) singing, (b) dancing, (c) painting. (    )

## Quiz

Write the letter that indicates the best definition.

1. (c)
2. (f)
3. (d)
4. (a)
5. (e)
6. (b)

(    ) 1. andante          a. elegant handwriting
(    ) 2. aria             b. a decorative wall hanging
(    ) 3. tempo            c. a fairly slow musical passage
(    ) 4. calligraphy      d. the rapidity of music
(    ) 5. choreography     e. planning of stage dances
(    ) 6. tapestry         f. a solo in opera

7. **ceramics** (sə-ram′iks): the art of making pottery, earthenware, and tile.
8. **monolith** (män′ə-lith′): a single large block of stone as used in architecture; an obelisk or memorial column.
9. **statuary** (stach′o͞o-er′ē): a collection of statues.

(a)

■ A *monolith* is a huge vertical shaft made of (a) one stone, (b) two stones, (c) several stones. (    )

(c)

■ In *ceramics* class you would probably make (a) watches, (b) dresses, (c) vases. (    )

(b)

■ *Statuary* refers to a group of (a) paintings, (b) statues, (c) legal regulations. (    )

monolith

■ The burial site of an ancient Pharaoh was often memorialized by a colossal granite *m*_____.

ceramics

statuary

■ An artist creates paintings; a potter creates *c*_____;
a sculptor creates *st*_____.

10. **collage** (ko-lazh'): an art composition in which bits of objects such as cloth, newspaper, and flowers are pasted onto a surface for their symbolic effect.

11. **mural** (myoor'əl): a painting done on a wall.

12. **surrealism:** the depiction of irrational, incongruous workings of the subconscious mind, especially as manifested in dreams.

surrealism

■ Salvador Dali's dreamlike drawing with its limp, melting watch is pure fantasy, an example of *su*_____.

(a)

■ A *mural* is painted on (a) a wall, (b) a small canvas, (c) a statue. (    )

collage

■ An artist pasted news captions, ribbons, and coins to her canvas, creating a *co*_____.

(b)
(c)

■ Marc Chagall's painting of "Fiddler on the Roof" is (a) realistic, (b) dreamlike. (     ). It is therefore classified as (a) a mural, (b) a collage, (c) surrealism. (     )

mural

collage

■ On one wall of artist Jose's garret was a large *mu*_____ depicting dying soldiers. Jose was now busy gluing war ribbons, bullets, and bits of flag to a drawing to create a *c*_____.

(c)

■ *Surrealism* has permeated motion pictures, poetry, sculpture, and other arts. The productions tend to be (a) true to life, (b) frightening, (c) dreamlike. (     )

---

## Quiz

Write the letter that indicates the best definition.

1. (b)
2. (e)
3. (a)
4. (f)
5. (d)
6. (c)

(    ) 1. ceramics     a. a collection of statues
(    ) 2. monolith     b. the pottery-making craft
(    ) 3. statuary     c. dreamlike art
(    ) 4. collage     d. a wall painting
(    ) 5. mural     e. a tall memorial stone
(    ) 6. surrealism     f. bits glued to a drawing

---

*Socrates discussed philosophy freely, and for that he was forced to take poison. You might wisecrack that you'd rather take poison than study philosophy, but that would be an uninformed attitude. You've been absorbing philosophy all your life, only you haven't been using the fancy words—like* apologetics, a priori, pragmatism—*to express your philosophic thoughts.*

13. **agnosticism** (ag-nos'ti-siz'əm): the doctrine that one cannot know about God or the hereafter, or of anything but material phenomena.

14. **deism** (dē'iz-əm): a belief in God based on reason but rejecting biblical revelation.

15. **fatalism** (fāt'əl-iz'əm): the belief that all events are predetermined and inevitable.

■ God definitely exists, according to followers of (a) agnosticism, (b) deism, (c) materialism. (    )

(b)

■ To believe that your life is predestined to have a certain outcome and that nothing can change it is *fa* _____ .

fatalism

■ The Bible proves the existence and omnipotent power of God, according to (a) deism, (b) Judeo-Christianity, (c) agnosticism. (    )

(b)

■ Unlike atheism, which says, "God does not exist," *ag* _____ maintains, "God may or may not exist—we have no way of knowing."

agnosticism

■ Benjamin Franklin and Thomas Jefferson were *deists.* Their belief in God was based on (a) the Bible, (b) miracles, (c) reason. (    )

(c)

■ Mr. Dingbat refuses to see a doctor, saying, "If I'm going to die I'm going to die." His questionable attitude is one of

*fa* _____ .

fatalism

16. **amoral** (ā-môr′əl): neither moral nor immoral; having no connection with morality.
17. **categorical imperative** (kat′ə-gôr′i-kəl): the doctrine of Immanuel Kant that one must do only what one would want others to do in the same situation.
18. **ethics:** a code of morals of a person or group.

amoral

■ Elmer decided to order toast. His decision was neither moral nor immoral but a_____.

categorical imperative

■ Very similar to the Golden Rule (Matt. 7:12) is Kant's so-called cat_____ im_____.

ethics

■ The psychiatrist won't reveal Lulu's intimate confessions to anybody else. He's bound by professional eth_____.

categorical imperative

■ Dying of thirst, Sir Philip Sidney gives a flask of water to a comrade, saying, "Thy need is greater than mine." Sidney lived and died by the ca_____ im_____.

ethics

■ Our country treasurer accepted sixty bribes. He didn't have a very lofty standard of e_____.

ethics

categorical imperative

■ Gang members who scream for vengeance and "an eye for an eye" have their own degraded code of e_____, one not at all in tune with Kant's ca_____ i_____.

amoral

■ Some religious sects regard dancing as immoral; though most shrug it off as a_____.

---

**Quiz**

Write the letter that indicates the best definition.

1. (d)
2. (f)
3. (e)
4. (b)
5. (a)
6. (c)

(   ) 1. agnosticism     a. standards of conduct
(   ) 2. deism     b. unrelated to morality
(   ) 3. fatalism     c. Kant's rule of morality
(   ) 4. amoral     d. uncertainty about God
(   ) 5. ethics     e. belief in inevitability
(   ) 6. categorical imperative     f. belief in a nonbiblical God

19. **a posteriori** (ā′ pos-tir′ē-ôr′ī): reasoning from particular instances to principles or from effect to cause; inductive; empirical; opposed to *a priori*.

20. **a priori** (ā′ prī-ô′rī): reasoning from general principle to particular instances or from cause to effect; deductive; based on theory rather than experiment.

21. **syllogism** (sil′ə-jiz′əm): a formula for deductive reasoning, consisting of a major premise, a minor premise, and a conclusion.

■ "*Major premise:* All men die; *minor premise:* Grandpa is a man; *conclusion:* Grandpa will die." Such a three-part formula is a

syllogism
(b)

sy_____. The deductive reasoning here is (a) a posteriori, (b) a priori. (    )

(a)

■ The ancients usually began with a major premise and reasoned *down* from that in a process of (a) deduction, (b) induction. (    )

syllogism

They produced a *sy*_____ involving *a*

priori

*p*_____ reasoning.

■ Modern scientists repeat experiments, and from particular instances reach a generalization—an inductive process known as *a*

posteriori

*p*_____ .

(c)

■ *A posteriori* reasoning is (a) deductive, (b) seductive, (c) inductive. (    )

(a)

■ On three different occasions Elmer ate chocolates and each time broke out with pimples. Elmer concluded that chocolate gave him pimples. Such inductive reasoning, whether accurate or not, is (a) a posteriori, (b) a priori, (c) a la mode. (    )

_____

22. **hedonism** (hē′dən-iz′əm): the doctrine that we should pursue physical pleasure every moment without taking heed of consequences.

23. **paradox** (par′ə-doks′): a situation that seems to have contradictory or inconsistent qualities.

24. **pragmatism** (prag′mə-tiz′əm): the doctrine that ideas have value only in terms of their practical results.

hedonism

■ The supreme aim of life is pleasure, according to *hed*_____. Unfortunately, those who pursue only pleasure—and this is the

paradox

*pa*_____—are least likely to find it.

pragmatism

■ The City Council decides to convert our beloved old memorial park into a mall which will provide more jobs and taxes. Theirs is an act of *pr*_____.

paradox

■ Sweden adopted socialism to help its people, yet the suicide rate shot up. What a *pa*_____!

pragmatism

■ Nation X, sensing future danger, demolishes the atomic bomb factory of Nation Z. Nation X has ignored peace pacts and international law, taking a course of *p*_____.

paradox

■ The shoemaker's children go barefoot—a *pa*_____.

hedonism

■ The Roman emperor ate grapes and eyed the dancing girls from his couch. His was a life of *h*_____.

---

## Quiz

Write the letter that indicates the best definition.

1. (b)
2. (e)
3. (f)
4. (a)
5. (d)
6. (c)

(     ) 1. a posteriori     a. pursuit of pleasure
(     ) 2. a priori     b. inductive
(     ) 3. syllogism     c. choosing what works
(     ) 4. hedonism     d. a seeming contradiction
(     ) 5. paradox     e. deductive
(     ) 6. pragmatism     f. premises and a conclusion

---

## REVIEW TEST

Write the word studied in this chapter that is defined at the left.

| DEFINITION | WORD |
|---|---|
| 1. the pottery-making art | *ce* _____ |
| 2. solo in opera | *a* _____ |
| 3. group of statues | *st* _____ |
| 4. fancy handwriting | *ca* _____ |
| 5. tall single-stone memorial shaft | *mo* _____ |
| 6. a painting on a wall | *m* _____ |
| 7. irrational, dreamlike art | *su* _____ |
| 8. ballet arrangements | *ch* _____ |
| 9. moral standards | *et* _____ |
| 10. belief that events are inevitable | *fa* _____ |
| 11. belief in God based on reason | *de* _____ |
| 12. unrelated to morality | *am* _____ |
| 13. two premises and a conclusion | *sy* _____ |
| 14. pursuit only of pleasure | *he* _____ |
| 15. an apparent self-contradiction | *par* _____ |

Write *True* or *False*.

_____ 16. A *collage* is a small university.

_____ 17. *A priori* refers to deductive reasoning.

_____ 18. *Agnosticism* denies the existence of God.

_____ 19. *Andante* is played at rapid *tempo*.

_____ 20. Kant's *categorical imperative* relates to ethics.

**Fine Arts and Philosophy    329**

## Key to Review Test

Check your test answers by the following key. Deduct 5% per error from a possible 100%.

| | | |
|---|---|---|
| 1. ceramics | 8. choreography | 15. paradox |
| 2. aria | 9. ethics | 16. False |
| 3. statuary | 10. fatalism | 17. True |
| 4. calligraphy | 11. deism | 18. False |
| 5. monolith | 12. amoral | 19. False |
| 6. mural | 13. syllogism | 20. True |
| 7. surrealism | 14. hedonism | |

Score: _____ %

## Fine Arts

1. **a cappella** (ä'kə-pel'ə): sung without instrumental accompaniment.
2. **aesthetics** (es-thet'iks): the study of beauty, especially as found in the fine arts.
3. **allegro** (ə-lā'grō): lively; faster than *allegretto* but not so fast as *presto*.
4. **atonality** (ā'tō-nal'i-tē): *music.* a lack of key or tonal center; a condition wherein no one tone holds a primary position.
5. **baroque** (bə-rōk'): involving fantastic ornamentation and theatrical effects, as in seventeenth-century art, architecture, and music.
6. **bas-relief** (bä'ri-lēf'): sculpture in which the figures project only slightly from the background.
7. **cadenza** (kə-den'zə): a showy musical passage, often improvised, by an unaccompanied instrument in a concerto.
8. **cantata** (kən-tä'tə): a composition involving arias, choruses, and recitatives, to be sung but not acted.
9. **chamber music:** music suitable for a small hall, as by an instrumental trio or quartet.
10. **coloratura** (kul'ə-rə-tyoor'ə): brilliant runs, trills, etc., to show off a singer's talents.
11. **cubism** (kū'biz-əm): art which uses cubes, cones, and other abstract geometric forms instead of representing nature realistically.
12. **dynamics:** *music.* the various degrees of softness and loudness in performance.
13. **étude** (ā'tood): a technical study for solo instrument.
14. **finesse** (fi-nes'): refined skill; adroitness in handling a delicate situation.
15. **forte** (fôr'tā): *music.* loud.
16. **fresco:** the art of painting on wet plaster.
17. **Hellenic** (he-len'ik): Grecian; pertaining to the ancient Greeks.
18. **impresario** (im-pri-sär'ē-ō): the organizer or manager of an opera company or of concert artists.
19. **intaglio** (in-tal'yō): a design carved below the surface, as on a gem: opposed to *cameo,* a design that stands out in relief.
20. **lapidary** (lap'i-der'ē): pertaining to cutting and engraving precious stones.
21. **little theater:** amateur or community theater; experimental or avant-garde drama playing to a limited audience.
22. **lyric** (lir'ik): a songlike outpouring of emotions and sentiment, as in sonnets, odes, elegies, and hymns.
23. **nocturne** (nok'tûrn): a dreamy, romantic musical composition appropriate to night.
24. **oratorio** (or'ə-tōr'ē-ō'): an extended composition for voice and orchestra, usually on a religious theme, without acting or scenery.
25. **overture** (ō'vər-chər): the orchestral introduction to an opera or other large work.
26. **percussion instrument** (pər-kush'ən): an instrument which produces its tone when a part is struck; for example, drums, triangles, piano.
27. **perspective:** the drawing of objects, exhibiting distance and depth.
28. **Stradivarius** (strad'ə-var'ē-əs): a violin or other stringed instrument made by the Stradivari family.

29. **string quartet:** a music group usually playing first and second violin, viola, and cello; a composition for such a group.
30. **symmetry** (sim′ə-trē): a balanced arrangement of parts.


## Philosophy

1. **animism** (an′ə-miz′əm): the belief that inanimate objects and natural phenomena, such as stones, sun, and rain, are alive and have souls.
2. **apologetics** (ə-pol′ə-jet′iks): the branch of theology which deals with the defense and proofs of Christianity.
3. **Berkeleianism** (burk-lē′ən-iz′əm): the philosophy of George Berkeley, maintaining that ideas are real and that material objects do not exist.
4. **determinism:** the doctrine that every action is the inevitable result of a sequence of causes.
5. **dialectics** (dī′ə-lek′tiks): the practice of examining ideas logically, usually by the method of question and answer.
6. **eclectic** (i-klek′tik): selecting what is considered best from various sources; not following any one system but choosing from all.
7. **empirical** (em-pir′i-kəl): depending on practical experience alone, not on theoretical reasoning: as, an *empirical* discovery.
8. **epistemology** (i-pis′tə-mol′ə-jē): the branch of philosophy that investigates the nature, limits, and validity of human knowledge.
9. **free will:** the doctrine that people have the power to choose between alternative courses of action: opposed to *determinism.*
10. **materialism:** the doctrine that physical matter is the only reality; also, a concern for worldly goods rather than spiritual goals.
11. **monism** (mon′iz-əm): the doctrine that there is only one kind of ultimate substance.
12. **nirvana** (nir-van′ə): In *Buddhism,* the blessedness achieved by absorption of the soul into the supreme spirit.
13. **ontology** (on-tol′ə-jē): the study of the nature of reality or being.
14. **oversoul:** the universal spiritual element which unites all human souls, according to Emersonian transcendentalism.
15. **positivism:** the system of Auguste Comte based on positive facts of sense experience and rejecting speculation.
16. **relativism:** the theory that truths are relative and that the basis of judgment varies according to persons, events, etc.
17. **subjectivism** (səb-jek′tə-viz′əm): the theory that all knowledge is subjective and relative, a reflection of one's own consciousness.
18. **Thomism** (tō′miz-əm): the dogmatic theology of Saint Thomas Aquinas, which became the basis of thirteenth-century scholasticism.
19. **utilitarianism:** the doctrine that ideas and things ought to be judged strictly by their usefulness rather than by beauty, tradition, etc., and that conduct should promote the greatest happiness for the greatest number.
20. **volition** (vō-lish′ən): the act of willing; a decision of the will.

# 23
# Foreign Expressions

1. *a cappella*
2. *ad nauseum*
3. *aficionado*
4. *à la carte*
5. *avant-garde*
6. *bête noir*
7. *c'est la vie*
8. *con amore*
9. *déjà vu*
10. *faux pas*
11. *hoi polloi*
12. *Homo sapiens*
13. *laissez faire*
14. *magnum opus*
15. *par excellence*
16. *persona non grata*
17. *potpourri*
18. *savoir-faire*
19. *sine qua non*
20. *status quo*
21. *sub rosa*
22. *tour de force*
23. *tout de suite*
24. *vox populi*
25. *Wunderkind*

*English has become a* smörgäsbord *(Swedish: "a buffet of assorted foods") of terms taken from at least fifty languages.*

*Many imported words have been used so much that they are now completely absorbed into the English language. Here are a few examples:*

American Indian: moccasin, moose
Arabic: algebra, magazine
Chinese: tea, typhoon
Dutch: cole slaw, sleigh
French: buffet, chauffeur
German: kindergarten, waltz
Greek: acrobat, alphabet

Hebrew: amen, kosher
Irish: slogan, whiskey
Italian: ballot, piano
Latin: cereal, report
Persian: pajamas, sugar
Russian: samovar, vodka
Spanish: alligator, cigar

*A second group of foreign expressions are often used but are not yet generally regarded as adopted. Such terms are written in italics until our language assimilates them. Meanwhile the status and popular pronunciation of these words keep changing. When in doubt, consult a good dictionary for current practice as to how best to pronounce a foreign expression and whether to italicize it.*

*Abbreviations used in this chapter include* Fr. *(French),* G. *(German),* Gk. *(Greek),* It. *(Italian),* L. *(Latin),* Sp. *(Spanish).*

*Master the twenty-five foreign expressions that are programed in this chapter. Then warm your acquaintanceship with the forty terms in the supplementary list.*

1. **a cappella** (ä′kə-pel′ə): *It.* singing without instrumental accompaniment. "The church choir sang *a cappella*."
2. **ad nauseum** (ad′nô′zē-əm): *L.* to a disgusting degree. "One tourist complained about food and plumbing and prices *ad nauseum*."

■ The chorus will now sing *a cappella,* so the orchestra will be (a) silent, (b) sawing away. (    )

(a)

■ My pianist was in jail that evening. Consequently, I sang my solo *a cap*_____.

*a cappella*

■ Our football captain kept referring *ad nauseum* to his own heroic achievements. He should probably have been more (a) modest, (b) detailed. (    )

(a)

■ The biology assistant, who hated snakes, had to handle them day after day *a*_____ *na*_____.

*ad nauseum*

■ When the sergeant took a shower, he sang *a ca*_____; and, ignorant of sharps and flats, he bellowed "Sorrento" tunelessly and endlessly *a*_____ *n*_____.

*a cappella*

*ad nauseum*

3. **aficionado** (ə-fish′yə-nä′də): *Sp.* a devoted follower of some sport or art. "Jose was an *aficionado* of bullfighting until he got trampled."
4. **à la carte** (ä lə kärt′): *Fr.* with a separate price for each dish on the menu; lit., according to the card. "Our guests, with an eye for expensive items, order *à la carte*."

■ An *aficionado* of soccer _____ [hates / loves] the game.

loves

■ The baseball sailed into the bleachers, where it was gloved by a young *af*_____.

*aficionado*

■ It's wise to order *à la carte* if you want (a) the standard full meal, (b) two or three special items. (    )

(b)

*à la carte*

■ Bill has a barrel of allergies and had to select his dishes *à la c*_____ .

*aficionado*

■ No, Joey, I won't push the fat worms onto your fishhooks. Better ask that *af*_____ of fishing to help you.

*à la carte*

■ My plump friend, with a tear in his eye, selected a spinach salad *à* _____ _____ .

---

5. **avant-garde** (a-vänt gärd'): *Fr.* the leaders in new artistic movements. "Walt Whitman was among the *avant-garde* to throw off the shackles of rhyme."

6. **bête noir** (bāt nwär'): *Fr.* a person or thing that one fears and dislikes; lit., black beast. "Algebra had always been his *bête noir.*"

*bête noir*

■ Rudy sometimes chased me home from school. He was my _____ [*avant-garde / bête noir*].

*avant-garde*

■ No fashions are too bizarre, if only they are created by the *av*_____*-ga*_____ among Parisian designers.

*avant-garde*

■ If not the first, Schonberg was among the *av*_____-*ga*_____ to compose in the twelve-tone technique.

*bête noir*

■ Speak softly and carry a big stick, especially if the neighborhood dogs are your *b*_____ *no*_____ .

*avant-garde*

*bête noir*

■ By the time my ancestor Gaspar started fooling around with impressionism, the *av*_____-*g*_____ was already into cubism. Gaspar might have painted ceilings, but he was deathly afraid of ladders. They were his *b*_____ *n*_____ .

---

## Quiz

Write the letter that indicates the best definition.

1. (b)
2. (d)
3. (c)

( ) 1. *a cappella*     a. each dish priced separately
( ) 2. *ad nauseum*     b. without accompaniment
( ) 3. *aficionado*     c. an ardent fan

4. (a)
5. (f)
6. (e)

(    ) 4. *à la carte*      d. to a sickening degree
(    ) 5. *avant-garde*     e. something one fears
(    ) 6. *bête noir*       f. the leaders in art

---

7. **c'est la vie** (sā la vē′): *Fr.* Such is life. "The prisoner had been making big money—a half-inch too big. *C'est la vie.*"

8. **con amore** (kän ä-mō′rā): *It.* with love; tenderly (used as a direction to musicians). "The lullaby is to be sung *con amore.*"

■ The musical instruction *con amore* is usually seen in sheet music involving (a) military marches, (b) love songs. (    )

*(b)*

■ Sophia kissed the gift box of chocolates where Giuseppe had written "c_____ am_____."

*con amore*

■ *C'est la vie* seems to suggest that we must (a) fight hard for improvements, (b) accept the things that happen. (    )

*(b)*

■ The sheepherder gambled his life savings on one throw of the dice—and lost. "C_____ l_____ v_____," he shrugged. "Too ba-a-a-ad."

*C'est la*
*vie*

■ "Yesterday Giuseppe nibbled my ear c_____ am_____," muttered Sophia. "Today he eloped with my best friend. Well, c_____ _____ v_____."

*con*
*amore*
*c'est la vie*

---

9. **déjà vu** (dā-zha vü′): *Fr.* the feeling that a new situation has happened before. "He first saw Lisa with a sense of *déjà vu,* as though he was reliving a dream."

10. **faux pas** (fō pä′): *Fr.* a social blunder; lit., a false step. "Asking the hostess how much she weighed was a *faux pas,* Clarence."

■ We entered Pokeville, and *déjà vu!* It was as though I had (a) been here before, (b) never seen such a lousy town. (    )

*(a)*

■ Kay had seen so many pictures of Mt. Fujiyama that her first sighting of it filled her with d_____ v_____.

*déjà vu*

■ A *faux pas* is (a) a pathway for forest beasts, (b) an error in etiquette such as sneezing into the punch bowl. (    )

*(b)*

■ Spilling soup on his necktie was bad enough but wiping his tie on the linen tablecloth was a definite *f*_____ *p*_____.

*faux pas*

*déjà vu*

■ With a terrible sense of *d*_____ *v*_____, I was sure that Uncle Louie was now going to tell Father Clancy the one about the priest and the rabbi—what a *f*_____

*faux*

*pas*

*p*_____!

11. **hoi polloi** (hoi pə-loi′): *Gk.* the common people: a somewhat contemptuous term. "The king sneered at the ignorance and sweat of the *hoi polloi*."

12. **Homo sapiens** (hō′mō sā′pē-enz): *L.* modern man; human being; lit., wise man. "Of all creatures, *Homo sapiens* is the only one who writes symphonies."

■ The scientific term *Homo sapiens* suggest that human beings have (a) wisdom, (b) a drinking problem. (    )

(a)

■ No animals had enough brains and ability to pollute the air, water, and earth except *Ho*_____ *sap*_____.

*Homo sapiens*

contempt

■ The masses, known as *hoi polloi*, were held in _____ [high regard / contempt] by royalty.

■ A truly democratic country has neither lofty aristocrats nor lowly

*hoi polloi*

*h*_____ *po*_____.

*hoi polloi*

*Homo*

*sapiens*

■ Ignorant *ho*_____ *po*_____ are, nevertheless, members of *Ho*_____ *sa*_____, and with education they can reach the stars.

## Quiz

Write the letter that indicates the best definition.

1. (c)
2. (a)
3. (f)

(    ) 1. *c'est la vie*     a. lovingly
(    ) 2. *con amore*     b. thinking man
(    ) 3. *déjà vu*     c. That's life.

4. (e)
5. (d)
6. (b)

(    ) 4. *faux pas*     d. the masses
(    ) 5. *hoi polloi*     e. a breach of etiquette
(    ) 6. *Homo sapiens*     f. the illusion of a replay

---

**13. laissez faire** (les′ā fâr′): *Fr.* the policy of non-interference in business or in individual conduct; lit., let do. "Government should try to keep its nose out of industrial or private affairs, according to the doctrine of *laissez faire*."

**14. magnum opus** (mag′nəm ō′pəs): *L.* the masterpiece of a writer or artist; lit., a great work.

very few

■ Under *laissez faire* our industries would operate with _____ [very few / numerous] government controls.

laissez faire

■ Some parents lay down rigid rules; others, more permissive, tend to practice *la*_____ *fa*_____.

(b)

■ A *magnum opus* is (a) a huge wine bottle, (b) an artist's masterpiece. (    )

magnum

opus

■ John Roebling and his son built several suspension bridges, but Brooklyn Bridge (1883) was certainly their *mag*_____ *op*_____.

magnum opus

laissez faire

■ Adam Smith wrote on economic theory, and in *Wealth of Nations,* his *m*_____ *op*_____, he developed the "let alone" doctrine of *la*_____ *fa*_____.

---

**15. par excellence** (pär ek′sə-läns′): *Fr.* excellent beyond comparison. "Benjamin Franklin and the others framed a constitution *par excellence*."

**16. persona non grata** (pər-sō′nə nän grät′ə): *L.* an unwelcome person; esp., a diplomat unacceptable to another government. "His cigar smoking made him *persona non grata* at the theater."

(b)

■ To be *persona non grata* means that one is (a) not a great big person, (b) not welcome. (    )

(b)

■ Anna Pavlova was a ballet dancer *par excellence*. This means her dancing was (a) up to par, (b) exceptionally good. (    )

■ If a diplomatic representative from Slobbovia is found to be operating a spy ring in Washington, D.C., our State Department would call

*persona non grata*

him *per* _____ *n* _____ *gr* _____ .

*persona non grata*

■ Jeff went to the men's room whenever a restaurant bill arrived, and soon he was *per* _____ *n* _____ *gr* _____ at the dinner parties.

*par excellence*

■ My barber is a mediocre stylist but he is a conversationalist *p* _____ *exc* _____ .

*par excellence*

■ Show me a freshman who reads one library book a week, and I'll show you a student *p* _____ *ex* _____ .

17. **potpourri** (pō-pōō-rē′): *Fr.* a miscellany or mixture of unrelated things. "Buster's pockets held a *potpourri* of his treasures."
18. **savoir-faire** (sav′wär fâr′): *Fr.* a ready knowledge of what to say or do in any situation; lit., knowing how to do. "Always smooth, always at ease, my friend was not lacking in *savoir-faire.*"

(a)

■ "Our junior high band will now perform a musical *potpourri.*" This announcement means we'll have the doubtful pleasure of hearing (a) a medley of tunes, (b) a symphony. (     )

*potpourri*

■ At noon Times Square was crowded with clerks, shoppers, laborers, bankers, and pickpockets—a regular *pot* _____ .

(a)

■ A person with *savoir-faire* tends to be (a) tactful, skillful, and adaptable; (b) flustered, awkward, and naive. (     )

*savoir-faire*

■ I was a country boy in Manhattan. I didn't have *sav* _____ *-f* _____ . In fact, I didn't have bus fare.

*savoir-faire*

■ Pierre stepped into the room where a woman was taking a bubble bath. "Sorry, sir," he said, retreating. Pierre had *s* _____ *-f* _____ .

*potpourri*

■ The *Reader's Digest* mixes short articles, anecdotes, quips, quotes, and quizzes; it presents a *po* _____ .

Write the letter that indicates the best definition.

1. (e)
2. (c)
3. (d)
4. (a)
5. (f)
6. (b)

(  ) 1. *laissez faire*    a. an undesirable person
(  ) 2. *magnum opus*    b. knowing always how to act
(  ) 3. *par excellence*    c. one's masterpiece
(  ) 4. *persona non grata*    d. supremely good
(  ) 5. *potpourri*    e. non-interference
(  ) 6. *savoir-faire*    f. a miscellany

---

19. **sine qua non** (sī'nē quā non'): *L.* something absolutely essential; lit., without which not. "The telephone has become a *sine qua non* of teenage romance."

20. **status quo** (stā'təs quō'): *L.* the existing condition; lit., state in which. "An ambitious executive will try to do more than maintain the *status quo*."

(b)

■ Defenders of the *status quo* in a society are likely to be (a) the underprivileged, (b) the wealthier class. (     )

*status quo*

■ Women were kitchen slaves until they decided to rebel against the

sta_____ q_____ .

*sine qua non*

■ A well-stocked library is the very _____ [*laissez faire* / *sine qua non*] of a college.

*sine*

*qua non*

■ "Idiot!" bawled bakery foreman Schultz, a slow man with a compliment. "You forgot caraway seeds! They're the *sin*_____

q_____ n_____ of a pumpernickel."

*sine qua non*

*status*

*quo*

■ Our labor union says that a paid vacation on Ground Hog's Day is

a *si*_____ q_____ n_____ of a new contract; but company officials support the *st*_____

q_____ .

---

21. **sub rosa** (sub rō'zə): *L.* secretly; confidentially; lit., under the rose, which was a symbol of secrecy. "The delicatessens agreed *sub rosa* to raise the price of salami."

22. **tour de force** (toor də fors'): *Fr.* a remarkable achievement; a stroke of genius; lit., a feat of skill. "Lindbergh's flight was a *tour de force* that won him instant admiration."

(b)

tour de force

(a)

sub rosa

sub rosa

tour

de force

■ The phrase *tour de force* describes an accomplishment that is (a) rather boring, (b) sensational. (     )

■ To ride a unicycle on a high wire and juggle five oranges—what a

t_____ d_____ f_____!

■ A *sub rosa* transaction is one that takes place (a) in secret, (b) on a TV network. (      )

■ Clym pops his cork when he learns that his wife Eustacia has been

meeting s_____ ro_____ with her old flame Wildeve.

■ "That's George Koltanowski," said an onlooker to me

s_____ ro_____. "He once played thirty-four simultaneous games of chess blindfolded, a real t_____

d_____ f_____."

---

**23. tout de suite** (to͞ot swēt′): *Fr.* immediately; right away; lit., all in succession. "I'm neck-deep in quicksand! Help me *tout de suite!*"

**24. vox populi** (voks pop′yə-lī′): *L.* public opinion; lit., the voice of the people; abbrev., *vox pop*. "Congress must not ignore *vox populi*."

(c)

(c)

vox populi

tout

de suite

vox populi

tout de suite

■ *Vox populi* refers to (a) a popular song, (b) our growing population, (c) public sentiment. (      )

■ "The sergeant returned *tout de suite*." This means he came back (a) with his sweetheart, (b) to the sound of bugles, (c) right away. (      )

■ Letters written to the editors of American newspapers are fairly

representative of vo_____ po_____.

■ Coach Cardiac was fuming: "We're trailing 14–13 with a minute

to go. Let's try that trick play to_____

d_____ s_____."

■ Governor Goofov expresses contempt for our state laws and for

v_____ pop_____. He should be impeached

t_____ d_____ s_____.

---

**Foreign Expressions    341**

**25. Wunderkind** (voon′dər kint′):  *G.* a child prodigy; lit., a wonder child. "This baby reads? She's a *Wunderkind!*"

(a)

■ A *Wunderkind* is (a) a brilliant youngster, (b) a thunderstorm along the Rhine. (     )

*Wunderkind*

■ Wolfgang Amadeus Mozart was composing music at age four and giving piano concerts at seven. Austria hailed him as a

*Wun* _____.

*Wunderkind*

■ She sang, she danced, she acted; and tiny Shirley Temple quickly became Hollywood's *W* _____.

---

### Quiz

Write the letter that indicates the best definition.

1. (c)
2. (f)
3. (a)
4. (d)
5. (g)
6. (b)
7. (e)

(     ) 1. *sine qua non*      a. secretly
(     ) 2. *status quo*        b. the voice of the people
(     ) 3. *sub rosa*         c. an indispensable thing
(     ) 4. *tour de force*     d. a remarkable accomplishment
(     ) 5. *tout de suite*     e. a wonder child
(     ) 6. *vox populi*       f. the current condition
(     ) 7. *Wunderkind*       g. immediately

---

## REVIEW TEST

Supply the missing words. The opening letters are given.

1. The Greek aristocrats sneered at the lowly *h*_____ *pol*_____.
2. Saying "Hi, babe!" to the mayor's wife was a horrible *f*_____

   *p*_____.
3. The rich get richer and the poor get babies. *C*_____ *la v*_____.
4. A country's leaders must listen to *v*_____ *pop*_____.
5. Nothing rattles Ronald. He has *sav*_____*-f*_____.
6. This wedding song must be sung sweetly and *c*_____ *am*_____.
7. I don't know soccer rules. Better ask an *afi*_____.
8. One official met *s*_____ *ro*_____ with members of the Mafia.
9. *War and Peace* was Leo Tolstoi's *mag*_____ *o*_____.
10. I don't want the full meal. I'll order *à l*_____ *c*_____.
11. Your accompanist has passed out. Just sing *a ca*_____.
12. *High Noon* was a western movie *p*_____ *exc*_____.
13. The closet held a *pot*_____ of shoes, tools, wigs, and apples.
14. Some old people resist change. They prefer the *st*_____ *q*_____.
15. I asked the boss for a raise and was turned down *to*_____ *de*

   *s*_____.

Write *True* or *False*.

_____ 16. A *Wunderkind* is a kid who wonders what's going on.

_____ 17. Hitting three home runs in one game is a *tour de force*.

_____ 18. A gorilla is a member of *Homo sapiens*.

_____ 19. The *avant-garde* often experiment with new art forms.

_____ 20. The *laissez faire* policy is permissive, not restrictive.

Write the foreign expression for each definition. The opening letters are given.

*Definitions*

21. *ad n*_____     to a disgusting degree
22. *b*_____ *no*_____     something feared

| | | |
|---|---|---|
| | *Definitions* | |
| 23. *d*_____ *v*_____ | the feeling of reliving a scene | |
| 24. *p*_____ *n*_____ *g*_____ | an unwelcome individual | |
| 25. *s*_____ *qua n*_____ | an indispensable thing | |

## Key to Review Test

Check your test answers with the following key. Deduct 4% per error from a possible 100%.

| | | |
|---|---|---|
| 1. *hoi polloi* | 10. *à la carte* | 19. True |
| 2. *faux pas* | 11. *a cappella* | 20. True |
| 3. *C'est la vie* | 12. *par excellence* | 21. *ad nauseum* |
| 4. *vox populi* | 13. *potpourri* | 22. *bête noir* |
| 5. *savoir-faire* | 14. *status quo* | 23. *déjà vu* |
| 6. *con amore* | 15. *tout de suite* | 24. *persona non grata* |
| 7. *aficionado* | 16. False | 25. *sine qua non* |
| 8. *sub rosa* | 17. True | |
| 9. *magnum opus* | 18. False | |

Score: _____ %

1. **ad hoc** (ad hok′): *L.* for this purpose only. "She appointed an *ad hoc* committee which later made its report and was dissolved."
2. **ad infinitum** (ad in-fə-nī′təm): *L.* to infinity. "Every creature has smaller creatures inside 'im, and so on and so on *ad infinitum.*"
3. **au courant** (ō kōō-rän′): *Fr.* well informed on current matters; up to date. "The old man read news magazines and so kept *au courant.*"
4. **bona fide** (bō′nə fīd′): *L.* in good faith; genuine. "Two park benches for ten dollars? Was this nice man making me a *bona fide* offer?"
5. **bon vivant** (bōṅ vē-väṅ′): *Fr.* a person who enjoys good food, drink, and luxury. "I have all the requirements of a *bon vivant* except money."
6. **carte blanche** (kärt′ bläṅsh′): *Fr.* full authority to do as one thinks best. "The governor of the island gave us *carte blanche* to shoot film anywhere."
7. **cause célèbre** (kôz′ sə-leb′r): *Fr.* a famous legal case or controversy. "The O. J. Simpson affair was a *cause célèbre* during the mid-nineties."
8. **caveat emptor** (kā′vē-at emp′tôr): *L.* Let the buyer beware; buy at your own risk. "Flea market sales are final, so it's *caveat emptor.*"
9. **coup de grâce** (kōō də gräs′): *Fr.* death blow; lit., stroke of mercy. "Our shop was losing money, and the workers' strike was the *coup de grâce.*"
10. **coup d'état** (kōō dā-ta′): *Fr.* a sudden, powerful political stroke, esp. the forcible overthrow of government. "In a bloody *coup d'état* the army leaders seized command of the young republic."
11. **cul-de-sac** (kul′də-sak′): *Fr.* a passage closed at one end; a blind alley. "Trapped in a *cul-de-sac!* They'd put all their Basques in one exit."
12. **de facto** (dē fak′tō): *L.* actually existing though possibly without legal sanction. "The *de facto* government is ruled by a tyrant and two lunatics."
13. **de jure** (dē joor′ē): *L.* legally so. "Democratic processes have set up a *de jure* government."
14. **dernier cri** (der-nyā krē′): *Fr.* the latest fashion; the newest thing. "Olga's gown is the *dernier cri* from Paris—from Paris, Texas, that is."
15. **e.g.** (abbrev. of *exempli gratia*): *L.* for example. "Grandpa collects various items, *e.g.,* beer bottle caps."
16. **entre nous** (äṅ-trə nōō′): *Fr.* between us; confidentially. "Let's settle this fender-scratching accident *entre nous.*"
17. **esprit de corps** (es-prē′ də kôr′): *Fr.* enthusiastic spirit and loyalty of a group. "Football games contributed to the *esprit de corps* at Acne Junior High."
18. **ex officio** (eks ə-fish′ē-ō): *L.* because of one's office or position. "The vice president is the *ex officio* president of the Senate."
19. **ex post facto** (eks pōst fak′tō): *L.* having retroactive effect. "Congress is not allowed to pass *ex post facto* laws."
20. **fait accompli** (fe-ta-koṅ-plē′): *Fr.* an accomplished fact, a thing already done, so that opposition is useless. "Mother hated the colors, but our paint job was a *fait accompli.*"
21. **gemütlich** (gə-mūt′lish): *G.* cheerful; agreeable. "The tavern was cozy and the atmosphere *gemütlich.*"
22. **hic jacet** (hik jā′sit): *L.* here lies. "*Hic jacet* Hy Fee, dentist, filling his last cavity."
23. **hors de combat** (ôr də koṅ-ba′): *Fr.* put out of the fight; disabled. "In six minutes our 'indestructible' fullback was *hors de combat.*"

24. **hors d'oeuvre** (ôr dûrv'): *Fr.* an appetizer. "I nibbled an *hors d'oeuvre* with my little finger extended."
25. **in absentia** (in ab-sen'shē-ə): *L.* in absence; although not present. "The philanthropist was awarded his honorary degree *in absentia.*"
26. **ipso facto** (ip'sō fak'tō): *L.* by that very fact. "A driver with high alcoholic blood level is *ipso facto* a lawbreaker."
27. **modus operandi** (mō'dəs op'ə-ran'dē): *L.* method of operating. "Zelda studied the new computer to figure out its *modus operandi.*"
28. **nom de plume** (nom də ploom'): *Fr.* a pen name; pseudonym. "George Sand is the *nom de plume* of a Frenchwoman who wrote novels."
29. **nouveau riche** (noo-vō rēsh'): *Fr.* a newly-rich person, possibly lacking in taste and culture. "One of the *nouveau riche* nailed up a Picasso in the bathroom."
30. **op. cit.** (abbrev. of *opere citato*): *L.* in the work cited. "The footnote reads 'Dingle, *op. cit.*, p. 99.'"
31. **pièce de résistance** (pyes də rā-zē-stäns'): *Fr.* the main dish of a meal; the principal work of a group. "The *pièce de résistance* of the program was 'Concerto for Tuba in Six Flats and a Basement.'"
32. **prima facie** (prī'mə fā'shē): *L.* at first sight before investigation. "Fudd's possession of the stolen jewels is *prima facie* evidence of his guilt."
33. **pro bono publico** (prō bō'nō pub'li-kō): *L.* for the public good. "Gumbo Center has dedicated its town hall *pro bono publico.*"
34. **pro tem** (abbrev. of *pro tempore*): *L.* for the time being. "Harpo will be chairman *pro tem,* until we get organized."
35. **quid pro quo** (kwid prō kwō'): *L.* one thing in exchange for another. "The oil companies got you elected and now they want their *quid pro quo.*"
36. **raison d'être** (rā'zôṅ det'rə): *Fr.* reason for existing. "The exploration of nature was John Muir's *raison d'être.*"
37. **rara avis** (rer'ə ā'vis): *L.* a very unusual person; lit., a rare bird. "Our new plumber is a *rara avis.* He brought all the necessary tools."
38. **sotto voce** (sot'ō vō'chē): *It.* in an undertone. "Moosehead explained his escape plan *sotto voce* to his cellmate."
39. **table d'hôte** (tab'əl dōt'): *Fr.* a complete meal as detailed on the menu. Cf., *à la carte.* "Vegetarian Vivian ordered *à la carte;* Hungry Harry, *table d'hôte.*"
40. **tête-à-tête** (tāt'ə tāt'): *Fr.* a private chat between two persons. "Ben and Agatha enjoyed their *tête-à-tête* at the Greasy Platter."